God's Arbiters

IMAGINING THE AMERICAS
Caroline F. Levander and Anthony B. Pinn, Series Editors

Imagining the Americas is a new interdisciplinary series that explores the cross-fertilization among cultures and forms in the American hemisphere. The series targets the intersections between literary, religious and cultural studies that materialize once the idea of nation is understood as fluid and multi-form. Extending from the northernmost regions of Canada to Cape Horn, books in this series will move beyond a simple extension of U.S.-based American studies approaches and engage the American hemisphere directly.

God's Arbiters

*Americans and the Philippines,
1898–1902*

Susan K. Harris

OXFORD
UNIVERSITY PRESS

OXFORD
UNIVERSITY PRESS

Oxford University Press, Inc., publishes works that further
Oxford University's objective of excellence
in research, scholarship, and education.

Oxford   New York
Auckland   Cape Town   Dar es Salaam   Hong Kong   Karachi
Kuala Lumpur   Madrid   Melbourne   Mexico City   Nairobi
New Delhi   Shanghai   Taipei   Toronto

With offices in
Argentina   Austria   Brazil   Chile   Czech Republic   France   Greece
Guatemala   Hungary   Italy   Japan   Poland   Portugal   Singapore
South Korea   Switzerland   Thailand   Turkey   Ukraine   Vietnam

Published by Oxford University Press, Inc.
198 Madison Avenue, New York, New York 10016

www.oup.com

Oxford is a registered trademark of Oxford University Press

Library of Congress Cataloging-in-Publication Data
Harris, Susan K., 1945–
God's arbiters : Americans and the Philippines, 1898–1902 / by Susan K. Harris.
   p. cm. — (Imagining the Americas)
Includes bibliographical references and index.
ISBN 978-0-19-974010-9 (cloth : alk. paper)
1. United States—Foreign relations—Philippines. 2. Philippines—Foreign relations—United States.
3. Philippines—Annexation to the United States. 4. Philippines—Foreign public opinion, American.
5. Racism—Political aspects—United States—History. 6. United States—Colonial question.
7. United States—Territorial expansion. 8. Political messianism—United States—History.
9. Christianity and politics—United States—History. 10. Imperialism—History. I. Title.
E183.8.P5H37   2011
327.730599—dc22   2010035133

1 3 5 7 9 8 6 4 2

Printed in the United States of America
on acid-free paper

The founders of the nation were not provincial. Theirs was the geography of the world. They . . . knew that where our ships should go our flag might follow. They had the logic of progress, and they knew that the Republic they were planting must, in obedience to the laws of our expanding race, necessarily develop into the greater Republic which the world will finally acknowledge as the arbiter, under God, of the destinies of mankind.

—Senator Albert Beveridge, January 9, 1900

When I . . . realized that the Philippines had dropped into our laps I confess I did not know what to do with them. . . . I walked the floor of the White House night after night until midnight; and I am not ashamed to tell you, gentlemen, that I went down on my knees and prayed Almighty God for light and guidance. . . . And one night late it came to me this way . . . (1) That we could not give them back to Spain—that would be cowardly and dishonorable; (2) that we could not turn them over to France and Germany—our commercial rivals in the Orient—that would be bad business and discreditable; (3) that we could not leave them to themselves—they were unfit for self-government—and they would soon have anarchy and misrule over there worse than Spain's was; and (4) that there was nothing left for us to do but to take them all, and to educate the Filipinos, and uplift and civilize and Christianize them, and by God's grace do the very best we could by them, as our fellow-men for whom Christ also died.

—President William McKinley, "Interview," circa 1900, Reported by General James
Rusling, 1903

I bring you the stately matron called CHRISTENDOM—returning bedraggled, besmirched and dishonored from pirate raids in Kiaochow, Manchuria, South Africa and the Philippines; with her soul full of meanness, her pocket full of boodle and her mouth full of pious hypocrisies. Give her soap and a towel, but hide the looking-glass.

—Mark Twain, "A Salutation to the Twentieth Century," December 31, 1900

TABLE OF CONTENTS

ACKNOWLEDGMENTS

No book is really single-authored. This one in particular is deeply indebted to the generosity of friends and strangers. My warmest thanks for their time, patience, skills, and generosity to Kevin Bochynski, Louis J. Budd, Ellen Gruber Garvey, John Gruesser, Barbara Hochman, Paul Lauter, Cheryl Lester, Laura Lomas, Stanley Lombardo, Gretchen Murphy, Sarah Robbins, Ann Carter Rose, Jean Pfaelzer, Bonnie Stretch, Vicky Unruh, and Priscilla Wald. A moment of silence and thanks for Jim Zwick, who gave the world *Boondocksnet,* a superb Web site, and *Mark Twain's Weapons of Satire: Anti-Imperialist Writing on the Philippine-American War* (1992). Jim critiqued some of my initial ideas and provided me with valuable information. His death is a loss to us all.

Special thanks for all the legwork to my two graduate research assistants, Nathaniel Williams and Carey R. Voeller (the latter now Assistant Professor of English at Wofford College, S.C.). Gwen Claassen and Paula Courtney, of the KU College of Liberal Arts Digital Media Services, did yeoman work in helping me prepare the manuscript; I am grateful for their cheerfulness, their patience, and their skills.

In addition to individuals, I am indebted to small groups who read drafts and chapters. First, many thanks to the anonymous readers for OUP, who pushed me to pull all my threads together; if I have not succeeded, it is my failure, not theirs. Although this book has been germinating since 2003, it was launched during a University of Kansas Hall Center Grant Writing

Workshop in 2006, under the able direction of Joane Nagel and Ann Cudd. I appreciate the efforts of all the participants who helped me develop my initial ideas. I am also grateful to the Midwest Americanists writing group, organized by Patricia Okker; to the Hall Center American seminar, especially Jorge Perez and Sherry Tucker; and most importantly, to my "Brooklyn Work Group," Ellen Gruber Garvey and Barbara Hochman, who brought keen analytical minds to my multiple drafts during the sabbatical year that we labored together in Brooklyn. I am deeply grateful to Sarah Robbins, who read through the whole manuscript at a crucial moment, and to Jean Pfaelzer, from whose generosity I have benefited before and whose hard labor on this manuscript infinitely improved the book. Thank you, Jeanie.

Many thanks also to the institutions and their staffs that made this research possible: to the Hall Family and the University of Kansas's Hall Center for support for research and travel; to the University of Kansas for a sabbatical leave to complete the book; to the New York Public Library Research Branch, The Library Company of Philadelphia, the Spenser Research Library at the University of Kansas, the Interlibrary Loan unit and the Watson and Anschutz Libraries at KU; to the Watkinson Library at Trinity College, especially Peter Knapp, Special Collections Librarian and College Archivist; to the British Library, the Arxiu Historic of Barcelona, and the University of Barcelona libraries, especially the Lletres Españoles and the Pavelló de la Republica; to the Sterling Library at Yale University, the Olin Library at Cornell University, the Center for Mark Twain Studies at Elmira College, and the Mark Twain Project at the University of California, Berkeley. At the last moment, the English Department at NYU gave me special permission to use the Bobst Library; I am deeply grateful for their collegiality. The good people of the Mark Twain Forum responded to my every inquiry with wonderful information; to them, and to the Mark Twain Circle, my thanks. Special thanks to Oxford editors Brendan O'Neill and Caroline Levander, who encouraged me to submit this manuscript to the Press, and to the Press staff who actually produced it. Portions of chapters 3 and 4 were previously published in *Transformations: The Journal of Inclusive Scholarship and Pedagogy,* vol. 20, no. 2 (Fall 2009/Winter 2010, 90–112). Portions of chapter 5 were previously published in *Comparative American Studies* (Fall 2007, 243–64). Thanks to the editors of both journals for permission to republish here. If I have neglected to mention any individual or institution, I beg forgiveness. I am humbled by the generosity shown me from all sides.

God's Arbiters

Introduction

A Christian Nation

> "What then is the American, this new man?"
> —J. Hector St. Jean de Crevecoeur, 1782

> "We are a Christian nation."
> —Senator Henry U. Johnson, 1899

"I am an anti-imperialist," Mark Twain announced to reporters in New York on October 15, 1900, upon arriving home after a nine-year sojourn abroad. "I am opposed to having the eagle put its talons on any other land."[1] But Twain immediately amended his declaration, noting that his anti-imperialism was new. "I left these shores, at Vancouver, a red-hot imperialist," he recalled,

> I wanted the American eagle to go screaming into the Pacific. It seemed tiresome and tame for it to content itself with the Rockies. Why not spread its wings over the Philippines . . .? . . . I thought it would be a real good thing to do.
>
> I said to myself, here are a people who have suffered for three centuries. We can make them as free as ourselves, give them a government and country of their own, put a miniature of the American constitution afloat in the Pacific, start a brand new republic to take its place among the free nations of the world. It seemed to me a great task to which we had addressed ourselves.

However, the *New York Herald* continued, Twain had changed his mind. "I have thought some more, since then, and I have read carefully the Treaty of Paris, and I have seen that we do not intend to free, but to

FIGURE I.1. "The American Lion of St., Mark's." *Life*, Life Publishing Company, New York, February 28, 1901.

subjugate the people of the Philippines. We have gone there to conquer, not to redeem. . . . And so, I am an anti-imperialist. . . ." (Zwick, 5).

Although he had made several short visits to the United States in the previous nine years, Twain had spent the majority of the time in Europe, living in Germany, Switzerland, France, Austria, Italy, and England. He also had undertaken a strenuous around-the-world lecture tour that profoundly affected his understanding of racial and colonial relationships. Popularly considered an expert on foreign affairs, he was given to tart commentary on international politics. Yet despite the acerbity, the national vision at the core of Twain's criticism of U.S. policies reflected most Americans' understanding of the country's mission. All three reports of Twain's interview that October day note that he had changed his mind about the legitimacy of U.S. policies in the Philippines. "Once I was not anti-imperialist," the *New York Tribune* reported him saying. "I thought that the rescue of those islands from the government under which they had suffered for three hundred years was a good business for us to be in." The *Chicago Tribune*'s version of his declaration had him remembering that the previous year "I thought it would be a great thing to give a whole lot of freedom to the Filipinos, but I guess now that it's better to let them give it to themselves. Besides, on looking over the treaty I see we've got to saddle the friars and their churches. I guess we don't want to" (Zwick, 4–5).

Although each newspaper phrases Twain's words slightly differently, all include the same major points: first, that he originally supported the U.S. invasion of the Philippines because he believed Americans wanted to help the Filipinos free themselves from Spanish colonial rule; second, that he believed it was America's duty not only to help free the Filipinos but also to encourage them to reshape themselves in the image of the United States; third, that on reading the Treaty ceding the Philippines to the United States he realized that the intent was to subjugate the Filipinos rather than to free them; and fourth, that a major flaw in the Treaty was that it obliged the Americans to continue supporting Catholic institutions as they had developed in the archipelago under Spanish rule. Signal words Twain is reported to have used include verbs such as "free," "rescue," and "redeem," and nouns such as "freedom," "duty," and "task." The understanding of the U.S. mission to which these words point is the focus of this book: I am using Mark Twain here as a measure of nineteenth-century Americans' understanding of who they were and how the government that represented them should be conducting itself on the global level. At the core of that understanding is a profound belief in the superiority of U.S. political and social institutions and a conviction that the United States had a divine mandate to help other countries follow its example. That Mark Twain, at the end of the nineteenth century, could assume that it would be "a good thing" to "put a miniature of the American constitution afloat in the Pacific" suggests that Americans believed they had a special mission to replicate themselves around the world.

Scholars of American history and rhetoric have long discussed twentieth-century doctrines of American exceptionalism, including Manifest Destiny, exceptionalism's nineteenth-century predecessor. Neither doctrine was systematic; historians use both terms loosely, as umbrella concepts to explain how nineteenth- and twentieth-century Americans imagined their country's relationship to the rest of the world. The doctrines were especially contradictory in their overlapping assumptions about religious and racial identity. Mark Twain was reared to believe that to be American was to be white and Protestant, and it was only after many years of travel and communication with people not born and reared in the United States that he came, painfully, to question those beliefs. Like Twain, most nineteenth-century Americans, no matter what their own race or religion, were taught that to be "American" was to be white and Protestant. Unlike Twain, not all of them came to question those assumptions. Internally, the issue of American identity and American citizenship played out in the tremendous post–Civil War conflicts over African American rights, immigration restriction, and Native American policy. On the international front, they were manifested first in popular assessments of the Spanish-American War and second (and more contentiously) in the debates over the Philippine-American War.

This book focuses on the debates over the Philippine-American War—a conflict that, as Thomas Bender has pointed out, history texts quickly subsumed into the Spanish-American War, with the result that the Philippine resistance to American rule was forgotten (Bender, 223–33). Although numerous scholarly books have been written about the Philippine-American War, they have not filtered into the public consciousness. Moreover, the Philippine-American War rarely has been taught in American schools in the last half century and few American citizens even know that it occurred.[2] I see the Philippine-American conflict as a significant moment in American history, not only because it signals the United States' emergence as a world power, but because the rhetoric of American identity employed to debate the costs of annexing the Philippines echo eerily in current debates over America's global responsibilities. The themes sounded in contemporary political rhetoric are rooted in nineteenth-century constructions of who we are and what our relationships with other nations should be.

If the Philippine-American conflict is the moment on which I focus my investigation of American identity, Mark Twain is the man who embodies the conflicting assumptions held by most white Americans. *God's Arbiters* uses Mark Twain to illuminate the debates over annexation because his stinging criticism of his country's course was founded in his fervent embrace of its special mission. In my reading, Mark Twain's own contradictions reflect the contradictions that characterized white America generally. Born in the Missouri backwoods in 1835, growing up among white Protestants who took white supremacy for granted, regarded Catholics as dangerous aliens, and taught children that America's civil liberties were invented during the Protestant Reformation, Twain's assumptions about race, religion, and national identity reflected those of his contemporaries. He came to his anti-imperialism only after judging that America was betraying its own principles by forcibly annexing the Philippines. But he did not relinquish his belief that the country, by virtue of its own history and institutions, should serve as a moral model for the rest of the world. The last decade of Twain's life was characterized by intense bitterness and misanthropy, most strikingly manifested in his attacks on religious and patriotic rhetoric. For many years, Twain scholars assumed that Twain's anger reflected the economic failures and familial tragedies of his private life. More recently, many have come to realize that Twain's ire was at least as much a response to his sense of national betrayal as it was to personal loss. For Twain, always keenly sensitive to cruelty and hypocrisy, both the U.S. government and the citizens who supported it had sold their honor for a back seat in the community of imperialist nations.[3]

This book, then, unpacks the sense of national identity that Mark Twain shared with his contemporaries, their deep-seated assumptions about what it meant to be an American citizen and their anxieties about the role that the United States should play on the world stage. In the process I show how a narrative of American identity, formulated over the course of the nineteenth century to impose unity on an ever-increasing multiplicity, was enlisted to support arguments over the annexation of the Philippines. I am treating this narrative not simply as "rhetoric," to be cynically exploited by politicians seeking emotional triggers. Rather, I am looking at the narrative itself: its loose and often incompatible elements, its evolution over time, its circulation across geopolitical borders, and its uses, in order to understand how a story that contains so many incongruities could play so powerful a role in the shaping of American policies at home and abroad.

Backgrounds: The Spanish-American and Philippine-American Wars

Americans appeared to have initiated the Spanish-American War from the best of intentions. In the beginning, it looked like the act of a friendly neighbor coming to the aid of Cubans in their struggle against Spain. This is not to say that the United States was entirely disinterested. Although Spain had controlled Cuba since the early sixteenth century, Americans had invested in the island since well before the Civil War, especially in the sugar and slave trades. American entrepreneurs and adventurers, many of them Southerners, had called for the annexation of the island at least since the 1850s. The U.S. government attempted to buy it from Spain in 1848, but the Spanish adamantly refused. The Ostend Manifesto, authorized by President Franklin Pierce in 1854, made a similar attempt, but Northerners, scenting a Southern strategy to extend the reach of slavery, virulently opposed it.[4] After that the government, at least officially, ceased its efforts. The Cuban economy remained heavily dependent on the United States, however, and throughout the nineteenth century interested entrepreneurs continued to demand annexation. They were opposed by anti-annexationists, many of whom feared the results of incorporating the islands' millions of Catholics and people of color into the United States.

Meanwhile, Cubans themselves were increasingly discontent under Spanish rule, and revolts occurred regularly in the latter half of the century. Some Cubans, seeing the United States as a bastion of freedom, suggested that the U.S. government should annex the island. Others sought U.S. aid against the Spanish, but rejected the idea of annexation. José Martí, a Cuban revolutionary who spent nearly two decades of the late nineteenth century in exile in the United States, urged the Americans to help the Cubans. In "A Vindication of Cuba," written in 1889, he excoriated the United States for having deferred to the Spanish rather than coming to the revolutionaries' aid. When the Cubans, with a "childlike confidence in the certain help of the United States," begged the Americans for support, he claims, the United States "'stretched the limits of their powers in deference to Spain.' They did not raise the hand. They did not say the word."[5] Martí, however, was opposed to annexation. "Cuba must be free," he wrote in his notebook, "of Spain and of the United States" (*Selected Writings*, 286).

In part because of a mysterious explosion that sank the USS *Maine* (February 15, 1898), an American battleship stationed in Havana harbor to lend stability to an increasingly volatile situation, the U.S. Army finally intervened in aid of the Cuban rebels. A majority of Americans supported the invasion. But they did not support the war because they wanted to annex the island, or because the yellow press carried inflammatory stories about Spanish atrocities against the Cubans and plots against the United States. Rather, as Martí had hoped, they responded to the Cubans' call for help on moral grounds. The Hearst papers are rightly accused of whipping up public enthusiasm for the war. But they could not have inflamed sentiment if it had not already existed. Americans supported the war because they saw the Cuban situation through the lens of their own national history—as a colony in which patriots were fighting for freedom from an oppressive mother country. From this viewpoint, the Americans' own colonial history made them natural allies for rebels against colonial rule throughout the world. The sense of moral obligation was so powerful that even men like William Jennings Bryan—an anti-militarist evangelical Christian politician—joined the army, announcing that "Humanity demands that we shall act."[6] Twain—at the time living in Italy—also believed that the United States had a moral imperative to aid the rebels, apparently defending U.S. intervention both to his family and his acquaintances. "I come across no end of people who simply can *not* see the Cuban situation as America sees it—people who cannot believe than *any* conduct can justify one nation interfering with the domestic affairs of another," he told his publisher in May of 1898. "From the beginning the family have been rabid opponents of this war & I've been just the other way," he added a few days later.[7] Neither Bryan nor Twain wanted the United States to annex Cuba however; for them justification for invading the island rested on America's duty to help struggling colonies achieve freedom and self-rule.

But few of those who supported the Cuban intervention anticipated that the "splendid little war" in Cuba would trigger a prolonged guerilla war in the Philippines. American possession of the archipelago, more than 7,000 miles off the Pacific coast, at first seemed almost an accident, a corollary to the Cuban adventure. But the United States' dual invasions—in the Caribbean and in the Pacific—made sense both historically and economically. Like Cuba, the Philippines had long been under Spanish rule. Magellan had claimed the islands for Spain in 1521, and the Spanish government, aided by friars from the Catholic church, had established a colonial system throughout the archipelago. Spanish—the official language—was spoken by the upper classes, who also took on the social trappings of Spanish culture. With the exception of the Muslim Moros in the south, native Filipinos were almost universally Roman Catholic, and what education existed for the lower classes was administered through the Church, which also controlled many local governments and owned huge tracts of land. Although many friars were seriously engaged in helping the Filipino peasants, overall they gained a reputation for corruption and exploitation, and the revolutionary movements of the late nineteenth century called for their removal. José Rizal, a nineteenth-century Filipino novelist and revolutionary, featured church corruption in both *Noli Me Tangere* (1886; *Touch Me Not*) and *El Filibusterismo* (1891; *The Subversive*). The books made him a national hero; widely translated, they also introduced the rest of the world to the Filipinos' point of view.

That point of view was increasingly self-conscious. Nationalism—the movement for national consolidation, identity, and autonomy that swept the Western world in the nineteenth century—also affected the Filipinos, and like the Cubans, they had grown restive under Spanish rule. At first they sought increased autonomy within the Spanish colonial framework. When the Spanish responded by exiling or executing the leaders and repressing political organizations, the reformers turned rebel and sought independence. *La Liga Filipina*, first formed by Rizal and other Filipino ex-patriots in Spain and brought to the islands by Rizal in 1892, had sought political change through peaceful means, but after Rizal was arrested and exiled by the Spanish, *La Liga* was replaced by the Katipunan, which called for armed conflict. Armed insurrection began in 1896; Rizal's execution by the Spanish that year gave the revolutionaries a martyr. By 1897 the rebels had declared a Philippine Republic, with Emilio Aguinaldo as its president. The revolutionaries' popularity alarmed the Spanish; at the end of that year they brokered a deal with the rebels, providing them with money and allowing them to go into voluntary exile in Hong Kong.

From the Americans' point of view, there were enough parallels between the Cuban and Filipino rebellions to make a case for going to war with Spain on behalf of all Spain's colonies, not just the Cubans. Moreover, a series of recent events in the United States laid grounds for augmenting American engagement in the Pacific. First, the Americans could argue that they already had a foothold west of California: American planters in Hawaii had gained power over the islands a decade earlier; and, like the American entrepreneurs in Cuba, had been agitating for the United States to annex them. Second, an economic depression during the early 1890s had sent American producers in search of markets abroad to absorb American surplus goods, and increasingly, they were looking westward. Third, the American navy had made a comeback, rebounding from a low point in the 1870s and 1880s. Alfred Thayer Mahan's *The Influence of Sea Power Upon History* (1890) had convinced both Presidents Harrison (1889–93) and Cleveland (1893–97) that the United States should rebuild its force, and by 1898 there were enough ships to enable it to patrol both the Atlantic and the Pacific oceans. Finally, Theodore Roosevelt, then assistant secretary of the navy, had the foresight to understand that these events could be used to the country's advantage and the audacity to act on his vision. Shortly before the outbreak of the Spanish-American War, Roosevelt maneuvered then-Commodore George Dewey into the command of the Pacific fleet. After the United States had invaded Cuba, Roosevelt took advantage of the illness of his boss, Secretary John Long, to order Dewey to take the warships from their berths in Hong Kong to Manila, and there to engage the Spanish squadron stationed in Manila Bay. Dewey sank the entire Spanish fleet. A month later the United States took possession of Guam, and in June, Congress approved the annexation of Hawaii.[8] The Treaty of Paris, signed by the United States and Spain in December 1898, forced Spain to give up Cuba, Puerto Rico, Guam, and the Philippines—almost all the remnants of its former empire. It was a defeat from which it would take the collective Spanish psyche years to recover.

But Dewey's success initiated pressing questions for the United States, chief among them the decision about what they were to do with their new possessions. Knowing that the United States might go to war with Cuba and foreseeing demands for annexation in the wake of an American victory, anti-annexationists in the United States had convinced Congress to pass the Teller Amendment the previous April, which prevented the United States from annexing Cuba in the event of a victory over Spain. However it said nothing about the political fate of other Spanish colonies that might end up in American hands. The Filipinos assumed that they would become independent, the goal for which they had been fighting and the only reason that they had accepted U.S. intervention. Although the Americans' superior battleships were the main instruments for destroying the Spanish ships, U.S. victories on land were dependent on the cooperation of the revolutionaries who were familiar with the terrain, its native inhabitants, and the Spanish. When Dewey was ordered to take the fleet to Manila, he was told to bring with him Emilio Aguinaldo, the Filipino revolutionary leader currently in exile in Hong Kong. Aguinaldo was out of town, but he hurried after the Americans as soon as he returned. The revolutionaries' understanding was that the United States was helping them achieve independence, as it had helped the Cubans. On that assumption, they helped the U.S. military secure Manila and other key Philippine positions. But events did not turn out the way the Filipinos expected. The treaty ceded them to the United States in exchange for a twenty million dollar reparations fee.

The treaty presented multiple problems. The most pressing concerned the islands' relationship to the United States: the Filipinos were outraged that they were now owned by the United States, and Americans were uncertain about their responsibilities toward their new possessions. The Filipinos made it clear that they wanted independence; from their viewpoint, the treaty had double-crossed them because Spain had ceded control of the archipelago to the United States rather than to them.[9] From the nationalists' perspective, this meant that they had simply traded one colonial master for another. Aguinaldo and his supporters felt betrayed: the Americans had explained their generosity in helping the Filipinos as an expression of a national belief that the United States had an obligation to help nations struggling for independence. According to Aguinaldo, Admiral Dewey had assured him that the Americans were not interested in taking over the archipelago and that U.S. forces would depart once the Spanish fleet was destroyed.[10] When it became clear that the Americans had no intention of leaving, the Filipinos, remembering their experience in resisting Spain, rekindled their struggle, this time against the Americans. The result was a prolonged guerilla war in the Philippines; enduring suspicion of the U.S. government by Latin American governments fearful that they, too, would be usurped; and the development of strong anti-imperialist sentiments within the United States.

From the Americans' perspective, the problem with the treaty was that it brought the United States to the brink of overseas empire, and many citizens were not at all sure that the country should take the leap. With the signing of the treaty, the United States suddenly found itself in possession of territories in two very disparate areas of the world, all of which featured Spanish as the official language and had developed their own forms of Spanish-inflected culture. Both Puerto Ricans and Filipinos demanded that the United States respect their independence, but American self-interest suggested that they might be more useful as American territories— a position urged on them by many Europeans, especially the British, who especially saw an American presence in the Pacific as a means of bolstering their own interests in the Far East.

But the Americans were daunted by the prospect of assuming responsibility for the islands. In the Philippines well over one hundred indigenous languages were spoken as well as Spanish, and only a small percentage of Filipinos had been permitted access to higher education or to European culture. The popular image of Filipinos in the United States painted them as savages, uncivilized and inassimilable. This left Congress furiously debating what it was going to do with the islands, a problem complicated by the fact that most U.S. citizens had little idea where Guam and the Philippines actually were. (Mr. Dooley, the celebrated political humorist, commented that Americans also didn't know whether the Philippines was a country or canned goods.) The period between the signing of the treaty in Paris, in December, 1898, and its narrow ratification by Congress on February 6, 1899, was thick with debates that centered on America's mission, racial pluralism, the role of commerce in the shaping of national identity, and the nature of citizenship. I am particularly interested in what I see as the core of all these issues: first, the fact that most speakers in the debates, no matter what position they defended, believed that the United States was a nation of white Protestants under a special mandate from God to represent freedom and fair dealing to the rest of the world; and second, the circulation of that belief in their arguments both for and against annexation. In the following pages I will examine Congressional speeches, editorials and letters-to-the-editor, sermons, essays, short stories, novels, and poems that spoke to the question of annexation from the standpoint of American religious and racial identity and argued about the changes that would transpire if the nation moved into the imperialist arena.

God's Arbiters: Americans and the National Narrative

As his interview with the reporters demonstrates, Mark Twain first supported the war, then changed his mind. So did William Jennings Bryan, the evangelical populist. "Is our national character so weak," Bryan asked in June, 1898, "that we cannot withstand the temptation to appropriate the first piece of land that comes within our reach?" After the United States invaded the Philippines, Bryan resigned from the army and took up the anti-imperialist cause. Both Bryan and Twain represent the sea-change that occurred in American conversations in the aftermath of Dewey's invasion. The prospect of annexing a country so far away, and about which most Americans knew so little, forced those who supported U.S. activities in Cuba on moral grounds to ask exactly what their national mission was, and how they should go about effecting it.

President William McKinley also changed his mind about annexation. But whereas Twain went from supporting U.S. intervention to opposing it, McKinley shifted from opposing annexation to supporting it. In 1903, nearly four years after the United States signed the Treaty of Paris, General James Rusling recalled an interview McKinley had held with Methodist Church leaders shortly after annexation. According to Rusling, McKinley told the churchmen that after a night of prayer and soul-searching he had concluded that it was the duty of the United States "to educate the Filipinos, and uplift and civilize and Christianize them, and by God's grace do the very best we could by them."[11] These lines are quoted frequently in discussions of the Philippine annexation, in large part because they crystallize the idea of religious mission deployed to justify continued American control of the islands in the face of clear Filipino resistance.[12] Here signal words are *educate*, *uplift*, *civilize*, and *Christianize*—action verbs implying that Americans should perform specific feats. But in addition to urging action, these particular words are value-laden, framing Americans' conception of the Filipinos and rationalizing U.S. activities in the archipelago as benevolent outreach. In calling Americans to educate the Filipinos, McKinley was suggesting that in their current state the islanders were ignorant; in calling Americans to uplift and civilize the natives he was suggesting that they were uncivilized and backward; and in calling Americans to Christianize the Filipinos he was suggesting that they were all pagans. Although many American commentators, especially those who had visited the Philippines, pointed out that, after 300 years of Spanish rule, most Filipinos were Catholic and that a complex, Spanish-inflected civilization was deeply rooted in most of the archipelago, McKinley's language echoed the dominant American view of the islands and provided a moral rationale for appropriating them.[13] In McKinley's words we can see how the argument that it was America's historic duty to help other countries achieve independence shifted ground. Suddenly, it was not only Americans' duty to help other nations achieve "freedom," it was also their mission to disseminate U.S. Protestant culture throughout the globe.

One way of understanding this vision is to recognize the conflict with Spain as a revival of the old antagonisms of the Protestant Reformation and a recasting, on a global scale, of U.S. antipathy to Catholicism generally. McKinley's call to Christianize the Filipinos implies that even those who were Catholic were not really Christian. For U.S. Protestants of the nineteenth century, the Roman Church represented a threat to their entire conception of what it meant to be an American. The version of national history most Americans imbibed at school was rooted in the ideological struggles of the Reformation. Students were taught that the Roman Church was a thoroughly corrupt, authoritarian institution that prevented its followers from achieving the level of independent thought and critical consciousness necessary for the exercise of American citizenship. Successive waves of immigration only fortified anti-Catholic sentiment. After the potato famine propelled Irish refugees into the United States in the 1840s, anti-Catholic rhetoric, compounded by longstanding English/Irish enmities, became rampant. By the 1890s, the power of New York City's municipal government—dominated by an Irish-American mafia and popularly known as Tammany Hall—had come to represent the corruption of the Roman Catholic Church generally and, more specifically, its threat to American moral and political institutions. Twain begins his most famous anti-imperialist essay, "To The Person Sitting in Darkness," with a review of Tammany Hall corruption that implies that Irish Catholics were its cause. The upshot of the history of Catholic-Protestant rancor in the United States was that by the late nineteenth century, for many Americans the word *Christian* was not synonymous with the word *Catholic*. Rather, the use of "Christian" during this period carries an implicit opposition to the Church of Rome. Hence McKinley's words lay out a plan of action that sees "civilization" as "Protestant" and "education" as inculcation into a national culture based in Protestant ideas.

The incorporation of "Christian duty" into Americans' conversations about overseas expansion was a logical consequence of these assumptions and a means of transcending the Constitutional issues raised by the struggle over annexation. It was a call that went well beyond the confines of that segment of the community that defined itself strictly within religious terms. Certainly the Protestant evangelical community—whom the Spanish had long forbidden to proselytize in the Philippines—urged annexation on missionary grounds, and major Protestant missionary organizations moved into hitherto forbidden areas of the Pacific as soon as the United States had secured the Philippines. But possibly the loudest proclamations of Christian duty came from the anti-expansionists, who opposed annexation on the grounds that it betrayed the Christian principles on which the nation was founded and would facilitate an influx of non-Christian, nonwhite immigrants to the American political and social terrain. As Matthew Frye Jacobson notes, the anti-imperialist movement contained so many disparate viewpoints that a unified statement of opposition was impossible.[14] What the anti-imperialists did have in common, among themselves and with the expansionists, was the argument from "Christian duty" and a desire to maintain the illusion that the United States was a white Christian nation. The debates, conducted in congressional chambers, in editorials and letters to the editor, in sermons, and in cartoons, show how intensely American conversations about national identity had become fixated on religion and race by the close of the nineteenth century.

Imperialism itself was not a new issue for the United States. The steady removal of Native Americans from lands designated for white settlement was already operating when the Constitution was signed. In 1803 Jefferson bought the Louisiana territory from the French, adding 828,000 square miles to U.S. borders; in 1848 the Treaty of Guadalupe Hidalgo, signed after a bloody war with Mexico and ceding nearly half the Mexican Republic's territory to the United States, added another 525,000 square miles. Throughout the nineteenth century, interest groups called for the annexation of contiguous or nearby states, from Canada to Nicaragua. The Monroe Doctrine, first promulgated in 1823, became a tool for national expansion after midcentury, and by the 1890s European observers increasingly had cause to note its dual function: to rationalize calls for U.S. annexation of other American countries as a means of "protecting" them from predatory European states, and to serve as a warning to those states whenever the United States scented the danger of outside interference in the hemisphere.

The Philippines were another issue, however. Despite American planters' calls for the United States to annex Hawaii, successive administrations had hesitated to extend the country's reach so far from home. Officially, U.S. western expansion ended at the Pacific shore.[15] Beyond that, economics, divorced from active governance, became the driving force. Moreover anti-Chinese sentiment was as strong as anti-Catholic sentiment among the general public. The United States had passed a stringent anti-immigration law aimed specifically at the Chinese in 1882, and subsequent laws refining it were passed in 1888 and 1891.[16] Chinese communities were often subject to violent attacks by whites; Twain pointed out that the police rarely came to the aid of Chinese individuals who were abused by white Americans.[17] Hence one powerful argument launched by anti-expansionists was that annexation of the Philippines and Guam would open the floodgates to immigration from Asia. Thomas Bailey Aldrich's 1895 poem "Unguarded Gates," which spoke of the "featureless features" of the "Malayan" and the "Hoang-Ho," and of "accents of menace, alien to our air," expressed a common sentiment when it invoked "Liberty, white Goddess" and asked, "Is it well to leave the gates unguarded?"[18]

At the same time that they opposed Chinese immigration, however, few Americans disputed the allure of economic ties with China. Throughout the 1890s Americans watched as Europeans divided up China's strategic cities among themselves—a process that would precipitate the Boxer Rebellion of 1899–1901, when the Chinese attempted, unsuccessfully, to retake control of their destiny. But until 1899, the United States was reluctant to assume the financial, administrative, and moral burdens of colonizer. American producers were ever on the lookout for new consumers, however, and the vision of China's teeming millions presented a strong temptation. Manila, capital of the Philippines, had served as the crossroad for Spanish-Chinese trade for three hundred years, and knowledgeable Americans knew that the power that controlled the Philippines would control access to commerce with China. For those engaged in trade, the sudden acquisition of the Philippines suggested that establishing a strong economic base there might be worth the burdens of colonial administration.

Roosevelt and his supporters also wanted to make sure that other European powers did not appropriate the archipelago. They pointed out the islands' appeal for the European Concert, a loose federation of powerful nations (Austria, Prussia, Russia, Great Britain, and France) pledged to act on areas of mutual concern. Several of the Concert's members already had outposts in China, and the United States perceived a danger to the Philippines from the potential interest the Europeans could have in acquiring a coaling station so close to Asia. They also fully understood the benefits of controlling it themselves. Their dream of expanding trans-Pacific trade was not new—during the construction of the transcontinental railroad some of the most animated conversations had envisioned the United States as a transportation artery between Europe and China. If the United States controlled the Philippines they could modernize the old Spanish trade routes, not only selling surplus American goods to Chinese merchants in Manila but also purchasing Chinese goods and shipping them to California, then across the continent via the railroad, and finally on to Europe. Moreover, there was always the danger that the Spanish would simply repossess the Philippines if the United States granted them independence.

The marketplace, then, was the stage on which the debates were initiated. And in the European press, which avidly followed the American debates, that is where they largely stayed. But as their moral justification for invading Cuba suggests, and their disputes over annexing the Philippines confirms, Americans struggled with multiple, and often contradicting, imperatives. Nineteenth-century Americans saw themselves within a fusion of Protestant Christian and Enlightenment identities, a collective self-imaging that left them vulnerable to charges that their actions might betray their destinies. In the popular understanding of American identity, the United States was a means toward a divine end, a country established to fulfill God's plan. But America's destiny could be accomplished only if her citizens continuously enacted the values on which their unique civilization had been founded. In practice this meant that any proposal for a radical change in national trajectory had to be carefully scrutinized to make sure it conformed to American ideals. Complicating this was Americans' sensitivity to racial differences. For white Anglo-Saxons and those identifying with them, the exceptional nature of American civilization was grounded in its religious and racial composition. This group saw itself at the top of hierarchical models of race and culture because they believed that their combined racial and religious histories had enabled them to develop the freest and most powerful civilization in the history of the world.[19] As a consequence, those seeing themselves within the Anglo-Saxon fold were extremely sensitive about the possibility of having their national destiny diverted, which seemed inevitable should there be another influx of radically different races. Well before the Spanish-American war, successive anti-immigration acts, beginning with the Chinese Exclusion Act of 1882, demonstrated Americans' worries about racial "amalgamation." The number of times the omnipresence of African Americans was raised in conjunction with the Philippine debates, and the frequent overlap of Congressional discussions about Native-American and Philippine affairs, are further signs of Americans' uneasiness about racial purity. Happy to expand American markets, at the same time many Americans—especially but not exclusively those who were actually white and Protestant— worried both about diluting the "American race" and compromising its moral principles.

The pervasiveness of racial anxiety in these debates has been extensively commented on. Less noted has been the role of religious rhetoric, which functions as a negotiating device between the three most prominent issues: capitalist desire, racial tension, and loyalty to fundamental principles. With the narrative of Christian-American history as the common foundation, the discourses of Protestant Christian capitalism, Anglo-Saxon Protestant racial superiority, and Protestant/Enlightenment values appear routinely in arguments both for and against annexation of the Philippines. One of the most striking facets of this discourse is its appropriation of Enlightenment ideals for religious ends. The valuation of human progress, of self-government, of individuals' ability to change and grow, and of the interdependence of politics and economics, all key Enlightenment ideas, are presented in these debates as Puritan inventions. According to the myth of American culture that evolved over the nineteenth century, not only did the Puritans invent individualism, consumerism, freedom, and democracy, their Protestant descendents were the only people really capable of demonstrating these values in everyday life. In *America's God: From Jonathan Edwards to Abraham Lincoln*, Mark Noll traces the emergence of "Christian Republicanism" in the antebellum period, noting that by the 1820s republican political ideology, commonsense moral reasoning, and evangelical Protestantism had merged, giving what he labels a "distinctively American shape to Christian theology."[20] Noll is primarily interested in the influence of American culture on the development of evangelical theology, whereas this study investigates the influence of Protestant ideology on the shaping of American identity. Noll's research, however, is germane to this study because in examining the role of religious discourse in the debates over the annexation of the Philippines, we are looking at the fusions Noll traces, focusing on a critical moment of American history.

Teasing out the significance of Protestantism as it overlapped with other economic, racial, and social discourses in the American mind is central to our understanding of U.S. imperial imaging. In carrying what had hitherto been a local identity into the global arena, in assuming that the culture that identity facilitated was intrinsically superior to other cultures and in arguing over the possibility that the process by which the United States came to that culture could be imitated by peoples with vastly different ideas about who they were and how they should live, the United States initiated a long-term debate over foreign policy and, arguably, a lasting mistake in imperial management. Examining the role of Protestant rhetoric in the disputes over the Philippines between 1898 and 1902, then, is a tool to help us understand patterns of U.S. imperialism both historically and in our own time.

It is also a tool for helping us understand other countries' responses to the United States, then and now. The final section of this book moves outside the United States to look at the American colonial experiment through the writings of spokesmen from Britain, Europe, Latin America, and the Philippines. Whereas the British pro-imperialist press actively encouraged the United states to annex the Philippines, and European governments tacitly condoned the act, representatives from Spain's former colonies vigorously opposed it. In the Philippines, Emilio Aguinaldo, President of the Philippine Republic until the Americans captured him, and Apolinario Mabini, architect of the Philippine Constitution, attacked the Americans for having broken their promises and articulated an astute critique of annexation as a betrayal of U.S. Constitutional principles. Latin Americans were equally appalled. In 1891 José Martí, the Cuban nationalist who had spent nearly twenty years in the United States and who was probably the foremost interpreter of Latin America to the Americans, published "Nuestra América," an essay that constructs a pan-Latin American culture in direct opposition to the sterile and aggressive Protestantism of the North. Martí's América is Catholic and spiritual, and its inhabitants are a mixture of indigenous peoples with the descendents of Europeans. Martí died in battle in Cuba in 1895, but two other Latin American writers in particular carried through his legacy: José Enrique Rodó, a Uruguayan; and Rubén Darío, a Nicaraguan. Rodó's essay "Ariel" (1900) calls for a unified Hispanic culture to counter the U.S. threat to Latin American spirituality. Darío's poems and essays indict the United States for dreaming of a "pan-American hegemony" and summon Latin Americans to unite in order to "counterbalance Anglo-Saxon America."[21] Both writers envision Latin America in specifically Roman Catholic terms, and, like Martí, juxtapose Latin spirituality to Anglo-Saxon sterility. Even more clearly than the American Protestants, the Latin Americans saw their battle against the Americans as a continuation of the religious struggles of the Reformation.[22]

Like the Latin Americans, Mark Twain understood the religious basis of the issue. Twain had been reared a Presbyterian, but early in his life he had rebelled against the doctrinally narrow Christianity of his childhood. That did not mean that he became an atheist, however, only that he was sharply critical of the ways that Christian rhetoric was enlisted to justify Christians' aggression. In 1972 Frederick Anderson published a sampling of Twain's protest writings, *Mark Twain: A Pen Warmed-Up in Hell*. The volume revealed a Twain hitherto little known, and the anger the selections reveal suggested that by his last decade, Twain had lost any faith he might have had. Recently, scholars have begun to probe Twain's relationship both to God and to organized religion, revealing a man deeply engaged by religious ideas even while furiously rejecting religious doctrine. Although Thomas Paine's *Age of Reason*, which Twain read while piloting the Mississippi River, began his liberation from the terrifying God of his childhood, he never really lost the sense that a God existed who enjoyed torturing his creations. In *Mark Twain's Religion* (2003), William E. Phipps reminds us that Twain had read through the entire Old and New Testaments before he was twelve.[23] Biblical verses, and the cadences of the King James Bible, came naturally to him. Joe B. Fulton traces these influences in *The Reverend Mark Twain: Theological Burlesque, Form and Content* (2006), arguing that Twain's writing "retains the forms of belief" and that those forms constitute the infrastructure of many of his works (Fulton, 34). Twain also maintained formal ties to religious institutions and personnel: for instance, he enjoyed a long friendship with the Reverend Joseph Twichell, pastor of the Asylum Hill Congregational Church in Hartford, to which Twain and his wife belonged. Twain and Twichell's friendship suggests that Twain continued to be interested in religious points of view, even if only to refute them. In *Mark Twain and the Spiritual Crisis of His Age* (2007), Harold K. Bush, Jr., argues that Twain was deeply spiritual, and that his career should be seen as "profoundly moral and religious" (Bush, 19). However Peter Messent remains convinced that the late Twain was profoundly disillusioned, and that even his ongoing religious debates with Twichell became formulaic, with Twichell affirming human potential and Twain denying it (*Mark Twain and Male Friendship,* 2009, 75).[24]

Clearly, Twain's relationship with God was neither settled nor simple. If he was not an active believer, he nevertheless had a profound desire for belief, and the desire fueled his frustration over what he perceived as gross injustices in the world, whether caused by human beings or by natural forces. Twain's desire for belief also framed his critique of the United States. Like his religious education, his education in American history had taught him that the United States was God's chosen country and that Americans therefore were held to a higher standard than the rest of the world. According to Phipps, Twain's "religion" rested on the conviction that the Declaration of Independence echoed the Book of Genesis in its insistence on the equality of all mankind. As a result, Phipps concludes, Twain "was ever alert to the way in which Americans disregarded either its international or its national implications. He advocated a higher patriotism that gave no favoritism to one's native country" (Phipps, 202–3).

Twain's disgust with the hypocrisy inherent in U.S. claims to Christian benevolence in the Philippines drives "To the Person Sitting in Darkness," the best known of his anti-imperialist writings. Dubbing the American enterprise in the Philippines the "Blessings-of-Civilization Trust," he notes bitterly that although America promises "justice," "Christianity," "law and order," and "liberty," to the peoples it invades, in practice these ideals are strictly reserved for "home consumption." Perhaps because he was himself deeply interested in the differences between "inside" and "outside" (many of his unfinished manuscripts involve characters who fall into microscopic or dream worlds and struggle to understand whether their inside/dream world or their outside/waking world is "real"), Twain clearly perceived the problem with which his compatriots were blindly struggling: in the end, the American story of freedom and civil liberties was a narrative generated by and applicable to only one ethnic and religious entity—an origins myth for white Protestants. Hence the struggle: the decision about what to do about the Philippines exposed the contradictions under which most white Americans lived. On the one hand they ardently espoused the exemplary narrative of American freedoms, and on the other, they fervently believed that those freedoms were generated from the Reformation, formulated by the Puritans, and could be fully enacted only by white Protestants.[25]

These contradictions are at the core of the national narrative that evolved over the course of the nineteenth century, in large part through the agency of American history, literature, rhetoric, and geography texts written for children. The narrative conflates Protestant and Enlightenment values, treating them as a unified entity. For example, over the first half of the nineteenth century American history texts implied that religious freedom, a distinctly Enlightenment idea, was a Puritan invention. Rather than pointing out that the Puritan colonists were at least as intolerant of religious diversity as the oppressors they fled, the story suggested that the Puritans had originated the idea that religious choice should be a fundamental value. As we shall see in chapter 4, the textbooks discussed the Bill of Rights as evidence of Protestant values, posited the United States as God's chosen nation, constructed the course of American history as the manifestation of divine will, and positioned the Founding Fathers as the directors of the national mission. After the Civil War, Northern commentators made Abraham Lincoln an honorary Founding Father. All of the heroes held up as role models were white, and nearly all were male and of British descent. The object was to produce citizens for whom the image of an "American" was a white Protestant descended from Puritan—or at least Anglo-Saxon—stock.

The ubiquity and flexibility of this narrative is striking. Because it compounded religious and secular values, it lent itself to arguments across political, economic, and social divides. No matter which side a partisan took on an issue that touched on American values, the likelihood was that he would refer to some element of this national myth to support his case, despite the fact that various parts of his story might fit uneasily with each other. For instance, many Americans believed the Cubans and Filipinos to be intellectually and morally inferior to whites and therefore unlikely candidates for self-governance. At the same time, they felt obliged to help them because they sympathized with their struggle to free themselves from Spain. Rather than resolve the contradictions inherent in these assumptions, they held them in tandem. Horace Davis, President of the Sperry Flour Company in San Francisco, presents a case in point: in 1904 Davis rejected an invitation from Edward Ordway, the Secretary of the Anti-Imperialist League of New York, to join the Anti-Imperialist League because, Davis explained, although he was opposed to "any further annexation of inferior races," he also believed that it was Americans' duty to see that the Filipinos are "fit for self-government before we thrust it upon them." For Davis, the Filipinos were the equivalent of the "uneducated negroes" of the South; he did not want the Philippines annexed to the United States because "We have too much load of that kind to carry now." Davis opposed citizenship for the Filipinos because he thought them racially unfit to carry out democratic responsibilities. At the same time, he believed the United States had a duty to prepare the Filipinos for statehood, which suggests that training might be able to overcome racial handicaps.[26] He did not see the contradictions inherent in his convictions. Felix Adler, educator and founder of the New York Ethical Culture society, also declined to join the League, noting that although "I am thoroughly anti-imperialist myself," "at the same time I am persuaded that the civilized races have certain duties toward the backward races."[27] For both these men, to be an American meant to bear an obligation to uplift, even if they considered the races they were uplifting inferior to themselves. Neither was certain how far the races could be uplifted, or how long it would take to uplift them. Nor was either certain if the Filipinos' disabilities were constitutional or cultural. Nevertheless they strongly believed that their country had a duty to perform.

The obligation to uplift others was intimately tied to an ongoing cultural effort to define the "American," an effort that existed in the face of the massive population shifts occurring in the United States during the period. As Davis's comments indicate, it also existed in the face of widespread conviction that people of color (and whites who were not Anglo-Saxons) were innately inferior. By the end of the nineteenth century, the story of who Americans were, where they came from, what they stood for, and how they manifested those values, became a prescription for racial, religious, and cultural homogeneity. At the same time, the optimism that animated many nineteenth-century evangelical sects suffused the general culture, suggesting that, with effort and the right training, it might be possible for individuals not born into the community of white Protestants to become enough like them to pass muster. One sign of the narrative's cultural power was the development of "melting pot" theories about immigrant assimilation. The logic of the melting pot implied that an immigrant could become an American by voluntarily shedding all evidence of difference from white Americans who had preceded him. The contradictions were clear—on the one hand, the story insisted that Americans were a particular racial and religious group, and on the other hand it suggested that immigrants of other races and creeds might become Americans by adopting white Protestant culture. Over time, the story of the U.S. special mission became a means of creating a community and specifying who belonged to it. The insiders were those who either were white Protestants or who had fully assimilated to white Protestant culture. The outsiders were everyone in need of uplift, from African and Native Americans to immigrants.

The Mission and the Philippines

The story of America's special mission was the common possession of both annexationists and anti-annexationists in their debates over the Philippines. Two senators in particular demonstrate how it could be used to plead their cause: Indiana's Albert J. Beveridge and South Carolina's Benjamin Tillman, both of whom, like Twain, will make appearances throughout this study. Although they spoke from opposite sides of the debate, both men argue from the same set of assumptions. An expansionist, Beveridge argued for annexation as the next step in a divinely mandated national trajectory. Tillman agreed that the United States had a divine mandate, but as an anti-expansionist and virulent opponent of African American rights, Tillman argued against annexation on the grounds that the national trajectory could only be effected by a white Christian population, which would become impossible if annexation diluted the national bloodstream. Here race is so tightly associated with religion that the two labels often function as a single idea.

Albert Beveridge painted national history as the progressive manifestation of a divine plan. In 1900, well after annexation had been effected, Beveridge, speaking to the Senate, responded to accusations that the forcible conquest of distant lands had betrayed the Founding Fathers' ideals. On the contrary, he maintained,

> [t]he founders of the nation were not provincial. Theirs was the geography of the world. They . . . knew that where our ships should go our flag might follow. They had the logic of progress, and they knew that the Republic they were planting must, in obedience to the laws of our expanding race, necessarily develop into the greater Republic which the world will finally acknowledge as the arbiter, under God, of the destinies of mankind.[28]

Here the driving message is that God has chosen the United States not simply to set an example of progress to other nations but to actively replicate itself around the globe. Moreover the divine mandate is also a racial mandate; references to what Beveridge calls "our expanding race" occur throughout the debates. Compacted into Beveridge's idea of America as Christian is also the idea that it is white. This "race" prides itself not only on its love of freedom and its republican principles, but also on its aggressiveness.

Beveridge's oration not only lays out the basic assumptions of the American story, it also follows a common narrative structure in the period's congressional speeches on annexation issues, one in which historical narrative substitutes for legal exegesis. Mindful of the lack of immediate precedents for what they were doing, U.S. legislators went to great lengths to examine the Philippine question within the light of U.S. history. The bottom line was the question of whether the Constitution sanctioned annexation of overseas territories.[29] But rather than closely reading the Constitution and related legislation, most lawmakers contextualized their constitutional reasoning within the national mythology, justifying expansion as the implementation of God's plan for America. Albert Beveridge was a master of that narrative; perhaps more than any other legislator of the period he knew how to appeal to Americans' sense of themselves as a people blessed in their own liberties and therefore obliged to export their culture to the rest of the world. "And so our fathers wrote into the Constitution these words of growth, of expansion, of empire . . ." he continued,

> unlimited by geography or climate or anything but the vitality and possibilities of the American people: "Congress shall have the power to dispose of and make all needful rules and regulations respecting the territory belonging to the United States."[30]

Rather than focusing on what specifically qualified as "territory belonging to the United States," which would have engaged the constitutional issue, Beveridge circumvents legal questions by engaging the popular narrative. The "divine mission of America," he concludes, is to "lead in the regeneration of the world" . . . in large part because the United States is uniquely qualified "to establish system where chaos reigns." For Beveridge, to be a master organizer was to be the Old Testament God, wresting order out of chaos without overmuch attention to legal details. Rather than seeing the Constitution as a broadly defined description and distribution of governmental duties whose specific applications were subject to interpretation, he sees it as both marching order and blueprint for action.

Beveridge's reading of the U.S. mission saw the United States as God's crack military unit, expressly commissioned to transform the world in its own image. His strategic recourse to the national narrative was calculated to trigger emotional rather than rational voting behaviors. But Beveridge could not have made the impact that he did had not he spoken to auditors who already believed that the United States had a special mission. Orators like Beveridge articulate rather than originate ideas, speaking into a pre-existing understanding of the rhetorical relationship of their words to a national mythology. And although Beveridge may have been one of the myth's most brilliant exploiters, he was by no means the only one. "Providence has given the United States the duty of extending Christian civilization, and we propose to execute it," Minnesota's senator Knute Nelson had announced during the contentious days prior to Senate ratification of the Treaty of Paris a year earlier.[31]

The American story was not the sole possession of the expansionists, however. Anti-annexationists, especially (but not exclusively) those involved in the various Anti-Imperialist Leagues, also called on the narrative to argue *against* annexation. For these Americans, a proper reading of America's Christian mission led to the conclusion that American ideals forbade the forced imposition of American government on other peoples. Like the expansionists, the anti-imperialists assumed that not only had U.S. civilization emerged from a unique coalescence of Protestant and Enlightenment ideas, but that civil liberties had been invented during that historical moment. Also like the expansionists, most believed that ethnic unity, social order, and personal self-control were prerequisites for modern nationhood. Many assumed that modernity was predicated on the principles of Free Trade, and most assumed that only Anglo-Saxons were capable of fully enacting this civilization.[32] Their difference from the expansionists lay in the conclusions they drew from their beliefs. Whereas expansionists spoke glowingly of bringing the benevolence of modern civilization to benighted peoples, a corollary to anti-expansionists' racial creed was the assumption that U.S. civilization could not be exported, especially to countries lacking an Anglo-Saxon majority.

Among anti-imperialist legislators, South Carolina's senator Benjamin Tillman may have most successfully encapsulated the complexity of this view in his address to the Senate on February 7, 1899, the day after the Treaty of Paris was ratified. In the speech, Tillman chided colleagues for first attacking the bill only to then turn around and vote for it. His assumptions about who Americans were and what they should be doing abroad appear in the conclusion of his speech. "We have within our grasp, and possible of attainment, a glory and honor such as has never come to another nation in the history of the world," he summarized: "the honor of having fought a war for the love of liberty and humanity, animated by no greedy, selfish purposes hidden under the declaration." And he continues, echoing the sentiments about national identity, race, religion, and responsibility expressed by his pro-expansionist colleagues:

> We are still an undegenerate people. We have not yet become corrupted. We have in our veins the best blood of the northern races, who now dominate the world. . . . [moreover] we have here a religion whose essence is mercy. We have had an experience in free government, government based on the will of the governed-for . . . and we have been taught by that government what so few people of this world have learned, both the firmness to rule and the power of obedience to that rule.[33]

Like his imperialist colleagues, Tillman sees American identity as Christian. "We are a Christian people," he reminds his auditors, "and our missionaries, or those imbued with the missionary spirit, clamor for the annexation of these islands for the purpose of shedding over them the light of the gospel." But he does not interpret that "spirit" as sanctioning forced conversions. "We are asked to do as Mahomet did with his creed— carry the Christian religion to these people upon the point of a bayonet, as he spread Islamism over western Asia and eastern Europe and northern Africa on his scimitar," he continues, and uses this comparison with Islamic proselytizing as the turning point in his critique:

> There are two forces struggling for mastery here, and the better instincts of every Senator . . . lead him to side with me in the proposition that we do not want to shoot people into a civilized condition if we know how to get around it. The two forces to which I have referred as struggling for mastery are liberty, light, and morality—in a word, Christianity—contending against ignorance, greed, and tyranny, against the empires of Mammon and Belial.[34]

For Tillman, annexation would put U.S. Christianity in the same category as the Mohametans, who had, according to popular Christian culture, only conquered through force, thereby earning the opprobrium of the world. Tillman is not arguing against a Christian reading of U.S. identity; rather, he is reading it *differently*, as forbidding outright imperialism. Tillman questions interpretations, not fundamental texts. When he accuses the missionaries of using Islamic techniques he is not only criticizing them for the assumption that forced conversion is a good idea, but also for the assumption that U.S. identity could be exported.

Tillman was not the only anti-imperialist to suggest that missionaries were the principle group urging annexation on religious grounds. As a result, historians have tended to treat the religious element in the debates as tangential to more pressing issues such as race and commerce, consigning specific religious language to the category of formal markers or assuming that specifically religious agendas were merely political responses to evangelical pressure groups. For instance in *"Benevolent Assimilation": The American Conquest of the Philippines, 1899–1903*, Stuart Creighton Miller explores support for annexation provided by the Protestant religious establishment generally and evangelicals particularly. Quoting the religious press, for whom Admiral Dewey's guns were "'God's own trumpet-tones summoning his people out of their isolation into the broad arena of the world's great life,'" Miller observes that "Almost in unison, religious editors across the nation . . . asked what God intended 'by laying these naked foundlings at our door.'" Miller's reading of the period highlights the pressure that the evangelical community brought to bear on the government: McKinley "had no choice but to take seriously the warning of the Presbyterian *Interior* that 'the churches will stand solidly against abandoning the islands,'" he argues.[35] And he quotes the Reverend Wallace Radcliffe, who proclaimed that

> [i]mperialism is in the air; but it has new definitions and better inventions. It is republicanism "writ large." It is imperialism, not for domination but for civilization; not for absolutism but for self government. American imperialism is enthusiastic, optimistic, and beneficial republicanism. Imperialism expresses itself by expansion. I believe in imperialism because I believe in foreign missions. Our Foreign Mission Board can teach Congress how to deal with remote dependencies. . . . [it can] give the President points on imperial republicanism. The peal of the trumpet rings out over the Pacific. The Church must go where America goes (Miller, 18).

Radcliffe was speaking to readers who supported Christian missions; *The Assembly Herald,* where this article was published, was the official publication of the Presbyterian Church in the United States.[36] In Radcliffe's reading of national mission, militarism and beneficence, republicanism and Christianity, merge in a fervid declaration of religious triumphalism. Here imperialist militarism becomes an agent for wholesale cultural transformations, with the American military paving the way and the missionary establishment giving the government lessons in imperial management.

Radcliffe's speech confirms Miller's claim that the evangelical establishment saw the Spanish-American War, especially the Philippines, as an opportunity to proselytize.[37] One hallmark of late-nineteenth-century U.S. culture was the influence of evangelical Christianity, which was widespread and generally favorably viewed. The social approval the evangelicals enjoyed buttressed missionaries' demands that the government facilitate their work and gave government officials and politicians reason to listen to them. However, I suggest that the religious elements in the debates are neither confined to specifically religious interests nor tangential to discussions of race and economics. In fact, the evangelicals' understanding of the U.S.'s role differed from nonevangelicals' understanding only in its greater emphasis on active spiritual outreach. Even the religious community needed a prior reading of U.S. history through providential history in order to be able to make its claims for a specifically national religious mission abroad, and this, as both Beveridge and Tillman's speeches demonstrate, already existed in the U.S. psyche. Consequently it is a mistake to assume that the religious elements in the debates were minor rhetorical tics, proffered to conciliate the evangelical lobby. Rather, religion, in tandem with race and commerce, was a major factor in Americans' deliberations over their national obligations regarding the Philippines. The idea of the United States as a Christian nation is intricately tied into Americans' understanding of their national history, identity, and mission.[38]

In the narrative of American history as it developed over the nineteenth century, national and Providential histories are one and the same. A good example of the homology between the two appears in a lecture given by the Reverend Newell Dwight Hillis in 1902, well after the United States had decided to annex the Philippines but still during the throes of the Philippine-American War. Delivered as the annual lecture for the American Board of Commissioners for Foreign Missions (one of the largest and most powerful of the missionary organizations), the talk begins by proffering the doctrine that "Christianity is leaven, and leaven, like the infinite God, works, and neither slumbers nor sleeps," a text that Hillis uses to justify U.S. imperialism as one arm of Protestant outreach.[39] In fact the lecture's narrative structure shows how nicely Protestant providential history provides a framework for American history.

Hillis begins with a review of the triumph of ancient Christianity over pagan civilizations. Moving through the centuries, he establishes a rhetorical pattern of mixing faux quotation and geopolitical location that leads inexorably to the Italian Renaissance, when the foundations for both Protestantism and democratic institutions were laid. At that point "the movement took on a new form," he declares.

> "Let the people have liberty and the laws"; the city was Florence, and the speaker was the monk of San Marco. "Let the people have direct access to God"; the land is Germany, and the speaker is Luther. "Let the people control their own church life"; the land is Switzerland, and the speaker is Calvin. "Let the people read the Bible for themselves, and own their own books"; the land is Holland, and the speaker is Erasmus. "Let each man present his own prayer to God"; the city is Paris, and the

speaker is Coligny. "There is only one King who rules by divine right, a sovereign citizen, to whom the monarch is responsible"; the land is England, and the speaker is Cromwell. "Let us have a new country, where we may lay the foundations free from the debris of past centuries"; the land is Massachusetts, and the speakers were our Pilgrim Fathers. And now has come the new era, when the old walls around China and the old cruelties in the islands of the sea have fallen, and the world is becoming one world, and the nations are becoming one people, and the strong tribes are helping the weak ones to make their government safe, and their laws just, their liberties secure. All this is history. All these are facts that cannot be denied, that cannot be minimized; that can only be confessed; verily, the leaven has worked; verily the light could not be hid. Events prove that Christianity has a self-propagating power (Hillis, 7).

"Having reviewed [all this]," Hillis continues, "It remains for us to ask, what is the meaning of Christianity's power to propagate itself and make its own way through the centuries and across the continents?" And he responds, "The answer to this question is not difficult nor far to seek. It makes states strong, it develops institutions for society without, by transforming the individual within" (Hillis, 11–12).

Two elements of this address are particularly relevant to Americans' sense of their national identity and their national responsibilities towards the Philippines. The first concerns Hillis's historical patterning. The penchant for seeing contemporary events in teleological terms characterized both the evangelical and the popular construction of American history, so much so that we could lay Albert Beveridge's speech about America's mission to arbitrate the destinies of mankind at the tail end of the Reverend Hillis's and see it as an elaboration of Hillis's contention that "the leaven has worked"—that is, as demonstration of the presence of divine history in contemporary time. The other important element of the speech is Hillis's conclusion that Christianity's power "makes states strong, it develops institutions for society without, by transforming the individual within." The individual "transformed from within" is the convert, the individual who believes that Protestant-Christian and democratic behaviors are the same thing. For Stuart Creighton Miller, such rhetoric was a way for the religious establishment to negotiate the apparent contradiction between colonialism and benevolence. For that reason, he notes that words such as "freedom" and "liberty" occur frequently in evangelical writings about the U.S. mission in the Philippines. The *Baptists Home*

Missionary Monthly, for instance, defined "freedom" as "soul-liberty"—a way of stating that in substituting Protestantism for Catholicism the United States would bring religious freedom even while maintaining political control over the islands for an indefinite period (Miller, 18).

But whereas Miller posits the influence of the evangelicals on legislators as a one-way street, I suggest that the language of divine mission transcends its particular usage by individuals or particular interest groups. Rather than "influencing" each other, both evangelicals and legislators drew from the same discursive pot. Certainly the evangelical community used the language of Enlightenment ideals in its effort to convince legislators that the United States had a duty to colonize the Philippines. But both expansionist and anti-expansionist legislators readily utilized evangelical language to the same ends. For both groups, the language of "freedom," "liberty," and "rights" was inseparable from religious concepts; the foundation of American liberties, in their view, lay in the narrative of Protestant progress toward an ever-more perfect civilization. "I have sometimes fancied that we might erect here in the capital . . . a column to American Liberty," declared Henry Cabot Lodge in a Senate speech *against* annexation on May 22, 1902.

> . . . I can fancy each generation bringing its inscription, which should recite its own contribution to the great structure. . . . The generation of the Puritan and the Pilgrim and the Huguenot claims the place of honor at the base. "I brought the torch of Freedom across the sea. I cleared the forest. I subdued the savage and the wild beast. I laid in Christian liberty and law the foundations of empire." The next generation says: "What my fathers founded I builded. . . . I declared and won the independence of my country. I placed that declaration on the eternal principles of justice and righteousness which all mankind have read, and on which all mankind will one day stand. I affirmed the dignity of human nature and the right of the people to govern themselves."[40]

Like the Reverend Hillis, Lodge constructs his historical landscape as a voice-added *tableau vivant*, where each figure represents a significant historical moment and steps forward to inform the audience of his or her role. Like both Hillis and Beveridge, Lodge employs careful repetitions, especially of opening subject/verb constructions, to create his rhythms. And with them both, he also speaks into, and out of, the national mythology: to "lay the foundations of empire" in a "liberty and law" that is distinctly

Christian is to claim the inseparability of "Christian" and "liberty," and to justify an American empire as divinely guided.

The Spanish-American War, best remembered by Americans as a showcase for Teddy Roosevelt's antics in Cuba, officially took place between April and August, 1898. The Philippine Insurrection, as the Americans originally called the Philippine-American War, began on February 4, 1899, two days before the Senate was scheduled to vote on the treaty, when Filipino and American soldiers began shooting at each other, an outbreak of violence between armies that had been living in uneasy proximity in and around Manila since the destruction of the Spanish fleet nine months previously. Reports of the incident, which wrongly credited the opening volleys to the Filipinos, reached Washington within twenty-four hours, and may well have been the deciding factor for several senators who had been wavering over whether or not to sign the Treaty. It passed the next day, by a margin of one.

The Filipinos were serious about fighting for their independence; despite superior American arms, the war lasted nearly three years.[41] Emilio Aguinaldo, who had been declared President of the Philippine Republic in January 1899, dissolved the regular Revolutionary Army into a network of guerilla fighters. The United States labeled the freedom fighters insurgents. Aguinaldo himself became a fugitive, pursued by American forces until General Frederick Funston captured him in 1901. Funston achieved his success through trickery; he hired Filipinos loyal to the Americans and directed them to masquerade as revolutionaries who had captured him and his handful of American troops. The Filipinos brought the Americans to Aguinaldo's men, successfully deceiving their revolutionary compatriots, who fed and succored the exhausted party before delivering them to Aguinaldo. When they arrived at the rebels' headquarters, the Americans whipped out their guns, killed several of Aguinaldo's men, and captured their leader.

This scheme was either an act of heroism or of perfidy, depending on one's point of view. For Mark Twain, it was perfidy; he labeled Funston "a satire on the human race,"[42] and in the biting essay "A Defense of General Funston," published in the *North American Review* in May 1902, he castigated Funston's methods, which abused the revolutionaries' humanity and hospitality. According to Twain the Americans and their Filipino "captors" begged food from Aguinaldo's men, then overwhelmed them. For Twain, that was the final act of treachery. "Every detail of Funston's scheme—but one—has been employed in war in the past and stands acquitted of blame by history," he declared bitterly. "By custom of war, it is permissible . . . to persuade . . . a courier to betray his trust; to practice treachery . . . to accept of courteous welcome, and assassinate the welcomers." However, Twain adds, Funston's unforgivable act was to ask for food and then to attack those on whose generosity he had depended: "When a man is exhausted by hunger . . . he has a right to make supplication to his enemy to save his failing life; but if he take so much as one taste of that food—which is holy, by the precept of all ages and all nations—*he is barred from lifting his hand against that enemy for that time*" (Zwick, 127, original emphasis). For Twain, Funston's act was dishonorable, marking both the General and the country he represented as treacherous. Mark Twain did not use the word "holy" lightly; for him Funston acted outside the parameters of civilized wartime behavior, implicating his entire country in the duplicity of his deed.

By 1902, Mark Twain was well launched on a philosophical inquiry into the possibility of moral action for individuals. Despite intensive reading in both philosophy and psychology he could never decide whether humans possessed a perverse moral sense that encouraged them to choose evil over good, or if they were devoid of innate moral controls and were simply products of their training. In "Defense of General Funston" he implies that a combination of training and innate disposition are the cause of Funston's perfidy. Yet even Twain's recourse to behaviorism here betrays his understanding of America's special mission. Twain began writing "A Defense of General Funston" on George Washington's birthday, and the framework for the attack on Funston is a comparison between the general and the Founding Father. "The proper inborn disposition was required to start a Washington; the acceptable influences and circumstances . . . were required to develop . . . him. The same with Funston," Twain concluded (Zwick, 124). Even though he portrays both men as products of their temperaments and their training, Twain finds in Washington a model for patriotic idealism: "Washington was . . . greater than the father of a nation, he was the Father of its Patriotism—patriotism at its loftiest and best; and so powerful was [his] influence . . . that that golden patriotism remained . . . unsullied for a hundred years, lacking one," Twain proclaims. And he predicts that Americans will transcend the current shameful moment and "be what we were before, a real World Power, and the chiefest of them all, by right of the only clean hands in Christendom, the only hands guiltless of the sordid plunder of any helpless people's stolen liberties, hands recleansed in the patriotism of Washington, and once more fit to . . . stand in [the presence of Washington's ghost] unashamed" (Zwick, 123–4).

Here Twain engages the American myth to justify his stance. With the ghost of Washington as the Founding Guide, Americans must return to their original destiny, which is to represent liberty and justice to the rest of the world. In 1902 at least, Twain had not given up on his country, but he did think it had taken a very wrong turn. His anti-imperialist writings are jeremiads to his countrymen, a rhetorical mode rooted in the Protestant tradition and woven into the country's history.[43] A jeremiad accuses the community of having transgressed, then demands that the members repent and resume their mission to follow in the ways of God. The underlying assumption of the jeremiad form is that the community actually has a history of virtue from which it has fallen. In his anti-imperialist writings Mark Twain accused his countrymen of transgression, but held out the possibility of redemption. Despite his attacks, he believed that America's core values lay in what Mark Noll calls a "Christian Republic," where Washington's ghost watched over "the only clean hands in Christendom," and to which it could be possible to return. For Twain as for his compatriots, the national myth articulated a core identity without which the very existence of the United States was inconceivable.

God's Arbiters explores the role that the story of America's special mission played in the debates over annexing the Philippines. The book is divided into three sections. The first section, American Narratives, is given to describing the religious, economic, and racial facets of the national narrative as they appeared in 1899. Chapter one, Citizenship and the Philippines Debates: The Religious Factor, continues the journey begun in this introduction, laying out the rhetorical landscape as it appeared in debates over the Philippines, and showing how Twain, Tillman, Beveridge, and other speakers marshaled their understanding of America's Christian mission as they argued their cases. Chapter two, Citizenship and the Philippine Debates: The Racial Factor, brings American racial dynamics into the picture: first, exploring the ways in which white Americans equated whiteness with Protestantism and the whole with capacity for citizenship, and second, showing how these assumptions affected arguments over whether or not annexation would lead to statehood for the Philippines.

Section two, Creating Citizens, focuses on questions of citizenship. Chapter three, A Connecticut Yankee in the Philippines, reads *A Connecticut Yankee in King Arthur's Court* in tandem with schoolbooks produced by Americans for use in Filipino schools in the first decade of the twentieth century. When Hank Morgan, the protagonist of *A Connecticut Yankee*, found himself transported to sixth-century England, he was convinced that he could turn medieval British Catholic culture into nineteenth-century American culture by introducing soap, scientific education, and multiple Protestant sects. Similarly, the architects of the American educational experiment in the Catholic Philippines stressed cleanliness, order, "rational" religion, and scientific education. In both cases, the reformers' faith in the power of "training" was undermined by their essentialist assumptions about religion and race. Chapter four, The National Christian, first glances backward at the literary formation of American history in textbooks created for American children throughout the nineteenth century. It was in these textbooks, I argue, that the fusion of American and Protestant identities evolved, in tandem with a set of moral prescriptions that dictated appropriate behaviors for American citizens. After the backward glance, I look forward, to the literary environment of the middle class American of the late 1890s and early 1900s, especially the ways that popular writers Charles Sheldon, Mary Fee, Captain Frank Steward, and Ernest Crosby treated questions of race and ethnic difference in their constructions of American citizenship.

Section three, The Eyes of the World, moves beyond U.S. borders to look at the Americans through English, European, Latin American, and Filipino eyes. These final three chapters of the book show how the U.S. annexation of noncontiguous lands was received in England and in Spain's former colonies. Chapter five, "The White Man's Burden," the Philippines, and the Anglo-American Alliance, studies the production and consumption of Rudyard Kipling's pro-annexation poem "The White Man's Burden: An Address to the United States." Here I argue, first, that the poem sprang from ongoing conversations being conducted in pro-imperialist British newspapers, all of which urged the United States to annex the Philippines and get on with the business of empire. Next, I look at how the poem was received within the U.S. narrative of Christian mission. The ambiguity of the poem, I suggest, made it amenable to interpretation from both sides of the annexation debate. Chapter six, "Saxon Eyes and Barbaric Souls": Non-Anglo Responses to the American Annexation of the Philippines, moves beyond both British and American borders, briefly surveying European responses to annexation and then looking at the ways in which Latin Americans constructed their own national identities in opposition to the white Protestant ideal. Here I discuss essays, letters, and poems by three of the great Latin American writers of the turn-into-the-twentieth-century: José Martí, Rubén Darío, and José Enrique Rodó. The final chapter, "Noli Me Tangere," shifts to the Philippines, examining the writings of Filipino nationalists Emilio Aguinaldo and Apolinario Mabini as they engaged American founding documents in their attempt to persuade the Americans that annexation was a profound mistake, both for the Filipinos and for the United States itself.

My hope is that this study, which explores the role of religion in the construction of American identity and the deployment of religious rhetoric in the debates over annexation of the Philippines, will help us understand some of the conversations that we are having in the twenty-first century, especially as those conversations rest on assumptions about religion, race, and what it takes to be an "American."

Section I

American Narratives

Chapter 1

Citizenship and the Philippines Debates

The Religious Factor

In both "The Stupendous Procession" and the last pages of *The Mysterious Stranger*—neither published during his lifetime—Mark Twain renders a dark history of the world through the medium of stage directions for a long parade. "The Stupendous Procession," composed during the opening months of 1901, addresses world imperialism specifically; the sketch opens starkly, without context: "At the appointed hour it moved across the world in the following order." What follows after the colon are all-cap introductions of the major allegorical figures with terse instructions for how each character should be staged. Throughout, Twain changes font type to lend emphasis to his specifications. The first figure to appear is "THE TWENTIETH CENTURY" ("a fair young creature, drunk and disorderly, borne in the arms of Satan . . ."), followed by "CHRISTENDOM" ("a majestic matron, in flowing robes drenched with blood . . ."),[1] followed by other figures calculated to show the new century mired in murder, greed, militarism, and imperialism. ENGLAND, for instance, is represented by "Mr. Chamberlain and Mr. Cecil Rhodes. Followed by *Mutilated Figure[s] in Chains*, labeled 'Transvaal Republic' and . . . 'Orange Free State.' *Ensign*—The Black Flag; in its union, a Gold Brick." (Zwick, 44). The full description of "CHRISTENDOM" includes a description, on the matron's head, of "a golden crown of thorns; impaled on its spines, the bleeding heads of patriots who died for their countries—Boers, Boxers, Filipinos; in

FIGURE 1.1: "William! William! The President's Speech." *Life*, Life Publishing
Company, New York, May 24, 1900. [artist: William Bengough]

one hand a slung-shot [*sic*], in the other a bible, open at the text, 'Do unto
others,' etc. Protruding from pocket, bottle labeled 'we bring you the
Blessings of civilization.' . . . *Supporters*: At the one elbow *Slaughter*, at
the other *Hypocrisy*." "AMERICA" is imaged as "a noble dame in Grecian
costume, crying. Her head bare, her wrists manacled. At her feet her Cap
of Liberty. *Supporters*. On the one hand *Greed*; on the other, *Treason*. Followed by *Mutilated figure in Chains*, labeled 'Filipino Independence,' and
an allegorical Figure of the Administration caressing it with one hand, and
stabbing it in the back with the other" (Zwick, 45–46).

Not surprisingly, the largest proportion of "The Stupendous Procession" is given to the United States. The procession includes a float occupied by Spanish Friars carrying banners advertising the privileges the Americans have allowed the Church to retain in the Philippines, led by a fat friar "wrapped in the Treaty of Paris—labeled 'This is Nuts for Us.'" It also features "THE AMERICAN EAGLE, ashamed, bedraggled, moulting; one foot chained. Placard, hanging from his tail: 'Washington revered me, the great hand of Lincoln caressed me: and now I am become policeman over this carrion!'" (Zwick, 46–47). Later images in the sketch include "THE CONSTITUTION, a giant figure, clothed in a ragged blanket full of holes"; "PATRIOTISM, On a float, two majestic female figures struggling over the Star Spangled Banner; the one is trying to pour a pail of Administration sewage upon it, the other is trying to prevent it"; "THE AMERICAN FLAG, Waving from a Float piled high with property—the whole marked *Boodle*." The sketch ends with the "STATUE OF LIBERTY, enlightening the World. Torch extinguished and reversed. Followed by THE AMERICAN FLAG, furled, and draped with crepe." And finally, the "SHADE OF LINCOLN, towering vast and dim toward the sky, brooding with pained aspect over the far-reaching pageant" (Zwick, 56).

Twain's sketch features nearly every image celebrated in the mythology of America's history and special mission. Like the Reverend Hillis and Henry Cabot Lodge, Twain dramatizes his concept, emphasizing its performative nature. Also like Hillis and Lodge, he builds rhythms from repetitions; here, of the pattern used to introduce each new figure: the title in capital letters, followed by a comma and a description. Most entries then feature the words "followed by," and have place markers titled *Supporters*, *Banners*, and *Floats*. Within this structure, he builds his case for a world consumed by greed and shame, headed by a United States in which the Constitution, the Declaration of Independence, the national bird, the flag, and other major national icons have been dragged into the mire.

But the darkness of this vision does not suggest that Mark Twain rejected the idea that the United States had been founded on the principles of liberty, justice, and Protestant Christianity. On the contrary; the bitterness of his satire points to the fervency of his belief. Twain's satiric writings, especially those produced in his last decade, have often been compared to Jonathan Swift's; the depth of moral awareness they exhibit reflects the bitterness of the disillusioned churchman. If he is to be believed, Twain himself once considered the ministry, but decided that comedy would better fit his sense of mission.[2] When he perceived the United States ready to trade its principles for a seat among the old, corrupt world powers, he used his satiric talents to protest his country's descent into shame. As we see in this dramatic sketch, as well as in those by Hillis and Lodge, the narrative of American liberties provides a rhetorical and ideological repository for imagery about the nature of Christian America, a communal source for figures and tropes that could be employed to argue more than one position.

Throughout the nineteenth century, claims for a Protestant basis to American liberties fed into assumptions about national identity generally and, specifically, into discussions about the religious and racial profile of those most fitted to participate in a democratic republic. A performative element emerges within the narrative of American identity when it was applied to the question of citizenship. A set of behavioral practices such as honesty, self-control, and orderliness, and of economic/social values such as thrift, gradually became synonymous with republicanism, providing defining marks of American identity. Judgments about an individual or group's capacity for citizenship depended on how well they could perform that identity. We see this network of associations throughout the debates about annexation, where virtually all parties, whether they are congressmen, clergymen, concerned citizens, or journalists, recite a list of behavioral practices that they define as uniquely American.

A word about this term, *behavioral practices*. The concept is a tricky one; on the one hand, the qualities I am pointing to designate values as well as behaviors. However, I am referring to the *performance* of values, the outward signs that an individual has internalized his or her culture's values. In *A Nation of Behavers*, Martin E. Marty speaks of the "profound," "integral" linking of religious belief with behavior in the United States, and traces the social history of American religions through the behavioral practices they valorize.[3] I am interested in a similar linkage; nineteenth-century Americans were highly sensitive to the performance element in public interaction, judging each other (as well as foreigners) on the ability to *manifest* "American" values. These values are economic, religious, and racial; they describe—and prescribe—the cognitive universe of the ideal American of the nineteenth century. One of the central contradictions in American life was the dual assumptions that on the one hand, it would be possible to assimilate nonwhite, non-Protestants into the American mainstream and, on the other, that a "real" American was a white Protestant of British descent.

The practice of "American" values may have had its roots in Americans' recognition that to operate successfully, the economic strategies of capitalism had to be enacted by individuals who were self-reliant, reasonably honest, and fond of keeping orderly accounts. Free Trade, the economic philosophy that holds that unrestricted trade (i.e., free of government controls such as tariffs) ultimately benefits its practitioners far more than do protectionist policies, has been a major ideological force in the United States at least since the Revolution. Emerging during the same era as the Reformation in Europe, the principles of Free Trade came to be associated with Protestantism itself and, especially in the United States, with modernity and civil liberties. By the late nineteenth century particularly, the freedom to buy and sell without restrictions—a specifically economic philosophy—had evolved into a cultural valuation of "freedom of choice" that could be applied to anything from religion to fashion.

The roots of the social application of Free Trade ideology go back at least to the seventeenth century: one example is John Milton's *Areopagitica* (1644), an essay arguing for freedom from prior constraint for the press, which operated as a metaphoric extension of the concept of Free Trade in its insistence on a "free and open encounter" of differing ideas within the public sphere. Milton's premise was that truth would always triumph. Evolving, under John Stuart Mill, into the concept of the Free Marketplace of Ideas, Milton's concept shows the application of Free Trade ideology to the cultural and theological realms. In the United States, Free Trade ideology dominated the economic sphere, despite opposition by Alexander Hamilton and his ideological descendents, and the ideology quickly became assimilated to the national narrative and to the providential reading of history in which the narrative was embedded. Even textbooks that endorsed Free Trade framed their economic principles within a religious narrative. For instance, a chapter on International Trade in Aaron Chapin's *First Principles of Political Economy* (1880), a text designed for high school students, argues for free trade on the basic assumptions that "the nations of men are of one blood, and constitute one family," and that "the happiest distribution of those blessings is secured by intercommunication and mutual exchanges, made as free as possible between all nations."[4] Chapin regards these assumptions as "the teaching of Christianity, confirmed by reason and common sense."

> The Golden Rule of Christ is full of wisdom and righteousness in its application to the intercourse of nations. We cherish the fond hope that the day is not distant when the nations will conform their policies to the rule, and "do unto others as they would have others do to them." Then

the theory of protection, with its false ideas of antagonism and selfish isolation, will have no place; but, instead, the brotherhood of nations as well as of individual men will be recognized, and the broad philanthropy which Christianity inculcates, and aims to make universal, will have free scope to work out the world's emancipation from all wrong and evil. In such a state the first principles of sound Political Economy will find their consummate application (Chapin, 211–12).

Free Trade, in other words, is God's will, mediated by the Sermon on the Mount; benevolently deployed, it will overcome all differences and reveal the true brotherhood of humankind. Chapin conflates economic theory and Protestant religion so fully that to argue against Free Trade is tantamount to arguing against the New Testament.

Chapin illustrates the process through which Free Trade ideology became intertwined with Protestant values in the United States. By 1899, Free Trade had become such a powerful cultural discourse that many Americans regarded the freedom to buy and sell unimpeded by government regulation as one of the sacred liberties invented during the Reformation and protected by the American Constitution. Free Trade arguments played a major role in the Philippine debates; despite President McKinley's embrace of protection prior to his election,[5] Free Trade ideology was central during his administration to debates over annexation, both as a specifically economic policy and as a general valorization of freedom from prior restrictions.

But as the recent history of Gilded Age capitalism proved, unrestricted economic landscapes furnished irresistible temptations to untrammeled greed. Free Trade cannot operate successfully for very long unless those engaging in it evince a basic level of social consciousness—the ability and *desire* to think about the social consequences of their acts. Even though Free Trade proponents believed that it was the best means of disseminating goods around the globe, they also believed that not everyone was fit to engage in it. According to this logic, in order for Free Trade to operate without exterior controls, individuals practicing it must develop interior constraints that would prevent them from committing the worst excesses possible under conditions of perfect freedom. These behavioral practices came under the rubrics of honesty, self-control, and orderliness. In time, and especially in regard to issues of Filipino independence, the ability to demonstrate these practices became prerequisites for self-government. In chapter three I will explore the emphasis on these practices in schoolbooks produced by the Americans for Filipino schoolchildren; here I only want to note that when

Americans of the period spoke of "capacity for self-government," they were often assuming the links between the ability to satisfactorily demonstrate honesty, self-control, and orderliness on the one hand, and capitalism and Protestant values on the other. For many, in fact, the associations were so strong that honesty, self-control, and orderliness became identified as Protestant values in themselves.[6]

The associative links between consumer capitalism and Protestant Christianity is evident in a 1910 address on missionary outreach delivered by Samuel Capen, President of The American Board of Commissioners for Foreign Missions, the major missionary organization in the United States. Like the Reverend Hillis, Capen believed that spiritual changes would be reflected outwardly. "When a heathen man becomes a child of God and is changed within he wants his external life and surroundings to correspond," Capen begins. "He wants the Christian dress and the Christian home and the Christian plow and all the other things which distinguish Christian civilization from the . . . life of the heathen. The merchant knows . . . that with the further spread of the Gospel, business will be largely increased."[7]

Here religious outreach, American material culture, and capitalist expansion are one and the same, and annexation becomes a means to disseminate "Christian civilization," an American way of life in which the practice of Christianity means consumerism and civil liberties means unrestricted commerce. In *Reforging the White Republic: Race, Religion, and American Nationalism, 1865–1898*, Edward J. Blum notes that the term *American civilization* "was shorthand for Protestant Christianity, consumer capitalism, and racial hierarchies." Blum quotes Josiah Strong, asking, in *Our Country*, "What is the process of civilization but *the creating of more and higher wants*? Commerce follows the missionary."[8] Additionally, in *Protestant Missionaries in the Philippines, 1898–1916* Kenton J. Clymer notes that the pervasive "theological language" in discussions of the Philippines was designed to communicate the American fusion of religious principles with hard work and thrift. Clymer quotes missionaries who encouraged these practices because, the missionaries claimed, they want "to help men possessed of bodies to create those outward conditions which will best enable them to use their bodies as instruments of the enlarged mind and soul which are the earliest gift of Christian conversion"—that is, to help the Filipinos become earners and spenders.[9] In this vision, Christianity is a tool for creating an ever-expanding and internally regenerating capitalist economy. Even Beveridge, who did not go so far as to believe that Filipinos were really capable of a change of heart, defended the U.S. "mission" as a divinely inspired fostering of trade: "most future wars will be conflicts for commerce. The power that rules the Pacific, therefore, is the power that rules the world," he stated in a 1900 speech to Congress that defended annexation on the basis of expanding markets. In a gesture toward the prevailing association of capitalism, capacity for self-government, and America's Christian mission abroad, Beveridge, despite claiming that "there are not 100 men among [the Filipinos] who comprehend what Anglo-Saxon self-government even means," nevertheless swore that Americans would "not renounce our part in the mission of our race, trustee of God, of the civilization of the world"—ensuring that the Filipinos would serve a long apprenticeship in preparation for self-government under American rule.[10]

One of the reasons expansionists could claim that "capacity for self-government" was a long hard road was because they had themselves been taught to associate capacity for self-government with Protestantism and with particular behavioral practices that, their teachers held, were prerequisites for republican virtue. Throughout the nineteenth century, American educators strove to fashion an American narrative that would teach children the basic values of American citizenship.[11] For the educators, the goal of an American education was not merely to teach basic literacy and numeracy, but to inculcate American ideals—ideals that rested on the assumption that the United States was God's favored nation; that honesty, self-control, orderliness, thrift, and other behavioral practices testified to those ideals; and that it was Americans' task to model those practices to the rest of the world. In *Looking Forward*, published in 1899, Arthur Bird advised that

> Each American must preserve his or her cultural identity by defining him or her self as a production and representative of the United States of America,—bounded on the north by the North Pole; on the South by the Antarctic Region; on the east by the first chapter of the Book of Genesis and on the west by the Day of Judgment . . . The Supreme Ruler of the Universe . . . has marked out the line this nation must follow and our duty must be done. America is destined to become the Light of the World.[12]

For readers of the New Testament, "The Light of the World" is a metaphor for Christ; in John 8:12, Jesus declares that "I am the Light of the World; he who follows Me will not walk in the darkness, but will have the Light of Life." Some readers would also be familiar with the English painter William

Holman Hunt's 1853–54 "The Light of the World," which depicts Jesus, holding a lamp, knocking at a closed door. Bird's fusion of American and Christian identities reflects decades of American efforts to teach citizens that the United States stood for Christ in the battle to redeem mankind.

The goal of producing an American citizenry in this mold is evident in textbooks written for nineteenth-century schoolchildren, especially U.S. histories, geographies, readers, and elocution and oratory texts. In these books, we see the incremental construction of citizens who, despite individual differences, are united by their participation in the values and behaviors that come to mark Protestant/American identity. In the Early Republican period, authors could envision their readers as already white and Protestant, but over the course of the century the texts had to adapt to an ever-growing, and increasingly diverse, student population. The pedagogy of educating Protestant Christians in Enlightenment values became, incrementally, the pedagogy of convincing non-Protestants to participate in an ideology in which Protestant and Enlightenment ideas were fused and which was signaled by specific behavioral practices. By the end of the century, when overtly religious references largely disappear from the textbooks, capacity for U.S. citizenship could be signaled by the practices alone. In *Schooling, the American Imperative, and the Molding of American National Identity* (2003), Douglas McKnight, speaking specifically of the urban Protestant middle class of the late nineteenth century, notes that

> [i]t was no longer necessary . . . to be explicit about what it meant to be an American or how an American should act because it believed it knew. The middle class looked into the mirror and saw America, that symbolic and imaginative legacy of the Puritans. The key . . . was to identify, control, and convey cultural knowledge to the young in a way that hid their political agenda. Morality was embedded in this knowledge and, as such, the child no longer had to struggle with individual morality because school would tell him or her how to act as well as how to think about his or her identity in terms of self, community, and, most importantly, nation. In some ways this was an updated form of . . . predestination. . . . The individual's . . . moral imperative was to reveal whether or not he or she was chosen (McKnight, 87).

Nineteenth-century textbooks—major agents in the creation of a national citizenship—reveal the process through which this "cultural knowledge"—the set of associations through which individuals came to identify as Americans—was communicated. Nineteenth-century American common-school texts work very hard to help children understand the centrality of behavior—that is, specific practices acquired over time and functioning as evidence that the subject responds positively to the culture's key values—to their standing in the community. What an earlier generation would have seen as outer manifestations of spiritual grace, and the later generation would come to see as "character," mid-nineteenth-century educators included under the rubric of moral education. For instance, although pioneer educator Horace Mann believed that religious education should take place in the home, he conversely argued that moral education was the province of the schools.[13] In practice, moral and religious education were identical; few writers of nineteenth-century textbooks imagined the possibility of moral action that was not motivated by Christian values, and the Christianity they imagined was specifically Protestant.[14] McKnight quotes the young Horace Bushnell, who, he suggests, took it for granted "that complete Protestantism is pure Christianity," that the highest form of Protestantism is congregationalism, and that "congregationalism is the author of republicanism." "We are the depositories of that light which is to illuminate the world," McKnight quotes Bushnell as saying (McKnight, 66). When Horace Bushnell and Arthur Bird use the reference in regard to the United States, then, they are associating America's mission to educate its citizens in republican principles with the Christian mission to educate American children according to the precepts of Protestant Christian ideology.

We see the program for communicating the practices and ideology of Christian republicanism most clearly in literacy texts for the very young, where children absorbed the behavioral practices as they learned to spell out the words that described them. Self-control, orderliness, and honesty were central to the project of creating American citizens in the Protestant mold. William Torrey Harris, U.S. Commissioner of Education from 1889 to 1906, called these practices the "mechanical duties" that were a necessary part of childhood education. "In a well disciplined school," he wrote in 1881,

> the pupil is first taught to be regular and punctual; to be cleanly in person; polite to his fellows; obedient to his teachers; he is taught to be silent and industrious, attentive and critical in his mental habits. To sum up all these in one word, he is taught to subordinate his capricious will and inclinations to the reasonable conditions under which he may combine with his fellow men, and share in their labors (McKnight, 114).

In *Outline of a Theory of Practice* (1977), sociologist Pierre Bourdieu contends that human societies inculcate their values through somatic—bodily—practices as well as through moral and intellectual ideologies because, he holds, bodily practices trigger memory, and hence, values.[15] Harris's emphasis on discipline, combined with Bourdieu's overview of the cultural work that education accomplishes, helps us understand why nineteenth-century pedagogical texts tend to stress not only what children should know and believe, but also what they should *do*. For instance, Herman Daggett's *The American Reader: Consisting of Familiar, Instructive, and Entertaining Stories* (1818) introduces itself as "composed of pieces which are moral and instructive, as well as entertaining," and anxiously notes that "It is by no means the wish of the editor, that the Bible should be excluded from our schools. It is proper that children should commence reading the New Testament at least once per day, at the same time that they begin this book."[16] Positing the Bible as a companion text, Daggett's reader is a compilation of stories featuring children and adults—primarily parents—in morally challenging situations.

Daggett's goal throughout is to inculcate a series of values and corresponding practices, including virtue, kindness, charity, obedience, and self-control. Kindness and charity in particular reinforce the social values that they illustrate. The text urges children to act out these values physically, going up to another child to comfort him or her, for instance, or visiting the sick and bringing food specially prepared to appeal to invalids. It also encourages them to practice cleanliness, which by the end of the nineteenth century had become the outward sign of the inner grace that it was to be "American."[17] Together, cleanliness, orderliness, honesty, and self-control became the leitmotifs of "true" American character, and these practices were believed to be rooted in Protestant values. Education historian Carl F. Kaestle notes that "when educators of the nineteenth century spoke of principles common to all religious denominations, they meant all Christian denominations, and when they said Christian, they meant Protestant" (McKnight, 89).

The success of this pedagogical agenda was signaled as early as the 1840s, when Catholic parents and religious figures moved to establish Catholic schools in order to remove their children from the Protestant ideology that, they felt, pervaded the "secular" American schools. But the proliferation of religious-based schools did not erase the cultural drive to associate American identity with Protestant identity and with the ability to manifest "Americanness" by demonstrating orderliness and self-control.

The set of associations became the cornerstone of the ideology of "Americanization" that we see in pedagogic and reformist writings from Noah Webster's *History of the United States* (1832), which insists that "the genuine source of correct republican principles is the BIBLE, particularly the New Testament, or the christian (*sic*) religion,"[18] to Jane Addams' writings about Americanizing immigrants at Hull House. It is the core of the narrative that posits the United States as an exceptional nation and the process through which the idea of normative American citizenship evolved over the nineteenth century.[19]

The multiple readings to which this complex fusion of social, religious, behavioral, and economic values gave rise is evident across the political divides in the debates over annexation of the Philippines at the turn into the twentieth century. Whereas the expansionists read the narrative as justifying their argument that annexation would bring "benevolence" and "civilization" along with expanded opportunities for Free Trade, anti-expansionists read it as forbidding aggressive annexation of noncontiguous territories. Often the debates seemed to depend on whether the speaker and his audience were willing to accept the national narrative as a totality or whether they felt compelled to point out the opposition's misreadings of its various parts. Neither, however, rejected the narrative outright; on the contrary, at some point in their argument even the most fervid opponents of "benevolent annexation" returned to the idea of America's special mission.

The anti-imperialists' response to expansionists' Christian capitalist vision of world mission was to decouple and denounce the association between religious mission and economic gain. They did not, however, jettison the idea of special mission. Their position was summed up most forcefully—and certainly most popularly—in Twain's "To the Person Sitting in Darkness," which skewered expansionism on its own rhetorical grounds. Twain uses the argument for American exceptionalism against what he saw as its wrongful interpretation. In the essay, Twain casts the entire Philippine mission in terms of a vast capitalist card game disguised as Christian outreach. "The Blessings-of-Civilization Trust," he admits, "wisely and cautiously administered, is a Daisy. There is more money in it, more territory, more sovereignty, and other kinds of emolument, than there is in any other game that is played." "But," he continues, "Christendom has been playing it badly of late years. . . . she has been so eager to get every stake that appeared on the green cloth, that the People who Sit in Darkness have noticed it . . . and have begun to show alarm" (Zwick, 28). One of the triggers for Twain's wrath was a recent incident in China, in which Protestant missionaries had responded to the murder of several of their members at the hands of Chinese nationalists by demanding infamously high reparations from innocent Chinese peasants. Critics suggested that the U.S. government control missionary groups trying to force Christianity on Asia. "*Shall we?*" Twain asks, rhetorically. "That is, shall we go on conferring our Civilization upon the peoples that sit in darkness, or shall we give those poor things a rest?"

> Shall we bang right ahead in our old-time, loud, pious way, and commit the new century to the game; or shall we sober up and sit down and think it over first? Would it not be prudent to get our Civilization-tools together, and see how much stock is left on hand in the way of Glass Beads and Theology, and Maxim Guns and Hymn Books, and Trade-Gin and Torches of Progress and Enlightenment (patent adjustable ones, good to fire villages with, upon occasion), and balance the books, and arrive at the profit and loss, so that we may intelligently decide whether to continue the business or sell out the property and start a new Civilization Scheme on the proceeds? (Zwick, 27–28)

Here, Twain attacks the uses of the national narrative, seeing the rhetoric about bringing "the blessings of civilization" to the Filipinos as a cover for capitalist aggression. When he adds hyphens to the phrase he de-naturalizes it, turning it into a compound modifier that demands readers' attention. The grammatical transformation highlights his skepticism and forces readers to pay attention to his critique.

However for Twain, exposing hypocrisy was not the same as rejecting the American narrative. Moreover attack is not this essay's only mode. Mark Twain excelled at sentiment, and he also understood the effectiveness of an abrupt tonal switch from anger to sorrow.[20] As in "Defense of General Funston," at the end of "To the Person Sitting in Darkness" he uses the popular narrative himself, via the symbolism of military uniforms, the flag, and the idea of honor. After satirically recommending that the United States "slip out of [its] Congressional contract with Cuba" (i.e., the Teller Amendment, which prevented the United States from annexing the island), Twain notes that the moment might also be a good time for "some profitable rehabilitating." "We cannot conceal from ourselves," he begins, that, privately, we are a little troubled about our uniform. It is one of our prides; it is acquainted with honor; it is familiar with great deeds and noble; we love it, we revere it; and so this errand it is on makes us uneasy. And our flag—another pride of ours, our chiefest! We have worshipped it so; and when we have seen it in far lands—glimpsing it unexpectedly in that strange sky, waving its welcome and benediction to us—we have caught our breath, and uncovered our heads, and couldn't speak, for a moment, for the thought of what it was to us and the great ideals it stood for. Indeed, we *must* do something about these things; we must not have the flag out there, and the uniform. They are not needed there; we can manage in some other way (Zwick, 38).

In this momentary break in the ongoing attack, Twain strikes a note of mourning, of grief; he touches the sorrow underlying the anti-imperialists' rage. For Twain as for many anti-imperialists, the U.S. narrative about its own special mission is not inherently false; rather, it has been *used* falsely, betraying the people who trust its promises. Suddenly the phrase "people who sit in darkness" points not to the pagan world but to Americans themselves, people who, like Twain, believe that the United States is somehow different from other nations.[21] To sit in darkness is to refuse to recognize that America's actions have destroyed its ideals. Hence the breath-catching moment about the flag, a memento of the homeland's promise for Americans living abroad, as Twain had for many years. Hence too the worry about military uniforms, which Twain uses to represent American identity. A master of parody himself, Twain understood the power of forms, both as shorthand for widely held assumptions and as vehicles for deception. The narrative of American exceptionalism is just such a form, a widely broadcast set of ideals, ritually couched in language that refers to "freedom," "democracy," and "rights," that is capable of soliciting a powerful emotional will to believe. When it is used falsely, as Twain well knew, it becomes itself parodic, creating a gap between the emotional pull that the form evokes and the rational recognition that actual events reveal a far different reality. Individuals experiencing the gap between ideal and real are so discomfited that they are moved to action—whether to expose hypocrisy, as Twain was doing, or to try to repair the damage. "To the Person Sitting in Darkness" is Twain's attempt to expose the gap between Americans' desire to believe that in annexing the Philippines they were bringing civilization, modernity, and Christianity to the Filipinos and the reality that the "civilization" of which they were so proud was predicated on Free Trade, consumer economics, and, frequently, untrammeled greed. Twain's essay, however, did not seek to destroy Americans' belief in their country's special mission. Rather, it sought to bring readers' consciousness to the need to restore national faith.

By 1901, when "To the Person Sitting in Darkness" was first published, the United States had been engaged in the Philippines for over three years, actively fighting Filipino nationalists who refused to acknowledge U.S. sovereignty or the benefits of its civilization. Increasingly, the United States had to make its case for keeping the archipelago and continuing to pour money, American lives, and its international reputation into the war. As Massachusetts senator George F. Hoar would note almost exactly one year later, "We have spent hundreds of millions of treasure; we have sacrificed thousands of American lives; we have slain 100,000 Filipinos; we have given away all the old ideals of the country in the past. The human intellect for us, so far as righteousness and liberty are concerned, has changed masters, and yet it has been no advantage to this country . . . that we went there." Moreover for Hoar, the gains for the Filipinos were also minimal: "Now then, what is the advantage to the Filipinos?" he asks, "You have substituted hate for love; you have substituted despair for hope; you have substituted despotism for a republic."[22]

Senator Hoar spoke for the anti-imperialists when he claimed that not only had the economic justification for the war proven false, but that on a moral level, the betrayal of the narrative of American "righteousness and liberty" was at least as costly as dollars and lives. If expansionists argued on the basis of Christian economics, fusing the missionary and capitalist errands to the Philippines, anti-imperialists tended to argue on the basis of American ideals, to show the world that personal liberties could coexist with Christian identity and sound republican government.[23] Like the expansionists, the anti-imperialists read American history as the invention of Protestant liberties. "Tortures of dearth and war our Fathers bore," protested the poet Frances Bartlett, "To live, and serve their God, in liberty./ We lift His cross upon a far-off shore, /And 'neath its arms slay those who would be free."[24] For Bartlett, American actions in the Philippines betrayed the bases on which the Puritans had founded their civilization. Caroline Pemberton accused the United States of actively fomenting a religious war. In a letter to *City and State* she noted that the United States was arming Philippine Muslims against the Tagals, native Philippine Catholics who had fought the Spanish occupation and were now prepared to fight the Americans. Claiming that the American Board of Missionaries for Foreign Missions—the chief Protestant evangelical organization in the area—would go to any lengths to destroy the power of the Roman Church, Pemberton prophesies the demise of American civilization: "The path laid out for you to walk in has been trod before; it is the highway of nations that walked that way to their death and are now lying in the dust of their own ashes."[25] Here betrayal of principles carries predestined consequences: The United States will join the list of empires, such as Egypt and Rome, who forgot the ideals on which they had been founded and that had given them a moral core. "White wing, white wing, /Lily of the air," sang the poet Katharine Lee Bates, author of "America the Beautiful," "What word dost bring, /On whose errand fare?/Red word, red word, /Snowy plumes abhor. /I, Christ's own bird, /Do the work of war."[26]

For these Americans, Christian morality forbade coercion, and a Christian nation should refrain from forcibly annexing a people whose fight for independence so closely reflected its own. William Jennings Bryan, who like Twain originally supported the war to free Cuba, resigned from the army in order to protest the annexation of the Philippines, claiming that it betrayed the principles on which the United States had rested their right to intervene in other country's affairs. An evangelical Christian, Bryan interpreted America's mission as a mandate to respect other nations' rights.[27] Anti-imperialists were also distinctly uncomfortable with the idea that their country could justify forced annexation as a benevolent form of Christian capitalism. "So, fellers, own up straight an' trew," concluded Aella Greene in her poem "Them Fillerpeans," "Thet ackshuns pruve you're greedy/An' don't preten' your objec' is/Befriendin' uv ther needy, /Nor tell erbauout the isluns whare/Your prairs an' teers air given/ Fer ederkatin' ignorance/An' fittin' souls fer heaven!"[28] Like the satirical columnist Mr. Dooley, Greene employs a dialect speaker as a truth-teller, suggesting that even characters on the margins of respectable society recognized the hypocrisy of justifying conquest as religious outreach.

Not only are both expansionist and anti-expansionist arguments laced with religious references, religious forms themselves, especially prayers and hymns, became public interventions into the debates, especially among those opposing annexation. The Reverend Herbert S. Bigelow prayed that God "grant us a Christian citizenship. . . . May we have too much faith in the sovereignty of Thy laws to fancy that we may lay the foundations of civilization upon the ruins of popular liberty."[29] For Bigelow, the word *Christian* designated the most moral form of American citizenship because it was the only way that American ideals could be fully realized. In praying for a Christian citizenship, he was trying to use a powerful communal tool to leverage his countrymen's return from hypocrisy to their rightful and righteous position as exemplars to the world.

Because anti-imperialists saw expansionists' alloy of Christian and commercial interests as rank hypocrisy, they attacked expansionists who claimed to be motivated by religious principles, accusing them of betraying fundamental American principles. Inverting the usual moral superiority of clergymen to capitalists, banker Gamaliel Bradford, in an address to an 1898 anti-imperialist meeting at Boston's Faneuil Hall, berated "the *clergy* of this country," who, he held, "have shown of late a painfully defective sense of proportion." Bradford, himself a descendent of one of the first families of Puritan New England, deploys the American narrative as a counter to the pro-expansionist clergy:

> In the name of the Pilgrims who planted at Plymouth the seeds of civil and religious liberty; in the name of Washington, who, after leading us through the war of Independence and seeing the Constitution launched in full glory, left us that noble legacy of warning, which has never had a deeper meaning than today; in the name of the martyred Lincoln, who sealed with his blood the work he had done; in the name of humanity, whose fate is bound up with our institutions, I appeal to the people of Massachusetts to protest against this rush of reckless and unbridled ambition (Foner & Winchester, vol. I, 277, emphasis added).

Here the repetition of "in the name of" evokes the pantheon of American heroes whose acts, and lives, had created the institutions that enshrined American values. Establishing American civilization as Protestant through evoking the Pilgrims, Bradford assimilates non-Puritans like Washington and Lincoln into the mythology. Synthesizing Providential history with Enlightenment ideas, he claims that U.S. history proved that the anti-imperialists were following in the true American grain. The Reverend Charles G. Ames, speaking to the same Faneuil Hall assembly, added that "[p]oor Christian as I am, it grieves and shames me to see a generation instructed by the Prince of Peace . . . shouting hosannas to the great god Jingo" (Foner & Winchester, vol. I, 280). Summing up the anti-expansionist clerical view at another meeting, the Right Reverend Henry C. Potter, one of the nation's most prominent Episcopal leaders, argued that "the Church of God is called upon, in the pulpit and by every agency at her command, to speak the words of truth and soberness, and to reason of righteousness, temperance and a judgment to come. . . . The things that this community and this nation . . . need are . . . a dawning consciousness of what, in individual and in national life, are a people's indispensable moral foundations, those great spiritual forces on which alone men or nations are built" (Foner & Winchester, vol. I, 259). Throughout these speeches, the anti-imperialist narrative of American identity rests on the assumption of Protestant Christian values, perhaps articulated most succinctly by Indiana senator Henry U. Johnson: "We are a Christian nation. We should not engage in a war of absolute extermination."[30]

Like Mark Twain, many anti-imperialists turned to satire and parody to illustrate their frustration with what they viewed as the expansionists' distortions of American Christian identity. Numerous parodies used familiar elements of the prayer form to expose the expansionists' unholy designs. Mark Twain's "The War Prayer"—which does not reference any specific war—may be the most famous of these satires, but in 1900 Charles Spahr also offered a "prayer," specifically dealing with the Philippines issue. "Oh Thou," the invocation begins, "who does exalt the mighty and put down those of low degree, crush, we beseech thee, the struggles of the Filipinos for independence. Force them to recognize that, although they are willing to die for freedom, they are not fit to live in freedom. May they and all men forget the declaration of independence. . . ." The prayer concludes by requesting that "All this we ask in the name of Him who said, 'Inasmuch as ye have done it unto one of the least of these my brethren, ye have done it unto me'" (Foner & Winchester, vol. I, 269–70).

Hymns, too, provided formal bases for parody. Julia Ward Howe's "Battle Hymn of the Republic," written to encourage Union troops during the Civil War, had become by 1899 a national hymn celebrating the country's divine mission to export freedom. Its concluding stanza—"In the beauty of the lilies/Christ was born across the sea . . . As he died to make men holy/Let us die to make men free"—articulated the national mission in explicitly Christian terms. Thirty years later, universal familiarity with the hymn's rhythms, melody, and sentiments made it vulnerable to parody. Twain's contribution attacked Christian economics, concluding that "In a sordid slime harmonious, Greed was born in yonder ditch, /With a longing in his bosom—and for other's goods an itch. /As Christ died to make men holy, let men die to make us rich—/ Our god is marching on" (Zwick, 41). William Lloyd Garrison, Jr. (son of the famous abolitionist), focused on religion and race, beginning: "The Anglo-Saxon Christians, with Gatling gun and sword, /In serried ranks are pushing on the gospel of the Lord"[31] (Foner, vol. II, 81). In "Our New National Hymn," William G. Eggleston trumpets the fact that "We are marching on to glory with the Bible in our hands, /We are carrying the gospel to the lost in foreign lands . . . We are robbing Christian churches with our missionary zeal, /And we carry Christ's own message in our shells and bloody steel" (Foner, vol. II, 96). Employing a different hymnal model but echoing the attack on Christian hypocrisy, Matthew Dix called on God in his "Imperialist Hymn": "Lord, from far-western lands we come/to save these heathen for Thine own. /We bring them bayonets and rum, /We bring them death and woe and moan / Sweet fruits that Liberty has grown" (Foner, vol. II, 115).

These parodies, only a handful of the many printed in venues ranging from small-town newspapers to major publishing houses, show perhaps more acutely than any other printed forms the tensions inherent in the issue of annexation for most Americans. Because, in their capacities as Americans, they identified with a complex that blended Christianity with Enlightenment values, they had difficulty making arguments about American ideals without recourse to language or images that reflected that fusion. Even labor leader Samuel Gompers, an immigrant and a Jew, turned to the rhetoric of Christian identity. Speaking to the Chicago Peace Jubilee in 1898, Gompers ended a passionate appeal to U.S. ideals by proclaiming that

> [t]he good sense, the conscience, the love of liberty and of justice and right of America's . . . citizens . . . will soon proclaim that this Republic of ours shall be true to its history, true to its declarations that 'governments derive their just powers from the consent of the governed,' true to its mission to spread the gospel and set the example of a free people governing themselves truly, safely, humanely, faithfully, with no purpose of conquest over other lands or other peoples, except as we shall conquer and shine . . . by our sense of justice, . . . industry . . . prudence . . . civilization . . . honesty and . . . humanity (Foner & Winchester, vol. I, 207–8).

Syntactically, the word "gospel" here refers to the gospel of "a free people governing themselves." Yet the resonance of the word "gospel" in Christian culture, together with its linkage to "set[ting] the example"—a latter day reference to the City on the Hill—and "conquering . . . by our sense of justice [and] civilization," exhibits the belief, so deeply rooted linguistically as to evoke a string of other associations, that American identity is grounded in Christian concepts. That Gompers should employ such rhetoric gives evidence of the power of the narrative; there are few ways to tell an American story without on some level employing the language of divine mission.

For those who believed that as a Christian nation, the United States should not subjugate other countries, the perversion of their cherished ideals was intensely painful. Perhaps more than any other form of protest, that pain is inherent in the parodies, which, because they summon familiar forms—forms that signal emotional allegiance to a set of ideals—create in the reader or auditor the contradictions the writers themselves are experiencing. Familiarity with form evokes a sense of shared belief; it is a way to make individuals think beyond their own parameters. Parodies violently undermine that agenda: they ask individuals to rethink the assumptions underlying group consensus. In the world created by parody, both parodist and reader are bound by a shared sense of betrayal: on the formal level, that the lyrics do not carry out the premises promised by the rhythmic patterns; on the ideological level, that the call to action the form embodies is violently contradicted by the new wording. The result is to force readers into a state of emotional contradiction, one that they will attempt to resolve. Hence parodies are calls to action: they ask readers to reinstate the comfort of the status quo. In this case, they ask believers to resolve the contradiction inherent in using Christianity as a cover for imperial designs. During the 1902 debates Tennessee senator Edward W. Carmack passionately and satirically attempted to unmask these designs on the Senate floor.

> There is one other little pretense to which I wish to refer. It is one that is intended to appeal to the religious people of the country, and that is that we are going there for missionary purposes. We are killing these people over there for the salvation of their souls. We are extending our Christian civilization in the Philippines over the dead bodies of the Filipinos. We are building up the Church of God out of human bones, cemented together with human blood. It is a pious, a holy, a religious war. Our very guns are supposed to be wadded with texts of Scripture; our rifle bullets sing psalms as they whistle through the air; our cannon balls are missionaries, bearing glad tidings of peace on earth and good will toward men.

"Mr. President," he concluded, "if the Church of God is to be established in the Philippines, it will not be by an Administration whose hands are red with innocent blood. It will be by some Administration that is to come after, bearing in its hands the gift of liberty and the blessings of peace."[32]

Carmack's speech illustrates the intensity of the dilemma many Americans were facing. Believing that they had a moral duty to help other peoples achieve a way of life similar to their own, they were also reluctant to see that civilization forcibly imposed. As the parodies and satires show, they were keenly aware of the irony of a nation that celebrated freedom only to wrest it from revolutionaries who were demanding the same liberties that Americans had demanded in 1776.

But there was another factor that helped Americans come to terms with their country's imperialist ventures, and that was their attitudes toward racial difference. In Americans' eyes, Filipinos did not qualify as "white," and this fact shifted the balance of the equation, recasting the relation between "training" (one of Mark Twain's favorite words) and capacity for self-government. At bottom, white Americans doubted that non-whites were capable of ruling themselves, and that made forcible imposition of "benevolent" U.S. rule far more palatable. In the end, these Americans told themselves, they were doing the Filipinos a great favor, because a U.S. administration in the archipelago would protect the Filipinos from the consequences of their hereditary incapacity for self-governance.

Chapter 2

Citizenship and the Philippines Debates

The Racial Factor

Race loomed large in the Philippines debates. For some Americans, the questions were social: would the Filipinos seek to marry into existing American racial groups, thus further diluting racial purity? Would they team up with the other "alien races" to outnumber white Americans, or, through interbreeding, create a "mongrel" race that would drag down the entire population? For other Americans, the questions were purely economic: Would the Filipinos constitute a new set of consumers for goods produced in the United States, as the expansionists envisioned? Or would they constitute competition as producers of cheap goods for the American market? One of the most publicized points of the debates concerned citizenship, long a troubled issue in the United States. Black males had been granted the franchise through the Fifteenth Amendment, ratified in 1870, though many whites believed them incapable of exercising it responsibly. American-born children of Chinese immigrants had been granted citizenship in 1896, but the state of California refused to allow those born in China to vote until 1926. Native American males were still excluded from the franchise, as were all women. Therefore one of the most vexing questions about Philippine annexation concerned the political status of the Filipinos. If the United States annexed, would the Filipinos become American citizens? Would they be able to vote? Would they have unrestricted access to the continental United States? And if the answer was

FIGURE 2.1: "Uncle Sam: 'How Can I Teach This Self-Government?'" *Denver Evening Post, also published in The American Monthly Review of Reviews*, vol. 19, no. 4, April 1899, p. 417. [artist: George Washington Steele]

"yes," could they actually carry out the responsibilities of American citizenship?

As many commentators have noted, the racial issue skewed the religious and behaviorist arguments.[1] Because racial polemics are essentialist, not behaviorist, factoring race into the debates over the Philippines disrupted the easy coupling of Christian mission with the belief that acquisition of self-control, orderliness, and honesty were viable avenues to citizenship. To believe that the civilizing mission would work implied that the civilization the expansionists sought to export was in fact exportable; that in learning to act *like* Americans, the Filipinos would *become* Americans. Both economic and evangelical arguments for annexation were predicated on the belief that individuals could change. For benevolent expansionists, the power of America's Christian mission abroad was that it would bring the Filipinos into the modern world and give them the economic tools to participate in it. During a 1902 Senate session over Filipino resistance to American rule, Maryland senator George Louis Wellington reminded his auditors how fiercely Mexicans had resisted American culture when they were forcibly incorporated into the United States after the 1848 Treaty of Guadalupe Hidalgo. By the turn into the new century, however, they had assimilated so far as to qualify New Mexico for statehood. From this precedent, Wellington concluded that "Liberty and participation in free government transform the savage into a patriot. They transform him from an anarchist into a good citizen. They make all people love the country which bestows upon them such blessings. The United States will redeem the Philippines, and in redeeming them will add vastly to the power, the growth, and prosperity of the whole country."[2] The "changes within" that the Reverend Hillis affirmed on the spiritual level appear here in the forecast that a redeemed Philippines will experience political and economic transformation. The evangelical strain in the pro-imperialist rhetoric facilitated an affirmation of Filipino capacity for, in American eyes, constructive change.

Senator John T. Morgan made a similar prediction when he forecast the future in *The North American Review* in June 1898, before the debates had begun in earnest. "The example of Hawaii," he remarked, "gives great encouragement to the philanthropist and the Christian who may look hopefully to the future of [the Filipinos]. When they are brought into living contact with the beneficent influences that have redeemed them from servile bondage . . . and have elevated them to the possibilities of a true and enlightened civilization, they will accept their new situation cheerfully."[3] Morgan suggests that U.S. tutelage will persuade the Filipinos to develop the values of U.S. citizens. Here "redemption" and "beneficence" (key religious terms) couple with "living contact" (close examples of American values in operation) to enable the Filipinos to recognize that their prior condition had been only "servile bondage." In Morgan's view, this association would lead to the "true and enlightened" pleasures of modernity, and eventually to the Filipinos' own ability to govern themselves.

But the issue, even for Morgan, did not remain that simple. As Matthew Frye Jacobson points out, throughout the nineteenth century, Americans had been taught to rank races, and people of African descent were inevitably placed on the bottom (Jacobson, 139). As a senator from a former slave state, Morgan was always conscious of racial tensions, and under pressure to resolve the phenomenon that whites were increasingly framing as "the Negro problem." In his view, racially inferior peoples had been granted citizenship, thus legally elevating them to equal status with whites. Morgan's solution was to get rid of the African Americans: two years after his cheerful prediction of Filipino "redemption" he proposed to export a sizeable portion of the U.S. black population to the Philippines. Black southern farmers in particular, he thought, could bring American agricultural techniques to the Filipinos. And African Americans would be natural mediators between the rebellious Filipinos and the American government. According to Morgan, the Filipinos accepted black Americans more readily than white, and therefore blacks could help Filipinos realize the beneficence of American rule. Not incidentally, the plan would also relieve the South of some of the "burden" of its black population, especially army veterans who (as they would increasingly do over the next fifty years) had returned to civilian life in the South only to rebel against the limitations imposed by systemic segregation.

However, according to R. B. Lemus, writing in *The Colored American Magazine* early in 1903, not even Morgan's southern colleagues supported him. Senator Benjamin Tillman noted the "enormity" of the expense of transporting and settling the African American population 7,000 miles. Morgan's Alabama colleague, Civil War veteran Senator Edmund Pettus, seconded Tillman on the cost. Acknowledging African Americans' new legal status, he also questioned the project's legality. Wholesale exportation of American citizens was "against the law," he noted. "We have no right to move citizens out of the country without their consent."[4]

The conversation among Morgan, Tillman, and Pettus illustrates the racial problem in the United States as it was conceived among some of the leading members of the white population and shows how it impacted the issue of the Philippines. Morgan's idea that transplanting African Americans to the archipelago would simultaneously "purify" the South by removing its "alien race," and facilitate the U.S. mission in the Philippines by deploying black Americans to serve as role models for Filipinos, contained its own contradictions: the race that was considered inassimilable at home could not, logically, become a tool for assimilation abroad. Elihu Root, Secretary of War, forwarded Morgan's proposal to Brigadier General George W. Davis, Commander of the Department of Mindanao. Davis's lengthy response acknowledged Morgan's motives and assumptions and carefully delineated what he saw as the strengths and weaknesses of "negroes" generally. He concluded that it was unlikely that African Americans could be induced to settle as farmers in the Philippines, where conditions were even more difficult than they were in the rural south.[5] In *The Colored American Magazine,* R. B. Lemus suggested that if the United States wanted to encourage Filipino loyalties, it might well do better to allocate twenty-acre farms to Filipinos rather than to Americans, whether black or white (CAM, 314).

Morgan's proposal signaled another issue that played into the debates: white Americans' discomfort with mixed-race individuals. The CAM article noted that Mississippi senator Anselm J. McLaurin favored the colonization scheme as long as it deported only mulattoes, keeping "our genuine black Negroes here." "We never had any trouble with the Negroes until the inception of the mulatto breed," McLaurin declared. "Our black Negroes are all right" (CAM, 318). Lemus, author of the article, tartly commented that McLaurin's discomfort with mulattoes was "due to the fact that they are his brothers and sisters" (CAM, 318). As Lemus discerned, for whites, the problem with mulattoes was that their very existence made visible the clandestine sexual relationships that had existed across the color line since the beginnings of slavery. Mulattoes also made too many claims to equality with their white relatives. For whites, the "American family" not only had distinct hierarchies, but only the white layers were supposed to be visible.

Lemus's article illustrates the role played by existing American racial issues in the debates over annexing the Philippines. The combination of ongoing arguments about human origins (Biblical/Darwinian) and descent (which group was created/evolved first, and which one had evolved/ degenerated from the original), with the palpable evidence that whites and blacks had been interbreeding for centuries, created an environment in which determination of racial status became a point of anxiety on both sides of the color line. Mixed-race characters appear in many of the literary works written during the period. Pauline Hopkins' lost-race novel *Of One Blood. Or, The Hidden Self*, serialized in *The Colored American Magazine* between November of 1902 and November of 1903, was one of many to feature a mixed-race protagonist in quest of his origins. One of the themes of Sutton Griggs's *Imperium in Imperio* (1899) concerns the importance of black racial purity. Other novels, such as George Washington Cable's *The Grandissimes* (1880), featured half-siblings relegated to opposite sides of the line. Mysterious characters of undetermined race haunt the literature of the period: in Kate Chopin's short story "Désirée's Baby" a young woman, an orphan, drowns herself when her baby turns out to be black; after her death, her husband discovers that the African blood had been a contribution from his own mother. Charles Chesnutt's *House Behind the Cedars* (1900) explores the split imperatives of mulatto siblings who can pass for white but must forsake their former friends and family in order to do so. And Mark Twain's *Pudd'nhead Wilson* (1894) not only features mixed-race characters but suggests that only science (in this case, fingerprints) can determine who—and what—an individual "really" is.

Clearly, Americans, both black and white, were uncomfortable with the idea that the American "family" was already mixed-race. Before emancipation, the social significance of color gradations was obscured by laws that designated anyone with African progenitors as black and therefore subject to enslavement. After emancipation, it became much more difficult to determine where on the social ladder the different hues belonged. Many whites, as Twain's ready description of one of the characters in *Pudd'nhead Wilson* as "one-sixteenth" black suggests, had already classified the genetic mixtures according to the proportion of black (never white) blood. Some commentators—the black lawyer/writer Charles Chesnutt was one of them—wanted to classify the lightest segment of the black population as a third race. Die-hard segregationists such as Benjamin Tillman vowed never to admit any nonwhite people into the body politic; others, more friendly, nevertheless were challenged by the prospect of assimilating the idea of blackness—even when it was indistinguishable from whiteness—into their understanding of what constituted "an American." "The shadow of the Ethiopian," as George Washington Cable noted in *The Grandissimes*, fell over many conversations ongoing in the United States at the turn into the twentieth century.

With racial fears running high among both whites and blacks—over racial and national identification, over family identification, over who could be classified as black or white and what those classifications would mean in the coming century—the argument that it would be possible to transform Filipinos into proto-Americans through a benevolent and responsible administration became increasingly untenable. The contradictions in white Americans' attitudes toward the outcome of annexation point to fundamental contradictions between Americans' professed belief in the possibility of transformation and their racial essentialism. They were uncomfortable with the idea of racial mixing because they understood race to be a fixed category, with specific character traits inherent to each racial group; consequently racial mixing—referred to as "amalgamation"—produced unpredictable offspring. Moreover they were confounded by the idea that Filipinos, themselves racially mixed, might become citizens of the United States. Rapid demographic changes within the United States had encouraged many whites to accept the conclusions of "racial science" that racial differences spelled distinct differences in mental and moral capability. Members of both the expansionist and anti-expansionist camps generally shared the assumption that irreconcilable differences existed between races that prevented nonwhites from achieving the level of moral and cognitive intelligence that made for responsible citizenship. The fixation on racial difference was the most obvious contradiction in expansionists' public stance. At the same time that they predicted that the American presence would redeem the Philippines from the feudal state in which Spain had kept them, expansionists also doubted that Filipinos could—or should—become American citizens.

The expansionists were not alone in their racial fears. Whereas expansionists such as Beveridge thought of the exportation of American culture as a one-way street, anti-imperialists such as Tillman feared an influx of Filipinos to the States, seeing the immigration implications of imperial rule against the backdrop of American racial anxieties. Three issues played into the anti-annexationists' concerns. The first, as we have seen, was the presence throughout the United States of African Americans who, no longer slaves and increasingly on the move, were widely perceived by whites as a dangerous, inassimilable subculture and a threat to racial purity. The second was the constant influx of new immigrant groups, the most prominent in the period being Eastern European Jews, Italians, and Chinese and Japanese. The final issue was the ongoing presence of Native Americans, subjects of the U.S.'s first, and arguably most brutal, expansionist move and still a major issue in legislative and judicial agendas of the 1890s. The threat that immigrants and African Americans posed to those who—without irony—saw themselves as "native" Americans is evidenced by the record number of lynchings, the rise of the KKK, the burnings of homes, stores, and neighborhoods, the growth of ethnic enclaves or "ghettos," the passage of legislation restricting immigration, and the increasing segregation of all facets of American life. One reason for widespread fascination with technologies (like fingerprinting or X-rays) or new sciences (like psychology) that claimed to uncover "hidden" information was that they seemed to make definitive racial identification possible. Among those seeking to guard the whiteness of America, the question of citizenship also loomed large: naturalization processes, voting tests, and identification papers all became ways to restrict access to active, efficacious citizenship. Tammany Hall, the visible emblem of the success of an earlier immigrant wave, became a code term for the corruption consequent on allowing non–Anglo-Saxons—specifically, Irish Catholics—to vote.

The state of perceived cultural crisis is the backdrop against which the arguments over the Philippines were staged. Because "capacity for citizenship" had been a contended category within the U.S. domestic arena ever since the Revolution, the potential political status of the Filipino became a focal issue (Jacobsen, 181). Legislators on both sides questioned the degree to which, as U.S. subjects, Filipinos would have the rights of citizenship. For legislators such as Tillman, who openly voiced his conviction that the country's African American population would never be prepared to exercise the full responsibilities of citizenship, the problems posed by the potential assimilation of seven million Filipinos (often inflated to ten million in political rhetoric) were paramount in his stance against annexation. In the midst of reading stanzas from Kipling's "The White Man's Burden" (itself an open intervention into the annexation debate) into the *Congressional Record,* Tillman noted that he wished

to call attention to a fact which may have escaped the attention of Senators thus far, that with five exceptions every man in this Chamber who has had to do with the colored race in this country voted against the ratification of the treaty. It was not because we are Democrats, but because we understand . . . what it is to have two races side by side that can not mix or mingle without . . . injury to both and the ultimate destruction of the civilization of the higher. We of the South have borne this white man's burden of a colored race in our midst since their emancipation and before. It was a burden upon our manhood and our ideas of liberty before they were emancipated. It is still a burden, although they have been granted the franchise. It clings to us like the shirt of Nessus, and we are not responsible, because we inherited it, and your fathers as well as ours are responsible for the presence amongst us of that people. Why do we as a people want to incorporate into our citizenship ten millions more of different or of differing races, three or four of them? [6]

In this speech, Tillman articulates Anglo-Saxons' fear that they would be outnumbered by other races, with a consequent loss of power. Seeing African Americans as "that people," an alien entity, despite their three hundred years of participation in the American experiment, he reminds his colleagues that American civilization as generally conceived would be destroyed by yet another influx of radically different peoples. In this speech Tillman fuses words deployed in the argument for expansion-as-benevolence, such as "civilization" and "liberty," to make it clear that these are white men's prerogatives. To this he adds the other threats to a unified populace: not only does the United States already have its own nonwhite populations with whom the dominant race cannot "mix or mingle," annexation would add three or four more inassimilable races. "We treat these people [Filipinos] as though they were a homogeneous people, like those of Cuba or Porto Rico," noted Mississippi senator Hernando de Soto Money in his recommendation that the treaty not be ratified, "when as a matter of fact there are four hostile races, totally different, speaking different dialects, perfectly dissociated in every respect."[7]

Tillman and Money both see the Filipinos as a threat to Americans' sense of themselves as a racially homogeneous and ideologically unified country.[8] We see this threat articulated as the indeterminacy of racial mixing in novels like *Puddn'head Wilson* or Chesnutt's *House Behind the Cedars*, as the possibility of subversive black political consolidation in novels like Griggs's *Imperium in Imperio*, and as the terror of black social and sexual aggression in openly racist texts such as Thomas Dixon's *The Leopard's Spots*—all works focusing on black/white tensions. But the same anxiety, articulated as an extreme case of cultural and political xenophobia, is evident in the Congressional debates. Even Americans willing to see the Filipinos as freedom fighters in the American mold could not also conceive of them as American citizens. So for Tillman, even though the Filipinos "are to-day patriots striving for what we fought for in our struggle with Great Britain in the last century," they are nevertheless a collection of peoples antithetical to the American ideal. That ideal is a compound of race, religion, and political values, the unique combination of which yields, for Tillman, a unified, undifferentiated whole, characterized by "a religion whose essence is mercy," a religion of "liberty, light, and morality."[9] Despite their similarity to Americans in their quest for independence and self-rule, for Tillman the Filipinos would never qualify as U.S. citizens because neither their race nor their religion fit this paradigm.

The emphasis on unity, or "homogeneity" as some senators phrased it, became a leitmotif of this conversation. A variation on the theme of racial purity, the call for homogeneity also was another locus for arguments over whether or not behavioral practices could be the outward manifestation of internal reformation. The national mythology envisioned the United States as an Anglo-Saxon Protestant entity undiluted in "blood" or values, a narrative constructed in the face of increasing racial and ethnic diversity. The public assumption that the United States was an Anglo-Saxon nation seemed ubiquitous. It pervaded textbooks published during the period, for instance, Edward Channing and Albert Bushnell Hart's scholarly *Guide to the Study of American History* (1896), a text for teachers, explains the genealogy of American history as "the study of the history of the English race in America"—a "race" clearly envisioned as white, Protestant, and English-based.[10] Theodore Roosevelt, who had already expressed his view that Anglo-Saxon civilization was superior to Native American cultures in *The Winning of the West* (published in four volumes between 1889–96), equated Filipinos with Apaches when he was not referring to them as "Tagal bandits" and "Chinese halfbreeds."[11] For Roosevelt, only the Anglo-Saxons had the "masterful instinct that alone can make a race great."[12] In *Following the Equator*, Mark Twain's account of his 1895–96 round-the-world tour, he noted that "We Americans are English in blood, English in speech, English in religion, English in the essentials of our governmental system, English in the essentials of our civilization." Despite having written numerous books and articles about racial issues within the United States, even Twain still viewed the normative American as white and Protestant.[13]

The ability to cling to the fantasy of homogeneity required increasing rhetorical skill, as the prospect of becoming a colonizing power forced Americans to clarify their understanding of what they meant by the terms *people*, *nation*, and *capacity for self-governance*. The year 1902 saw an outcry against American interrogation methods with Filipino prisoners, especially the method commonly referred to as "the water cure," in which prisoners were forced to drink several gallons of water, after which an American soldier would jump on their stomachs until they confessed—or died.[14] During the Senate investigation, John C. Spooner, senator from Wisconsin, supported U.S. strategy by way of a line-by-line exegesis of the Declaration of Independence. Using Native Americans as a foil, Spooner insists that the "people" the Declaration designates only refers to Americans of English descent because only they manifested the homogeneity necessary for self-government. "Scattered tribes do not constitute a people," he declares. "The Declaration of Independence did not apply to the Indians. They were great nations . . . they were not peoples, however."[15] In contrast Spooner describes the American colonies as of "one people;

they were a part of the English people; they were children of England; they had the education and the conditions of England; they had here the best of England's institutions; they were no less one people with the English in ties of blood, association, education and love of liberty than the Southern people, and we were one people in the old days, as we are today, and as we always, always hereafter will be; and Jefferson wrote of that situation" (Spooner, 41–42).

Spooner inveighs against the Filipinos because, like American Indians, they consist of more than one race and culture, marking them as neither a "people," nor even capable of becoming a "nation."

> The Filipinos are not a nation, and there can be no "political being that we call a people," one people, in the language of the Declaration of Independence, which lacks the sentiment of nationality and which is not capable, by acquirement and characteristics, of cohesion, power for organization, and conception of right and law and order equal to the formation of a nation, which can be called a people in the sense in which that language is used (Spooner, 38).

Insisting that "the Filipinos are . . . a variegated assemblage of different tribes and peoples, and their loyalty is still of the tribal type," Spooner cites a recent publication, Archibald Ross Colquhoun's *The Mastery of the Pacific*. Of the Filipino Malay, Colquhoun claims:

> Other deficiencies in their mental and moral equipment are a lack of organizing power. No Malay nation has ever emerged from the hordes of that race which have spread over the islands of the Pacific. Wherever they are found they have certain marked characteristics, and of these the most remarkable is their lack of that spirit which goes to form a homogeneous people, to weld them together. The Malay is always a provincial; more, he rarely rises outside the interests of his own town or village (Spooner, 39).[16]

After quoting Colquhoun, Spooner resumes his comparison. "Who," he asks, "would compare our people with the tribes in the Philippines?" Capacity for nationhood "presupposes a people so far educated in love of liberty and in the science and capacity for government, as to be able to form a nation entitled upon principles of international law and usage. . . . Will any one tell me that there was such a people in the

Philippines? Will any one deny that there was such a people in the colonies?" (Spooner, 42)

For Spooner, as for many Americans, homogeneity is not only a prerequisite for nationhood, it is also a prerequisite for U.S. citizenship. A genuine "people," in Spooner's eyes, is ethnically, religiously, and culturally homogeneous; for them nationhood is the relatively simple formalization of already accepted principles into universally recognized rules and regulations, with a unifying narrative to accompany the formal details. Non-homogeneous groups, like the American Indians, could amalgamate into "nations" provided the different tribes agreed to accept a common set of governing principles—but they would be a federation of different peoples cooperating for a common goal rather than the homogeneous nation that Spooner celebrated. According to Spooner, the Filipinos differed from the Indians in that they lacked even the Indians' limited capacity to transcend their tribal confines to participate in an extra-local organizational structure. In this view, the Philippine mix of Malay, ethnic Chinese, Negrito, and Moro tribes, with the added onus of mixed-race individuals resulting from three hundred years of Spanish occupation, presented insurmountable obstacles to the collective mentality necessary for nationhood.

Spooner's meditations on the prerequisites for national unity point to the peculiarities of U.S. nationalism in the nineteenth century. Americans, Thomas Bender reminds us, tend to segregate their national history from contemporary events in the rest of the world, whereas in fact what happened within the United States had a great deal to do with what was happening elsewhere.[17] During the nineteenth century European countries—most notably Italy and Germany—consolidated provinces into nations, a difficult process because many of the provinces were longstanding enemies. Americans were sharply aware of these struggles and of the need for unifying narratives, in large part because they needed similar histories to reunite their own population after the sectional hostilities of the Civil War. According to Amy Kaplan, the Spanish-American War was the apogee of that unification effort. During that war white Northerners and Southerners remembered that for all their sectional disagreements, both sides were white and Protestant. They confirmed their commonality by fighting for American principles against a common U.S. enemy in Cuba.[18] But by 1899 the problem lay in how to make the story of American identity in some way work for the Philippines. What would happen to the already contested idea of American homogeneity if the idea of "nation" also signified "the Philippines"?

For a country still agonizing over the significance of black male enfranchisement, this was an especially fraught concern. It was compounded by immigration issues, which turned Americans' attention from nonwhite populations internal to the United States to foreign populations coming from outside U.S. geopolitical borders. In addition to black/white and white/Native American relations, ongoing disputes over immigration restrictions, especially of the Chinese, also frame the Philippines debates. Comparisons were constantly drawn, both explicitly and implicitly. One of the strategies used to argue against annexation was to raise the specter of Filipinos, elected to the U.S. Congress, legislating for white Americans—a flashback, in different guise, to the much-lampooned specter of African Americans in control of Congress during the Reconstruction era. As Senator Money observed,

> I do not believe there is a man here who dares to say that he would take the Filipinos as citizens of the United States. . . . Does any man in the Senate say that he is willing that the Filipinos shall determine who shall be the next President of the United States? Is he willing that the Filipinos shall determine the foreign and domestic policy of the United States? . . . Immediately the Filipinos will . . . want accession to their power in this and the other House, and they would demand that we should make war from one end of the Orient to the other, that they might sit here, the supreme arbiters of the destinies of the American people. We want no possibility of that sort.[19]

Three years later, in a speech in which he framed opposition to Filipino citizenship as a defense of American labor, Maryland's senator George Wellington picked up the same strain, arguing that a nation occupied in passing bills to prevent Chinese immigration would not tolerate a Philippine state. The expansionists, he claims,

> demand that you give [the Filipinos] a local State government, that you let them build up their own government, free and independent, as one of our States, sovereign in itself, and then under the protection of the American flag let them become a State in this Union. . . . But, sir, is the majority party, is the Administration, willing to concede to the Filipinos this sort of a government? They dare not avow it. They can not do so. There would be an uprising against them from every end of the country.[20]

Wellington continues to believe that contact with Americans can help "redeem" the Filipinos, but he also refuses to support passage of any bill that will open the possibility of U.S. citizenship.

Like Tillman, Virginia senator John W. Daniels saw the African American presence as the major exception to a national identity that was otherwise white and Protestant. In Daniels's reading of recent American history, the Civil War had been caused by the threat to homogeneity posed by the importation of the African Other:

> Mr. President, when we contemplate the one hundred and twenty-five years of the history of the American Republic . . . we discern that there has been but one impediment to our national harmony and to our national growth. For that impediment the generation that founded this Republic . . . were not responsible. They were the unwilling heirs of unwilling and protesting ancestors. The Dutch ship that landed at Jamestown bringing here another race brought also Pandora's box. The interjection of a race nonassimilable with the American people has been the fly in the ointment of American institutions, of American peace, of American history.

"That one ingredient in the American commonwealth," he continues, "turned brother against brother, sowed the seeds of discord into that which otherwise would have been a perfect Union. Without that we were a homogeneous people."[21]

Despite his avowal that only the presence of African Americans prevented the United States from homogeneity, Daniels instantly moves on to cite U.S. experiences with its own indigenous peoples as an example of why the treaty should not be ratified:

> Mr. President, there is one thing that neither time nor education can change. You may change the leopard's spots, but you will never change the different qualities of the races which God has created in order that they may fulfill separate and distinct missions in the cultivation and civilization of the world. The Indian of one hundred and twenty-five years ago is the Indian of to-day—ameliorated, to a certain extent civilized, and yet the wisdom of our forefathers, when, in the Constitution, they set them apart as one people, separate and distinct from the great dominant race which had come to take this land and to inhabit it is indicated in what we are still doing and must forever do with them so long as they

maintain their tribal relations and so long as they are Indians. Racial differences, differences of religion, differences in mode of thought, differences in psychology, the subtle analyses of man have put them asunder.[22]

Despite his claim to seamlessness, Daniels lays out an American landscape laced with fissures, a homogeneity built over the remnants of indigenous cultures. He opposes annexation because it will introduce the likelihood of uncontrolled eruption of yet another foreign race into that landscape. To enforce his message he uses the language of miscegenation— not only, in its suggestion of black lust for white women, one of the most inflammatory rhetorical constructs of the turn into the twentieth century— but also, as we have seen, a focal point for American anxieties about the dilution of racial purity during the period. Daniels insists that once the treaty is ratified the Filipinos will become American citizens in all but the right to vote. "To-day we are the United States of America," he begins.

To-morrow . . . we will be the United States of America and Asia. . . . It is proposed to make citizens of the United States, with all the rights of citizenship which attach to the inhabitants of an American Territory, a large and miscellaneous and diversified assortment of people . . . The treaty is the thoroughfare, and through . . . that thoroughfare a million of Filipinos march into the open doorway of the American Republic. More than that, 70,000,000 Americans march into the Philippine Islands as the Filipinos march here. *It is a marriage of nations. The twain become one flesh. They become bone of our bone and flesh of our flesh. . . . I trust yet, Mr. President, that before this marriage is consummated the spirit of American constitutional liberty will arise and forbid the bans.*[23]

Speaking as a Southerner, Daniels chooses his images carefully. Eager to operate in a national arena, he calls on racial fears shared by Northerners and Southerners alike. Moreover he raises the specter of miscegenation knowing full well that on the domestic front, white campaigns to take away the civil rights of African Americans were most successful when they were grounded in the imagery of sexual threat. In a country where black men could be lynched for even looking at a white woman, where the process of institutionalizing anti-miscegenation laws was ongoing throughout the states, the idea that a million Malays might become "married" to the white majority was calculated to terrify his white auditors about the safety of their families and about their very definitions of themselves. For these congressional representatives, the most frightening aspect of imperialism is its potential to dilute the purity of Anglo-Saxon America.

The pattern of association in these speeches links racial hierarchies to religious affiliations, which in turn are linked to patterns of values and the behaviors that give evidence of those values. The result is an ongoing loop: race, religion, and appropriate practices all point to each other in a continuous round of associations, creating the foundation for the national narrative that linked Christianity, whiteness, liberties, and capitalism, and bundled the whole under the rubric "civilization." Essentialist and behaviorist assumptions coexist in these speeches. When in 1898 John Morgan suggested that after the Filipinos had been "brought into living contact with the beneficent influences that have redeemed them from servile bondage . . . and have elevated them to the possibilities of a true and enlightened civilization, they will accept their new situation cheerfully," he meant that when the Philippines became a U.S. territory the Filipinos would take on the values of U.S. citizens. Existing in tandem with—and direct contradiction to—essentialist arguments over the racial inferiority of the Filipinos, this behaviorist argument suggests that on some level Americans perceived that capability for citizenship was performative. And performance, as social theorist Judith Butler reminds us, is one of the avenues through which human beings understand the world.

Performance creates the illusion of stable identities because we internalize and assign significance to repeated acts. Butler's famous example focuses on gender identity, which, she claims, is socially constructed; "a stylized repetition of acts through time."[24] People playing out gender roles believe that their roles are inborn, inherent, "natural" expressions of their essential "selves." I suggest that this understanding of how gender is performed in culture also serves as a model for understanding how late nineteenth-century Americans understood both religion and capacity for democratic citizenship. The notion of "gender" is predicated on sexual characteristics: according to cultural norms, genitalia dictate how we act, and those acts, repeated over time, constitute gender. Only when gender norms are disrupted, when gender-related behaviors actually change (Butler uses the example of drag) do we begin to perceive the cracks in what we had taken to be a seamless identity (Butler, 115). In the late nineteenth century, "capacity for citizenship" was predicated on both biology and behavioral practices. The biology was whiteness, specifically racial descent from what was commonly known as Anglo-Saxons—people of English/Scottish stock.[25] To this was grafted Protestantism, a category even less stable than race (Protestants tend to shift between sects) but nevertheless enhancing race with a set of values that came to be seen as inseparable from it. To be both Anglo-Saxon and Protestant was to exist as a value-added set of possibilities. That potential was realized in behavioral practices, understood as learned but believed to be most readily learned by those bearing the right bio-cultural mix. What the nineteenth century commonly referred to as "character" was, as James B. Salazar reminds us, a code word for a scheme to produce particular kinds of citizen-subjects.[26]

"Capacity for citizenship" then was, for turn-into-the-twentieth-century Americans, a linguistic sign pointing to a compound of essentialist *and* behaviorist assumptions—a shifting mix leading to colorful if self-contradicting pronouncements and dire warnings about the threat that an influx of Filipinos would create within the American landscape. "When we shall have, as we will, driven [the Filipinos] at the point of the bayonet to submit to the authority of the American nation," Maryland Senator Arthur Pue Gorman forecast, "the whole archipelago will then be a pest to the American Union. I believe that it will open the door for a flow from the Chinese Empire and from the islands themselves of a host of men, untold in numbers, who will not assimilate with, but will tend to degrade, the American people."[27] For Gorman, Filipinos and Chinese both would be incapable of performing the values associated with citizenship; worse, their example would undermine Americans' own performance. In chapter 5 of this book I will discuss the influence of Rudyard Kipling's poem "The White Man's Burden, The U.S. and the Philippines," on these debates; here I will only note that when Senator Tillman read the poem to the Senate he interpreted it as forecasting the destruction of the United States if the archipelago was to be annexed. "I have fallen in love with this man," he avowed to his colleagues. "He tells us what we will reap." At the end of his reading he concludes, like Gorman, that the Filipinos lack the capacity to become American citizens: "Those peoples are not suited to our institutions. They are not ready for liberty as we understand it. They do not want it. Why are we bent on forcing upon them a civilization not suited to them and which only means in their view degradation and a loss of self-respect, which is worse than the loss of life itself?"[28] Supporting the Filipinos' desire for independence at the same time that he judges them unfit to be Americans, Tillman offers racial difference as a sensibility so foreign that the very effort to imitate "Americanness" would destroy them.

With a general agreement that the Filipinos should not become American citizens, Americans also debated Filipinos' capacity for self-rule, on the premise that they would at some point become independent. Interestingly, few of the congressional speakers seemed willing, or even interested, in spelling out exactly what capacity for self-government actually would look like within Filipino culture. Instead they skirted the issue, focusing on timing and outcomes rather than precise definitions of what Filipinos would have to do to prove themselves worthy. A year after Tillman's speech Albert Beveridge spelled out his understanding of the time needed to generate self-governing peoples. "Let men beware how they employ the term 'self-government,'" he warned.

> It is a sacred term. It is the watchword at the door of the inner temple of liberty, for liberty does not always mean self-government. Self-government is a method of liberty—the highest, simplest, best—and it is acquired only after centuries of study and struggle and experiment and instruction and all the elements of the progress of man. Self-government is no base and common thing to be bestowed on the merely audacious. It is the degree which crowns the graduate of liberty, not the name of liberty's infant class, who have not yet mastered the alphabet of freedom.

The Filipinos not only had not yet reached that pinnacle but were constitutionally incapable of doing so: "Savage blood, Oriental blood, Malay blood, Spanish example-are these the elements of self-government?"[29]

In contrast Senator Shelby Moore Collum defined the *fruits* of self-government, if not how to get them. In "a bird's-eye glance at the history of the world," he finds

> . . . the wheels of progress stopped where civil and religious freedom do not abide; but where these blessings fall men lift their eyes, and looking about them, span continents with the iron rail, chain the mighty waters and the electricity of the air to do their bidding, and open the doors of learning and make education free to all.

The fruits of self-government are modernity, imaged in concrete technological terms: as railroads, dams, electricity, and mass education. But these fruits are restricted to the special few, who have paid their dues in struggles over time: "These strides in civilization come only in self-governing countries, and self-government can be learned only by experience," Collum concluded.[30]

Modernity, clearly, was the key to proving capacity for self-government, but no one quite knew how it was to be obtained. To the Americans, however, it was clear that it was going to be a long time before the Philippines would be ready for independence. In 1901 the U.S. Supreme Court began deciding a series of cases that would come to determine the political status of the Philippines. Known as the *Insular Cases*, these decisions redefined "territory" from its earlier significance as a geographical area in which the population was being prepared for eventual statehood, to an area owned by the United States but by definition not on trajectory for statehood. Eventually, these laws came to apply to Puerto Rico, Guam, American Samoa, the U.S. Virgin Islands, and the Northern Marianas as well as the Philippines. The *Insular Cases* resolved the dilemma of citizenship for U.S. territories acquired after 1899; by the time the last was decided in 1922, the Court had decided that in fact the Constitution did not follow the flag. As long as a territory was "unincorporated"—not slated for statehood—the United States had no obligation to extend full U.S. Constitutional rights to its inhabitants.[31]

With Filipino citizenship beginning to be taken out of the question, and independence indefinitely deferred, the United States found itself saddled with dependencies that were increasingly expensive to administer, vulnerable to foreign attack (the Japanese occupied the Philippines for the better part of World War II), and more often in conflict with their colonial masters than grateful for their masters' benevolence. Perhaps most painfully, Americans discovered that their blunders in imperial management had been staged on a global platform, provoking sharp criticism from other former colonies—especially in Latin America—and knowing smiles from European imperialists, who noted that the Americans had acted out of self-interest rather than out of solidarity with struggling new nations. Americans did not enjoy the discovery that their claim to special moral status had lost credibility. "What a spectacle we have presented to the less favored and despotic nations of the world!" lamented Massachusetts representative John R. Thayer in December of 1901.

> We have overpowered the organized resistance of these people . . . but we have not conquered them. The same spirit is there, the same desire for liberty and independence animates and controls them now that did

when the first shot was fired. They are simply biding their time and waiting for an opportunity to realize their much-cherished purpose. They have been told . . . that we are interested for their present and future welfare; that our ways, like those of the Lord, are to them past finding out, but that in the end everything we do will inure to their uplifting and eternal good; that we are anxious to grant to them so much of liberty and independence as is good for them and as they are capable of receiving and appreciating, but reserving to ourselves the right to decide as to the amount, the quality, and the time when it shall be bestowed. . . .[32]

Thayer's outburst suggests the country's new dilemma. Eager to make its mark in the world, the United States had embarked on an imperial adventure without planning for its aftermath. Imagining itself within a mythic national history that credited the country's material success on its unique fusions of Enlightenment and Protestant thought, it incorporated an evangelical mission to broadcast its formula to the rest of the world. At the same time, its own racial ideologies rejected the possibility that non–Anglo-Saxon Protestants could ever emulate the American story. "These people will always remain strangers and foreigners to us," pleaded Henry Dickinson Green, Pennsylvania's representative to Congress. *"We can not make them white. We can not make them like our citizens."*[33] Green's comment strikes at the center of U.S. self-contradictions. For all their efforts, Americans could not replicate themselves in the Philippines, nor, at bottom, did they wish to do so. In June, 1900, William Howard Taft, recently appointed Governor-General of the Philippines, wrote to Supreme Court Justice John M. Harlan that "The idea that these people can govern themselves is . . . ill founded. . . . They are in many respects nothing but grown up children. . . . They need the training of fifty or a hundred years before they shall even realize what Anglo-Saxon liberty is."[34]

In 1901 Mark Twain was drafting "The Secret History of Eddypus, the World Empire," intended as an attack on Christian Science and on the course of U.S. world conduct generally. Unfinished and never published in Twain's lifetime, the "Secret History" looks back on U.S. history from a perspective cast well into the future. "Civilization is an elusive and baffling term," Twain's narrator comments meditatively.

It is not easy to get at the precise meaning attached to it . . . In America and France it seems to have meant benevolence, gentleness, godliness, justice, magnanimity, purity, love, and we gather that men considered it a duty to confer it as a blessing upon all lowly and harmless peoples of remote regions; but as soon as it was transplanted it became a blight, a pestilence, an awful terror . . . The strength of evidence . . . seems to indicate that it was a sham at home and only laid off its disguise when abroad.[35]

By 1901 Americans could maintain the fantasy of homogeneity at home only through strenuous rhetoric accompanied by repression of its own minorities and increasing legislation against immigration. Abroad, the fantasy could not hold. In seeking to spread the "blessings of civilization," the Americans revealed themselves—both to themselves and to others—as a nation of hypocrites. As Twain remarked in jottings for "Notes on Patriotism," an address he was preparing in 1902, events were proving that "the Great Republic is not just exactly and precisely a republic at all, but only a qualified despotism" (Zwick, 115).

Section II

Creating Citizens

Chapter 3

A Connecticut Yankee in the Philippines

I. Educating Britons: Hank Morgan in Arthurian England

The outbreak of hostilities between the Filipinos and the Americans in 1899 was not the first time Mark Twain had thought about Americans who set out to transform other cultures. More than a decade earlier, he had created an American booster in the character of Hank Morgan, the protagonist of *A Connecticut Yankee in King Arthur's Court.* Hank is a nineteenth-century jack-of-all-trades who finds himself transported to sixth-century England and decides to transform the monarchy into a republic modeled on nineteenth-century America. He fails, but his adventures on the road to failure gave Twain a wide field for rumination about human nature. It also gave him a chance to demonstrate a typical American's response to the lure of absolute power. Hank Morgan is an American inventor whose certainty in his own rectitude makes him a prototype of the self-confident American who engages in well-meaning "uplift" without calculating the amount of damage he can cause.

Although *A Connecticut Yankee in King Arthur's Court* is popularly regarded as a humorous novel, it also lends itself to historicist readings.[1] Hank's cocky, self-conscious "American" attitudes and the havoc he wreaks invite readers to interpret it either in terms of Twain's own historical contexts or as a parable for the reader's own times. The story seems especially prescient from the vantage point of 1900; examined through the perspective of the U.S.'s early policies in its new territories, Hank becomes

FIGURE 3.1: "School Begins." *Puck,* Keppler & Schwarzmann, New York, January 25, 1899. [artist: Louis Dalrymple]

an extraordinarily accurate representation of the American imperialist. In *Mark Twain and Human Nature,* Tom Quirk comments that "however able a social engineer the Yankee may be, his grand plans for republican reform founder on his optimism, misapprehension, or conceit," and notes that Hank is constantly having to scale back his grand plans to rapidly transform the monarchy into a republic.[2] Hank's strategies for creating his "civilization" look like blueprints for the dogmatic investments in Protestantism, public education, and commerce that characterized the first years of American rule in the Philippines, and his failure to effect his program anticipates American failures in the archipelago. As both John Carlos Rowe and Quirk suggest, Twain is wiser than his protagonist; Hank thinks he can work wonders overnight; Mark Twain knows that it takes many years to achieve genuine reform.[3] Hence Hank Morgan's story becomes a lesson in the destructive powers of American civilization when it is forcibly transplanted.

Like many Americans of his time, Hank Morgan is an economic, cultural, and religious Free Trader, and he moves quickly to implement Free Trade ideals throughout Arthurian Britain. "I had started a teacher factory and a lot of Sunday schools the first thing," he tells us after he has been in England for several years. "As a result, I now had an admirable system of graded schools in full place . . . and also a complete variety of Protestant congregations." Like his nineteenth-century compatriots, Hank equates "Christianity" with "Protestantism": "Everybody could be any kind of a Christian he wanted to; there was perfect freedom in that matter," he proudly records. Benevolently eschewing the possibility of privileging his own Presbyterian sect, he declares his faith in free choice, reasoning that "spiritual wants and instincts are as various . . . as physical appetites," and that individuals do best when their religion suits their individual character.[4] But Hank doesn't include Catholicism in his designation "Christian," and it's clear that benevolence isn't his only motive: he wants free competition among the various sects because "I was afraid of a united Church; it makes a mighty power" (CY, 81).

One of the legacies of Mark Twain's childhood was his distrust of the power of the Catholic Church, and Hank combines Twain's uneasiness about the Church with the character's own enthusiasm for Free Trade. Hank valorizes Protestantism not for its theology but because it is decentralized; it encourages individuals to "shop" among its multiple sects, and the shoppers' ability to change sects at will hinders formation of a consolidated religious power. Joe B. Fulton, in his study of theology and form in Twain's writings *The Reverend Mark Twain,* notes that for Twain, the existence of fringe "wildcat religions" was "a small price to pay for the political freedom that results from a fragmented church."[5] Fulton suggests that for Twain, Roman Catholic culture "symbolized . . . a 'pre-modern' world of universal tyranny, a world he understood from the sermons he heard in childhood against the Catholic menace" (Fulton, 23). In *A Connecticut Yankee in King Arthur's Court* Hank regards the Roman Catholic establishment as tyrannical precisely because it is centralized, able to control all facets of medieval life. Consequently he opposes it from his first days in Camelot and makes defeating it a major objective: "I had two schemes in my head," he tells us. "The one was, to overthrow the Catholic Church and set up the Protestant faith on its ruins." The other is to establish universal suffrage and to move toward making Britain into a republic (CY, 398). But in his efforts to vanquish the enemy, Hank becomes him: he discovers that he likes authoritarian power. Four years into his sojourn he celebrates his success: "my works showed what a despot could do with the resources of a kingdom at his command. Unsuspected by this dark land, I had the civilization of the nineteenth century booming under its very nose!" (CY, 82)

Hank projects utmost confidence in the righteousness of his cause. "Unlimited power is the ideal thing, when it is in safe hands," he tells us.

"The despotism of heaven is the one absolutely perfect government" (CY, 82). Although he claims to oppose earthly despotism, his assertion seems to have no effect on his own stealthy agenda to remake the sixth century in the image of the nineteenth. He devotes his energies to clandestinely establishing schools, churches, factories, and military and naval academies that would—"one candlepower at a time"—transform the British populace from monarchical subjects to republican consumer-citizens and make him sole architect of their social and economic agendas.

But transforming subjects into citizens is not an easy task. Hank discovers that adults do not easily shed life-long training in cultural values. In the end, he realizes, his program will be effective only if he begins with children, subjecting them to his educational system before they can be socialized into their own retrograde culture. Consequently, he gathers a group of English boys and puts them through a rigorous course that includes modern military tactics, the principles and practices of electricity, and the manufacture of bicycles. Throughout the novel he uses the boys as his tactical team—stringing telephone and telegraph wires throughout the kingdom to connect its parts with Camelot, sending in five hundred knights on bicycles to rescue Hank and King Arthur when they are threatened with execution. In Hank's own eyes, he is England's most important figure because his activities had made it "the only nation on earth standing ready to blossom into civilization" (CY, 373).

But as Americans would continually rediscover throughout the twentieth century, technology, scientific training, and Protestant values do not automatically transform individuals from dissimilar cultures into Americans. Hank's plan to supplant medieval psychology with modernity by saving young hearts and minds does not triumph, even among his chosen few, who protest his expectation that they will turn on their own people. "We have tried to forget what we are," they explain, "we have tried to put reason before sentiment, duty before love; our minds approve but our hearts reproach us . . . These people are our people, they are bone of our bone, flesh of our flesh, we love them—do not ask us to destroy our nation!" (CY, 429) In the short run, Hank's will triumphs over the boys' national sentiment, but medieval culture prevails in the end. The boys help him build an electrified fence around their headquarters, and it electrocutes twenty-five thousand knights. But although the fence keeps the knights out, it also keeps Hank and his troops in, and the dead bodies trap them. The corpses rot, sickening the men, and Hank himself is wounded.

When everyone is off guard, Merlin—who has epitomized the medieval mentality throughout the novel—disguises himself as a nurse and puts Hank to sleep for thirteen centuries. In the end, Hank's campaign to replace medieval civilization with nineteenth-century American culture is destroyed by the very forces that it sought to supplant.

II. Educating Filipinos: The Americans in the Philippines

In light of the U.S. educational experiment in the Philippines, Twain was extraordinarily prescient. Hank's optimism that he can transform sixth-century Britons from subjects to citizens is remarkably similar to Americans' conviction that they could teach Filipinos how to be self-governing. When they assumed control over the Philippines, the Americans sought to export American values as the foundation for their project of "benevolently assimilating" the Filipinos. Unlike the British in India, who dealt with the subcontinent's large and extremely diverse population by creating a class of Indians specifically assigned to mediate between the masses and the British colonial government, leaving traditional structures largely intact among the other classes, U.S. officials believed that they should spread American civilization throughout their new colonies.[6] Based on their experiments with Native Americans, African Americans, and immigrants at home, they assumed that they could transplant nineteenth-century American culture to the Philippines by replacing Filipino traditions with American culture and technologies. Like Hank, they encouraged the growth of Protestant communities; like him they believed that the principles of Free Trade could apply to cultural as well as economic forces; like him they believed that modernity—which was what they meant by the word "civilization"—could only come about through adoption of a set of social and moral practices that included honesty, self-control, and orderliness. Finally, like Hank, the Americans focused on education, especially of young children. Hank, however, never spells out exactly how he is re-educating his Britons, whereas the Americans in the Philippines left ample records of their strategies. Unlike their Congressional representatives, who talked about bringing freedom and civilization to the Filipinos but rarely specified the means of effecting the transformation, the Americans who actually worked in the Philippines developed clear, well-articulated agendas and strategies for implementing them. At the same time, however, they also revealed their suspicion that much of their effort would be wasted because the Filipinos' racial constitutions and colonial histories would prevent them from fully appreciating the superiority of U.S. culture. We can see both their goals and their doubts manifested in the schoolbooks that they wrote specifically for Filipino children.

During the three hundred years through which they had controlled the Philippines, the Spanish had established a rudimentary system of primary schools that taught basic literacy and religion.[7] Many of the schools taught in indigenous languages, barring access to Spanish—official reasoning being that the fewer Filipinos having access to the colonial power's language, the less chance there would be that they would seek power themselves. In effect, the Spanish kept the Philippines in a semifeudal state of dependence, a major factor in the complaints lodged by successive waves of Filipino nationalists. As soon as the Treaty of Paris was ratified, U.S. policy makers felt forced to differentiate their form of imperialism from the Spanish model by committing to teaching the Filipinos how to enter the modern world.

American educational efforts in the Philippines began with the passage of the Education Act of 1901, which established Fred W. Atkinson, formerly a high school principal in Springfield, Massachusetts, as superintendent of Filipino Education. Under Atkinson the Americans set the goal of establishing free universal public schools, instruction in English, and the training of native teachers. To jumpstart the program the United States brought in over one thousand American teachers. In the beginning, they also imported textbooks used in U.S. schools, but teachers quickly realized the irrelevancy of books that featured blond children eating strawberries or playing in the snow, so they commissioned texts to be written specifically for Filipino children.[8] These textbooks show how the tensions inherent in the congressional debates over annexation were translated into educational policy. During the debates, congressmen had discussed America's goals regarding the archipelago: whether the United States should ready the Filipinos for independence, prepare them for U.S. citizenship, or perpetuate their status as colonials. In the end, the politicians waffled: the rhetoric about "benevolent assimilation" boiled down to annexation with the long-term goal of preparation for independence and the short-term goal of colonizing. To implement this the American educators adopted a progressive approach to change, vigorously employing modernization as a stick and independence as a carrot while making it clear that it would take a minimum of a generation before Filipinos would be fit for self-government. As "trustees" of the archipelago, the Americans quickly demonstrated how little faith they had in their wards' capacity to assume control of their own interests.

The first step the Americans took was to change the official language from Spanish to English because, as one teacher recalled, "The basic reason for using English was that in teaching a people democracy it was wise to use the language to which most great democratic principles were native." They believed that democracy could only develop within an Anglo-Saxon environment.[9] The new textbooks spanned many subjects, from arithmetic to histories of the Philippines to guides for Filipino teachers. The foremost task of these texts was to teach the art of republican citizenship; they did so by modeling the set of social and personal practices that, for Americans, signaled capacity for self-government. In insisting that capacity for republican citizenship could only evolve from American Protestant culture, the textbooks enabled the United States to declare that it was preparing Filipinos for independence even while deferring it until the majority of the Filipino population was able to imitate white American Protestants.

Like the British in India, the Spanish had already created a privileged elite among the Filipinos, a process that eventually backfired because many of the revolutionaries originated within its ranks.[10] The Americans were not interested in simply creating a class of imitation Americans. Rather, the men and women who designed the first educational policies for the Philippines assumed that they could train the entire archipelago for self-government in the American mold. However, the texts they developed betray their assumption that it would be impossible for Filipinos to fully manifest "Americanness," first because of what Hank would have called their "inherited ideas"—the deeply rooted legacy of Catholic training, largely rote, combined with indigenous cultures—and second, because in white Americans' eyes, most Filipinos were racially unfit for self-government. For instance, Mary H. Fee, one of the first wave of American schoolteachers to be shipped to the island, opined that "Our own national progress and that of the European nations from whom we are descended have been so differently conceived and developed that we can hardly realize the peculiar process through which the Filipinos are passing. . . . All the natural laws of development are turned around in the Philippines, and motives which should belong to the crowning years of a nation's life seem to have become mixed in at the beginning."[11]

Fee's attempt at historical relativism is hampered by her assumption that European Protestants bear a history so unique that only descendents of the original racial group can enact their civilization. She concludes that the Filipinos are not simply at a different stage of national development from the Americans, but have a different racial and historical trajectory altogether. Declaring bluntly that "there is not room for Protestantism in the Philippines," Fee claims that "the introspective quality which is inherent in true Protestantism is not in the Filipino temperament. Neither are the vein of simplicity and the dogmatic spirit which made the strength of the Reformation" (Fee, 202). For Fee, the Filipinos are interesting, charming, talented people, but they lack the English Protestant's intellectual rigor and emotional willpower, both prerequisites for productive participation in modern society. Three hundred years of Spanish misrule had only compounded the difficulties. Representative Green's observation that no amount of training could "make [Filipinos] white" was only a blunt statement of many Americans' conviction that non Anglo-Saxons were constitutionally handicapped when it came to enacting American civilization.

According to Glenn May, in *Social Engineering in the Philippines: The Aims, Execution, and Impact of American Colonial Policy, 1900–1913* (1980), U.S. priorities were to prepare the Filipinos for self-government, to establish a public school system, with emphasis on primary education, and to bring about the economic development of the archipelago. Speculating on U.S. motives, May suggests that

it must have been obvious to [the commissioners] and to most Americans that U.S. policy in the Philippines was designed primarily to remake the colony in the image of the United States. . . . This is not to say that they believed the Filipinos capable of attaining the intellectual level of Americans or of running their own government, but they still were determined to transfer American values and institutions in some form to the new colony. . . . To provide Filipinos with experience in self-government surely made sense to men who had learned from grade school that the roots of U.S. democracy could be found in New England town government. To educate the Filipino masses made sense to citizens of a nation which, since its inception, had placed inordinate faith in the powers of education. To develop the Philippine economy by means of American investment made sense to men who, in their own lifetime, had witnessed the dynamic growth of their own country's economy. One can understand U.S. social engineering in the Philippines only if one realizes that it was . . . an experiment in self-duplication.[12]

The schoolbooks Americans designed for the Philippines urge Filipino children to develop American values and to manifest those values through specific moral and social practices. At the same time they advise the children that it will be many years before the Philippines will be ready for self-government. The question of citizenship—what it was, who was capable of embodying it, and how it could be taught—demonstrates the contradictions of the American vision even while showing how earnestly U.S. authorities sought to bring the benefits of U.S. civilization to a people they neither knew nor understood. Like Hank Morgan, the United States mistakenly assumed that cultures could be changed by educating children in modern science, democratic practices, and Protestant values. Like Hank, they were leery of the power of the Catholic Church. And finally, like Hank, they eventually discovered that their "experiment in self-duplication," as May termed it, could not overcome the power of entrenched custom and belief—either their own or the people they sought to transform.

What we see most forcefully in the textbooks written for Filipino children is an emphasis on inculcating a set of social and moral practices that the writers believed were foundational to self-government. The pedagogical project went well beyond teaching literacy, science, and mathematics. Much as they had attempted to do with Native American children, who were kept in boarding schools until their teachers determined that white culture had supplanted Native culture, American educators attempted to supplant Filipino culture with American social, political, and economic values.[13] One of the means through which they taught these values came under the rubric of "character development"—lessons in moral conduct, spelled out in a series of positive and negative prescriptions.

In *A Question of Character: Scientific Racism and the Genres of American Fiction, 1892–1912* (2000), Cathy Boeckmann discusses the effect of post-Darwin evolutionary theory on the assessment of political behavior, suggesting that models based in Enlightenment concepts gave way to "anthropological understandings of which people have the character to be allowed to participate in enlightened government and which do not."[14] She also notes that to demonstrate character in the United States was to demonstrate capitalist values: that in American eyes, "the very best evidence for the development of character is the acquisition of money and its investment in property" (Boeckmann, 41). Boeckmann's study links the development of character studies to race, suggesting that the word, and its associated concepts, came to stand for racial differences. I suggest that they also came to stand for religious and cultural differences; that references to "character" during the first decade of the twentieth century mask intense anxieties over difference. In *Bodies of Reform: The Rhetoric of Character in Gilded Age America*, James B. Salazar notes that during the early national period U.S. educators explicitly linked "the project of 'building character'" to the production of a unified citizenry.[15] Salazar's historicizing of the concept of character as a unifying agency in the service of national identity helps us understand why the idea carried so much weight for the American architects of Filipino education. Because they believed that character was instrumental in nation-building, they made it central to pedagogical agendas. The problem was that the "character" they were seeking to create was predicated on values they understood as inseparable from both whiteness and Protestantism.

The goal to produce Filipino citizenship through behavior modification is evident in Harry Couch Theobold's *The Filipino Teacher's Manual* (1907), a pedagogy text produced for native Filipino teachers. Here we see a two-fold pedagogical effort: on the one hand, to indicate the administration's educational goals and suggest strategies for achieving them, and on the other, to enlist native Filipinos in the enterprise.[16] "The national importance of the school comes from its power to form the characters of the boys and girls," the manual advises. "As we consider that the school's greatest work is the moulding [*sic*] of character, we feel that the school is a sacred institution. It comes next to the church in its influence upon our national life."[17] With this opening statement, the manual then situates "character" as central to creation of a national consciousness and the teacher as the agent for national rebirth. "When these boys have become strong, healthy men, understanding the true meaning of citizenship, and knowing their duties as well as their rights and privileges," it suggests, "the teacher will look with joy upon the new nation he has helped to create" (Theobold, 2). Not only are the students to be taught to think of themselves as part of a national enterprise, the teacher is encouraged to think of him or herself as a key civilizing agent. In co-opting the native teachers' energies, the manual also co-opts their loyalties; once they have effectively produced young republicans, they will most likely feel compelled to defend the product they have created.

In keeping with the philosophy that the teacher's primary task is to create citizens, "character" construction becomes the leitmotif of *The Filipino Teacher's Manual*. "The purpose of moral instruction is to influence the child's character," it informs the native teachers. "We want the child to become a person who always tries to do what is right. To do right includes being fair, honest, kind, truthful, obedient, helpful, and unselfish" (Theobold, 98). The manual lists avenues for moral instruction that range from role modeling to restructuring daily physiological routines. All examples are generated against an American rather than a Filipino background, exposing children to American history and ideals but teaching them little Filipino history. In a section recommending that teachers present models for emulation as part of the classroom environment, for instance, the manual suggests that "Pictures of such great men as Washington, Lincoln, Franklin, Magellan, Columbus, Rizal, and others [might] be placed on the schoolroom walls. Reprints of famous pictures and of statues also make good subjects for decoration" (Theobold, 12). With the exception of José Rizal, the Filipino writer and freedom fighter martyred by the Spanish in 1896, and Magellan, the first western European to reach the Philippines, these are all standard heroes from the pantheon presented to U.S. schoolchildren, with little relevance to Philippine history. To American educators, however, they presented much needed exemplars. "Stories from history and biography will provide the teacher with much material to be used in the teaching of morals," the text advises the Filipino teacher, "Children can tell us why they like to read about Lincoln or Washington. They can tell us why everybody admires such men and calls them great men. The question may be asked, 'Are we hard workers and honest like Lincoln?' Or, 'Can we not be as truthful as Washington was?' Such lessons as 'How Benjamin Franklin became Famous' will contain many truths for every boy and girl to think about and act upon" (Theobold, 106–07).

That all these lessons are intended to lay the groundwork for responsible citizenship is clear from the text's admonitions to the instructor. "It is the forming of right sentiments in the minds of the pupils that shows the influence of a good teacher," the instructor is told. "If he has learned to be honorable, just, kind, and industrious, he will be a good citizen" (Theobold, 106). The manual also encourages children to see themselves in relation to republican structures. The chapter devoted to "Civics in Primary Schools" advises that the child's "relation to the government should be taught as soon as he is old enough to grasp the idea. He knows what a barrio is, and he should be led step by step to grasp the meaning of 'pueblo,' 'province,' 'nation,' and 'government'" (Theobold, 224).

If we remember that Senator Spooner had insisted that Malays could never understand the meaning of *nation* because they were incapable of transcending the tribal (as discussed in chapter 1), then we can see the emphasis on civics in the manual as an attempt to encourage national consciousness. The chapter on civics focuses on representative government, suggesting that students organize the school into a small city and elect officials to run it. According to the authors, the exercise will encourage students to think of themselves as responsible members of a larger organization. "The child should be taught to think to himself, 'I am only a pupil of the barrio school, but even as such, I am also a citizen of the Filipino nation. There are duties for me to do, rules for me to keep every day. I must try to become a clean, orderly, active, and useful citizen. Especially must I be honorable in all things.'" The manual then spells out the processes by which these characteristics may be attained: "To become orderly, I must do the things promptly and well that are given to me to do every day. To become active and healthy, I must exercise by working and playing every day. To become useful, I must not only learn and think about the studies that are given me, but I must learn to do something useful with my hands; for my country needs men who can do useful work. To be honorable means to tell the truth at all times, no matter if I suffer for it, and to keep my promises faithfully, trying hard never to deceive others in word or action" (Theobold, 229).

The agenda laid out here testifies to the intensity with which Americans associated honesty, orderliness, industry, and honor with the idea of citizenship. The constant emphasis on these social and moral practices suggests underlying anxieties about their absence—the suggestion being that Filipinos at the time of conquest were cheating, lazy, and dishonorable, and that they would not change of their own accord. It is easy to see why Americans believed this: first, the Filipinos had vigorously resisted the imposition of U.S. colonial rule, often thwarting U.S. intentions through petty acts as well as through outright hostility. Second, as we have seen, the palpable racial differences of Filipinos from the idea of the normative American, their long servitude under Spanish rule, their overwhelming Catholicism, their Muslim minority, and their large influx of ethnic Chinese could be seen as a mirror image of demographic changes taking place in the United States, especially in cities where massive immigration was radically altering the racial landscape. In confronting the

Philippines, U.S. authorities were confronting two issues: American anxieties over their own increasing internal diversity,[18] and equal anxiety over a new territory that Americans regarded as both racially and culturally chaotic.

Textbooks by Prescott F. Jernegan, intended both for the Filipino schoolroom and for the Filipino general public, demonstrate Americans' contradictory imperatives in the Philippines. Jernegan clearly saw himself as creating textbooks to educate a new people. In many ways, his texts epitomize U.S. educational strategies in the Philippines in the first decades of colonial rule. They are clearly written, well-researched, and generally informed, and they communicate American social, economic, and political values both thematically and structurally. They also demonstrate the Americans' ambivalence about the mission they had undertaken. On the one hand, Jernegan points to a democratic future by suggesting that the Filipinos are inherently freedom-loving and will eventually attain independence; on the other hand, he constantly points out the number and diversity of tribes and religions in the Philippines and openly voices his doubt they can become unified enough to form a representative democracy.

In Jernegan's texts, racial, social, and religious homogeneity are the paramount requisites for self-government. Additionally, to operate efficiently a nation must have transportation and communications systems that will allow all parts of the country to be in contact at all times. In *A Connecticut Yankee,* Hank Morgan dispatched topographical teams to map the country and communications specialists to string ground wires for telephone and telegraph systems to ready Arthurian England for the leap to the nineteenth century (CY, 84). Jernegan too regarded the gathering of information, and the construction of roads, railways, telephones, and telegraphs, as agents of modernity because the promulgation of information about the country and the ability to move around it easily encouraged individuals to imagine themselves as members of communities larger than their own tribes. Part of the American strategy in the Philippines was to encourage Filipinos to imagine themselves as parts of a national community.

There is a cognitive shift implied here. Like Hank Morgan, the Americans in the Philippines believed that the people they were retraining not only must know *more,* they must also know *differently.* Feudal individuals, as Hank discovered, perceived the world as unknowable. A prime example in *A Connecticut Yankee* is Hank's response to a petitioner who tells him that it is impossible to give him directions to the place she wants him to go because the miles "do so lap the one upon the other, and being made all in the same image and tincted with the same color, one may not know the one league from its fellow" (CY, 92). Twain understood that for the inhabitants of the sixth century, the world did not break down into distinct parts and categories; it was unknowable because it was all of one piece. Similar experiences with other denizens of Arthur's realm lead Hank to conclude that "these animals didn't reason. They never put this and that together" (CY, 40). Breaking wholes into constituent parts and then "putting this and that together" constitutes the kind of analytic approach to problem-solving that nineteenth-century Americans revered.

In contrast to the medieval worldview, modernity assumes the world can be known. The modern mind breaks the objects it perceives into discrete pieces, reducing them to manageable portions that can be apprehended in relation to each other. Moreover relational knowledge facilitates control. Hence an educational program intended to lead medieval minds to modernity must teach students how to cut, chop, categorize, and analyze so that they can exercise dominion over their human, physical, and social environments. Textbooks must convince students not only that they should want to master these processes, but that they are capable of doing so. Hank Morgan called his schools "man factories"—in his mind, to be a "man" meant to be capable of exercising control and to be eager to do so. But Hank does not treat us to his curriculum or his textbooks, whereas Jernegan does. And Jernegan's texts contradict themselves: they celebrate independence but fail to teach students to trust themselves.

Jernegan's analysis of Filipino cultures suggests that the author himself doubted that Filipinos could surmount their racial and cultural handicaps. In his *A Short History of the Philippines, For Use in Philippine Schools* (1905), diversity is the cause of all national disabilities. "Everything great in this world has been done by the united efforts of people who spoke the same language and believed the same things," he avers. And the Filipinos he surveys are "not a nation, but the wandering fragments of many different tribes" (Jernegan 1905, 29). Until the Philippines overcomes this fragmentation, it will not be ready for independence.

Jernegan's texts exhibit the problems created by the Americans' insistence on cultural unity in a country populated not only by many cultural forms but also many races. In keeping with modernity's emphasis on categorizing and analyzing, the nineteenth century had seen the

proliferation of theories about racial origins, and most geography textbooks of the time had at least one chapter describing the major races of
the world. These descriptions tended to be arranged hierarchically, with
Northern Europeans at the very top of the hierarchy and black Africans
at the bottom. Asians ranked below whites but well above Africans and
aboriginals. Jernegan's *History* reflects this convention in its hierarchical analysis of Filipino races. The opening of the *History* categorizes
Filipino tribes from the least to the most civilized. Negritos, for Jernegan an uncivilizable race, occupy the bottom rung, while the rest of the
Philippine racial groups occupy ascending rungs, with those of Malay-
sian descent at the top. Jernigan describes Negritos as "little black savages who now dwell in the mountains. Most of them are less than five
feet tall. They have woolly hair, thick lips, and broad noses. Clad in
little or no clothing, they wander from place to place" (Jernegan 1905,
21). The "woolly hair," "thick lips," and "broad noses" match the distortions commonly used in cartoon depictions of African Americans
and—not incidentally—in cartoons of Filipinos created for the American market. Like much racial analysis of the nineteenth century, Jernegan's description is highly inflected by the social norms of the
nineteenth-century United States. His distaste for many of the racial
groups is thinly disguised, and the racial landscape he portrays is far
from homogeneous.

Nevertheless, Jernegan's *History* insists that only a homogeneous
population can be self-governing. His discussion of Filipino racial and
cultural landscapes suggests that the entire archipelago is hopelessly het-
erogeneous, a situation that will require centuries, rather than years, to
remedy. It also suggests that until the individual tribes learn to cooperate
and to assimilate the nation will never reach the first rung on the developmental ladder. The flip side to teaching Filipinos how to become citizens of a republic is teaching them to devalue any sign of cultural
difference.

Jernegan's texts rarely mention religion directly, largely because the
Education Act had forbidden religious teaching in the public schools.[19] It
was, however, very much an underlying theme. The uneasy balance
between demands for homogeneity and order, on the one hand, and the
celebration of individualism, on the other, was especially evident in
nineteenth-century discussion of the differences between Protestant and
Catholic sensibilities, at least as portrayed by the Protestant mainstream.
For Protestants, as Hank made abundantly clear, multiple sects were to be

valued because they gave individuals choice (Free Trade), and also prevented the development of a centralized power (antimonopoly). In this reading, the Catholic Church was a monopoly, dangerous because centralized and univocal. At the same time, Protestants also saw Catholicism as philosophically unruly, with too many kinds of deities and too many options. Moreover, in the Philippines, the Americans perceived the Church as too tolerant of native customs, which the Americans regarded as mere superstitions. For Americans, to civilize meant to put everything in order, which entailed creating orderly habits, including a religion in which all the parts fit together and worked toward a common goal. Jernegan's text insists that in addition to honesty, industry, and the other personal virtues, a people needed a religion that would facilitate progress. "The most important fact about any people is its religion. The religion of a people tells us what they value most, and how well they can think," he tells his readers (Jernegan 1905, 47).

Never overtly suggesting that American Protestantism best facilitates modernity, Jernegan does suggest that religions are as hierarchical as races and that peoples who have inherited their traditions from the Spanish—such as the Filipinos and the Cubans—are less capable of practicing democracy, in large part because they have been reared within the overlapping hierarchies of the Spanish and the Catholic systems. Even Spain itself, he points out, could not establish a republic, presumably because the Spanish could not imagine a form of government based on popular consensus rather than originating at the top. The evidence points to the fact that "Peoples who have lived in oppression and ignorance for centuries need a very long preparation for freedom" (Jernegan 1905, 247)—the implication being that "oppression and ignorance" are coded references for subjugation to the Catholic Church. For Jernegan, it would be impossible to establish a republic in the Philippines without the "orderly" combination of character, religion, and industry offered by U.S. models.

The textbooks written for Filipino children transform Americans' own desire for a unified American culture into a prescription for nation building in other countries. Jernegan concludes his chapter on Philippine diversity by returning to his original point about the necessity of homogeneity as a precursor for representative government. Without it, he suggests, the Filipinos will find it impossible to form a coherent and progressive government. "People of the same blood, language, and religion are often torn apart by civil war. How could people of a hundred different tongues, living on hundreds of scattered islands, remain at peace? When will the Macabebe love the Tagalog, or the Moro the Christian?" His answer to his rhetorical questions is to advise a long period of indenture to democratic traditions, accompanied by technological developments that will physically unite the archipelago, through roads, railroads, communications, and, eventually, new family ties:

> Some day the Filipinos will all know the same language and possess the same education. Railroads will help unite the people. Business, travel, and marriage will make friends of Filipinos who now distrust each other. Perhaps an independent Philippine republic will then be possible. There are many intelligent Filipinos who know it is now impossible. There is no country in the world where so many different peoples, as in the Philippines, with different customs and religions, live in peace under a government of their own making (Jernegan 1905, 281).

Despite his clear objective of enticing Filipinos to change their ways by changing their values, Jernegan, like most of the progressive reformers at the turn into the twentieth century, delivered a message rife with contradictions. To achieve independence—the stated goal of the Filipino freedom-fighters—the peoples of the Philippines would not only have to be united politically and economically, they would also have to share the same value system, including their religious values. They would have to develop transportation and communication systems that would link all parts of the archipelago and would bring hitherto unknown peoples in contact with each other. Then, intermarriage would "unify" the Filipinos through racial amalgamation. Since not even the United States actually manifested this degree of homogeneity—nor would it tolerate the suggestion of racial mixing within its own borders—the demand that the Philippines mimic the United States through amalgamation posed an irresolvable contradiction.

The insistence on a unified Philippines as a precursor to independence points to a fundamental flaw in Americans' understanding of modernity. Over the course of the nineteenth century Americans had learned to see themselves within a rhetorical framework evoked by specific associations of Protestant Christianity, Anglo-Saxon racial heritage, Enlightenment political values, and culturally sanctioned moral and social practices. National feeling—patriotism—encouraged conformity, giving an illusion of national unity. Even within the United States, however, this illusion was fragile. The white Protestant culture that was advertised as the national norm was daily challenged by the evidence of other races and religions thriving in American soil and beginning to make their presence felt economically and socially. Increasingly, the description of the United States as a white Christian nation appeared to be a rhetorical construct, useful as a political rallying call but without relation to reality. Transported to foreign soil, the rhetorical strategies that fostered U.S. nationalism appeared not only arrogant, but hypocritical and parochial. As Twain suggested in "The Secret History of Eddypus," seen from abroad, American civilization appeared to be "a sham at home" and a "blight" when it was transported.[20] In retrospect, the U.S. experiment in the Philippines illuminates one of the foundational missteps in early twentieth-century U.S. foreign policy. In failing to understand that the civilization they were at pains to export was predicated on a national identity rhetorically associated with white Protestantism, in clinging to a racialized conception of modernity even while they assumed that changes in social and moral practices would encourage cultural and cognitive transformations and recreate Filipinos in the image of Americans, American educators and other social engineers not only illustrated the limitations of their vision of their own national identity but also the limitations of their understanding of modernity itself.

When sixth-century Britons resisted Hank Morgan's policies he retaliated, often violently; he had a penchant for dynamite and a tendency to cuss out his opponents, calling them "animals" and "savages." Although he insisted that "training is everything," he also made essentialist judgments. Bringing order, communication, transportation, and economic and religious Free Trade, in addition to a belief that adoption of American institutions should be the goal of all right-thinking peoples, he also permitted his canvassing knights to "remove" anyone who rejected the civilization-goods they were peddling (CY, 398). And he wanted, needed, absolute authority to effect his agenda. For all his talk of a republic, The Boss, as he labeled himself, reveled in being the nation's only real power, and in the end, his own self-confidence defeated him. Similarly, in assuming that modernity could only be effected in the American mold, and in insisting that cultural and racial diversity was a handicap rather than an adjunct to development, the United States initiated one of its most enduring mistakes in imperial management. The rhetoric that could produce the illusion of unity within U.S. geopolitical borders depended on specifics of U.S. cultural history that could not be duplicated, and its vision insisted on homogeneity rather than accommodated diversity. For all their reputation as a pragmatic people, the United States formulated imperial policies that were founded in a fantasy of national identity, where the "genuine American" was both white and Protestant. American educational policies in the Philippines failed not only because the Americans failed to understand the Filipinos, but because they also failed to understand themselves.

Chapter 4

The National Christian

Americans' assumption that the United States could and should dupli-cate itself in the Philippines originated in nineteenth-century formulations of American history. Textbook writers understood that citizens produced by the nation's schools would recognize themselves as participants in its destiny, and they taught children that God had brought the Puritans from old to New England in order to found a nation that would lead in the redemption of the world. Jernegan's contradictions—his desire to teach Filipinos how to participate in the modern world coupled with his convic-tion that they would never be capable of fully understanding it—had their roots in cultural beliefs that Protestants of Anglo-Saxon descent were the originators of modernity and therefore the best capable of practicing it. We see these convictions both in textbooks created for American school-children and in popular literature produced for adults. Both pedagogical and popular texts participated in the creation of a "national Christian"—a figurative representation of an American who embodied the culture's racial, religious, and behavioral values.

I. Textbooks and the Creation of American Identity

Textbook production exploded in the nineteenth century, one sign of the country's enthusiasm for universal education. At first the center of the publishing industry was located in the Northeast, particularly in New England, but later, publishing houses sprang up across the country. Despite the shift in venue, however, textbooks, especially American history, basic literacy, and elocution texts, maintained a national vision grounded in

PEACE ON EARTH
GOOD WILL
TOWARD MEN

FIGURE 4.1: "The Higher Civilization: For Full Particulars Inquire of the Filipinos and the Boers." *Life*, Life Publishing Company, New York, June 28, 1900. [artist: Frederick Thompson Richards]

New England history.[1] What Hank Morgan knew, and how he understood what he knew, can be taken as paradigmatic of American education during the second half of the nineteenth century. One of the most prominent early educators to instruct U.S. schoolchildren in their country's Christian mission was Noah Webster. He is most famous for his *American Dictionary* and the "Blue-Backed Speller," a basic literacy text widely used through the first half of the nineteenth century, but he wrote many other books, including one we have already seen, his *History of the United States; To Which Is Attached a Brief Historical Account of Our England Ancestors, from the Dispersion at Babel, to Their Migration to America; and of the Conquest of South America, by the Spaniards*. The *History*'s first definitive edition, published in 1832, was reprinted numerous times over at least the next decade. Together, the dictionary, speller, and history texts show Webster's conception of an American citizenry: men and women whose consciousness of human moral life was rooted in biblical precepts and for whom "republican" meant citizen of a self-consciously Christian nation.

Webster's central premise is that republicanism and Protestantism are inseparable. "Almost all the civil liberty now enjoyed in the world owes its origins to the principles of the christian (*sic*) religion," he advises in the *History*. "Men began to understand their natural rights, as soon as the reformation from popery began to dawn in the sixteenth century; and civil liberty has been gradually advancing and improving, as genuine christianity (*sic*) has prevailed."[2] "Genuine Christianity" here is defined as specifically Protestant; only those Europeans who broke from the Roman Church were capable of formulating modern political ideals. The upshot, Webster concludes in his closing homily "Advice to the Young," is that "the christian [*sic*] religion" is "the real source of all genuine republican principles" (Webster 1832, 339). For Webster, the American citizen was a product of a distinct line of god-fearing, freedom-loving people who needed only to realize the happy conjunction of ancestry and duty to bring about the millennium.

Webster's education texts set a pedagogical model for American schools, both north and south. The Reverend K. J. Stewart's *Geography for Beginners* (1864), produced for children of the Confederate States of America, shows that the religious basis of American education transcended sectional divides.[3] Despite writing in different eras, from very different geographical terrain, Stewart and Webster share a distinctly Protestant worldview. In Stewart's geography, God is first cause, and "Nature" is defined as "God's handiwork."[4] Within this divinely created landscape, Stewart ranks peoples and cultures along racial and religious lines. The opening chapter consistently associates "Christian" with "civilization" and other religions, races, and cultures with falsehood and ignorance: "Christendom, the civilized and Christianized parts of the world." "Pagan, Heathen, a superstitious worshipper of idols." "Mohammed, the false prophet of Mecca." The true/false dichotomy built into the description of people is followed by descriptions of places of worship: "Church, a temple consecrated to the worship of God." "Cathedral, an Episcopal Church." "Synagogue, a Jewish Church." "Mosque, a Mohammedan Church" (Stewart, 9). Here the reiteration of the word *church* functions to emphasize the centrality of the Christian sacred space the word implies. Chapter quizzes include questions such as "Do savage people surpass civilized people in intelligence? In knowledge? In happiness? In wealth? Have they the Bible?" (Stewart, 35)

Clearly Stewart's book, like Webster's, is predicated on a readership committed to a basic Protestant Christian comprehension of the world, its origins, and its teleology. It would be easy to marginalize these books, to see them as beyond the ordinary boundaries of textbook discourse in the nineteenth century. However, they establish the premises even of those that never, overtly, bring a religious worldview into the picture. Copies of the books could be found across the country—Mary Prior Lynch, reared a slave in North Carolina, learned to read by studying her mistress's copy of Webster's speller.[5] We do not know what texts young Sam Clemens read, but we do know that the pedagogical culture in which he was raised encouraged children to read the Bible as part of their education, a practice so culturally embedded that a Hannibal newspaper of 1853 recommended the Bible as the best preparation for life, referring to it as "wisdom's inexhaustible mine."[6] Both the young slave in North Carolina and the young master (Clemens's family owned slaves) in Missouri came to literacy through instructional materials grounded in Christian principles.[7]

In *The Story of A*, Patricia Crain suggests that the "rites and rituals, both individual and institutional," that surround absorption of the alphabet "permeate" subject formation because memory is, in the end, a process of training, or retraining, the part of the body that we call the brain. What we learn and how we learn it becomes integral to our cognitive framework—how we understand the world.[8] Like the works of his English predecessor Thomas Dilworth, whose eighteenth-century *A New Guide to the English Tongue* Webster revised to create a specifically "American" primer, Webster's textbooks begin by imprinting Christian moral regulations on the brain of the neophyte reader.[9] For instance, his "Blue-Backed Speller"—the one Mary Lynch studied in her mistress's house—reinforces moral identification with Christian precepts by ample quotation from the Bible, inculcating cultural values in tandem with syllabification.[10] The self-consciously "American" element occurs in the suggestion that the culture into which the child is being socialized is both a model of Christian society and a major agent in God's plan to evangelize the world. Together, the speller and the *History* succeeded in imprinting the image of an American landscape in which church and state, even if legally separate, walked hand-in-hand toward national and global redemption.

While not all American textbooks announced their grounding in Protestant Christianity as loudly as Webster's, nevertheless most rested on the same assumptions, and continued to do so throughout the nineteenth century. They created a pedagogical environment in which God was first cause, making it difficult to discuss any theories that did not ultimately return to biblical principles. The struggle to teach Darwinian evolution illustrates the impediments this set of beliefs presented, both to scientific education and to cultural progress. In 1891, Frederick W. Dodell translated *Moses or Darwin?: a school problem for all friends of truth and progress,* a book originally published in Switzerland. In his preface to the American edition, Frederick Dodell lambastes the permeation of the schools by religion:

> The use of the Bible in the public schools, and the use of text-books in reading which contain surreptitiously incorporated religious and dogmatic tenets, is absolutely objectionable. There is so much religious reading matter in the public-school readers that the statute prohibiting religious instruction in the public-school has become *utterly nugatory.*[11]

Dodell was especially concerned about the state of science teaching in American schools, but his observations on the omnipresence of religion in common-school texts extend to the teaching of basic literacy. He believes that the church has a stranglehold on the state: "Although Church and State are theoretically independent of each other, we must not for a moment think that they can exist in neutral juxtaposition for any length of time," he warns. "The Christian Church, ever since she usurped part of the State authority, has ever acted the part of the wolf in the fable, and the State that of the lamb" (Dodell, 19-20).

Even a brief perusal of common-school texts suggests that Dodell was right about the permeation of the school environment by religion. The goal of *American Education: Its Principles and Elements* (1877) was, according to its author, Edward Deering Mansfield, "to excite attention to what should be the elements of an American education; or, in other words, what are the ideas connected with a republican and Christian education in this period of rapid development."[12] Here "American," "republican," and "Christian" are interlocking parts of the American whole. As Dodell sensed, the philosophy behind what we have come to call Creationism also stood behind the construction of American history, suggesting that national interests and religious mission were inseparable. The doctrine of American exceptionalism is, at base, a creationist reading of the national past in terms of its mission into the future—a doctrine suggesting that individuals absorbing its principles would be vulnerable to calls for patriotic action that were couched in religious terms.

The exceptionalist reading of national history permeated the pedagogical environment of the nineteenth-century common-schools. While most American history texts eschew Webster's strategy of beginning the story of the United States with the Book of Genesis, they nevertheless structurally foreground the Protestant reading of American teleological history. Readers and elocution texts were participants in the enterprise. Because they asked students to work out textual meanings and then to memorize and perform them, readers and elocution texts were major players in the project of creating "national Christians"—Americans who conceived of themselves, in their capacity as citizens, at the intersection of Protestant and national identities. This process began in primary school, where readers built on the primers' foundations. For instance, G. S. Hillard's *The Franklin Fifth Reader, for the Use of Public and Private Schools* (1871), an elocution text for young children, begins with the 23rd Psalm and then moves through a collection of old and new pieces that include poems on the Liberty Bell, narratives from American history, and a series of Old Testament tales. Throughout, patriotism and Christianity are treated as inseparable. In the "History of our Flag," a sermon reprinted in the book, students learn that "wherever [the U.S.] flag has gone, it has been a herald of a better day,—it has been the pledge of freedom, of justice, of order, of civilization, and of Christianity. Tyrants only have hated it, and the enemies of mankind alone have trampled it to the earth. All who sigh for the triumph of truth and righteousness, love and salute it" (Hillard, 173). The mix of religious and national sentiment here is the stuff of patriotism; they are hard-wired into the child's cognitive structure through memorization and performance.

Readers intended to teach literacy and literary consciousness also fused lessons in Christian piety to national identity. Henrietta Christian Wright's *Children's Stories in American Literature, 1660–1860* (1896) opens with a story about John Eliot, the Puritan evangelist to the Indians who translated the Bible into one of the Indian languages and created catechisms for Indian children. Speaking to a primary school audience, Wright's text suggests that the story of America begins with the Protestant Christian mission to convert the heathen. It also situates the origins of national literature in "New England literature," and in the Puritans, who she claims were the first to defy the king "and openly declare[d] for freedom of conscience."[13] Religious liberty is emphasized in these texts, coming to stand for the freedoms embodied in the entire Bill of Rights and suggesting that the Puritans were the originators of American civil liberties. Throughout most of the books designed for primary school students, carefully chosen elements of New England history are presented as the markers of a uniquely American national narrative, while the consistent interweaving of Biblical tales, didactic sketches, and essays on the superiority of Christianity urge the reader to imagine his or her best self as the legatee of English Protestants who fled oppression, invented civil liberties, and created a national identity in which patriotism was inseparable from faith.

Texts aimed at older students taught them how to argue the case intellectually, introducing selections from English and classical literatures but maintaining the focus on creating a national citizen. The *McGuffy Readers*, widely used throughout the northern states for more than half a century, are most often cited as the major players in the project of inculcating national and Christian identity in the process of teaching literacy, but they were not alone in the enterprise. Oratory texts especially seek to create citizens who see themselves at the intersection of English, classical, and Protestant identities. For instance, Caleb Bingham's *Columbian Orator* (1821) and Increase Cooke's *American Orator* (1819) both feature classical, English, and American selections, with religion existing as a kind of *a priori* glue. Thus *The Columbian Orator* features not only Cato's "Speech Before the Roman Senate" and Washington's "Address to the People of the United States," but also addresses and essays by famous writers and orators on religious themes, such as Blair's "On the Creation of the World," Cumberland's "Christ's Cruxifiction," and Milton's "Christ Triumphant over the Apostate Angels."[14] *The American Orator* threads religious and national issues throughout the book, juxtaposing essays such as "Religion and Superstition Contrasted" and "Portraits of Mahomet and Jesus Contrasted" with a "Disquisition on Patriotism," "Extracts from Washington's Farewell Address," and eulogies on Washington, Hamilton, and Fisher Ames.[15]

Both *The Columbian Orator* and *The American Orator* suggest that successful orators are men (not women) descended, either lineally or metaphorically, from classical times to the recent past and that the stuff of eloquence links Christian and American manhood. These were the books that inspired Frederick Douglass, the African American slave who taught himself to read through *The Columbian Orator*. The adult Douglass's manliness, his oratorical eloquence, and his familiarity with classical,

English, and Christian writings show just how effective the textbooks could be in creating a citizen who came to self-consciousness through reading. Most importantly, Douglass exemplifies the process by which the neophyte citizen, in learning *how* to read, also absorbed the sentiments that brought him to identify himself as an American legatee of precisely those classical, English, and Christian histories that the texts celebrate. That Douglass was most certainly not the *Columbian Orator*'s intended reader testifies to the texts' power in the shaping of an American citizenry.

Part II: Deploying American Identity:
Popular Writing, Racial Challenge, and
Imperialist Quandaries

If nineteenth-century textbooks sought to create a citizenry that thought of itself at the intersection of Protestant and Enlightenment ideologies, popular adult literature of the turn into the twentieth century demonstrates their success. It also shows how race complicated popular understanding of what it took to qualify for citizenship. Four works in particular exhibit these issues: Charles Sheldon's 1896 novel *In His Steps*, Frank Steward's *Tales of Laguna* (1902–03), Mary H. Fee's *A Woman's Impressions of the Philippines* (1912), and Ernest Crosby's *Captain Jinks, Hero* (1902). Sheldon's novel vigorously advocates the practice of Christian values in the public sphere. Fee's memoir about teaching in the Philippines, and Stewart's short stories about American soldiers stationed there, introduce racial matters, suggesting Americans' attitudes toward the Filipinos they had been sent there to uplift. And Crosby's satiric novel, written out of a passionately anti-imperialist stance, proves the power of the national mythology by attacking it, accusing Americans of using the rhetoric of Christian benevolence as a cover for pillage and commercial aggression.

   First published in 1896, *In His Steps* was and remains one of the most popular novels within the United States in the last 100 plus years, selling over 30 million copies and still counting. Numbers like that suggest that the book supplied readers with a means of actively deploying their conviction of American identity by practicing Protestant Christian values in the public sphere. The novel's central figure is a small-city minister, Henry Maxwell, and its plot details the adventures of Maxwell and a number of his parishioners who pledge to spend a year asking themselves "what would Jesus do?" before embarking on any action. The book is openly evangelical, frequently preaching outright: structurally, each chapter begins with a New Testament quotation, and there are numerous calls and addresses to the reader throughout, usually toward the ends of chapters. There's also plentiful preaching within the fictional framework: in dramatic representations featured in the plot, in letters, and in conversations between people struggling to understand their duties. The novel, in other words, directly addresses its readers; its goal is to force them to practice the Christian values that they claim to affirm.

In "'What Would Jesus Do?' Practical Christianity, Social Gospel Realism, and the Homiletic Novel," a study of the entire genre of evangelical novels of the late nineteenth century, Gregory S. Jackson notes that St. Paul's call to followers to imagine themselves "crucified with Christ"—to be always envisioning themselves walking with Jesus in the "ever present now"—was a central tenet of the Social Gospel.[16] *In His Steps* provides a prime example of the Social Gospel creed: the novel valorizes suffering as the prime mark of an individual's *imitatio Christi*. The authorial assumption seems to be that men and women cannot imitate Christ unless they suffer as Christ did, on the moral and psychological levels if not the physical. Seeking to convince his readers that everyday middle-class life can present serious religious challenges, Sheldon features numerous examples of familial discord and social ostracism suffered by the pilgrims as they launch their year-long journeys. One character, hitherto president of the local college but now about to embark on a project to clean up local politics, admits to Maxwell that he knows he has used the ivy tower to hide from his true responsibilities, but that now he is determined to engage the political arena in order to act out Jesus' commands. "This is where the suffering comes to me," he tells his minister.

> It would not hurt me half so much to lose my position or my home. I loathe the contact with this municipal problem . . . But the call has come to me so plainly that I cannot escape; "Donald Marsh, follow me. Do your duty as a citizen of Raymond at the point where your citizenship will cost you something." . . . Maxwell, this is my cross. I must take it up or deny my Lord.

To which Maxwell replies,

> I am now at a point where, like you, I am driven to the answer the question "what would Jesus do?" one way. My duty is plain. I must suffer.

All my parish work, all my little trials and self-sacrifices, are as nothing to me compared with the breaking into my scholarly, intellectual, self-contained habits of this open, coarse, public fight for a clean city life. . . . The answer to the question, "What would Jesus do?" in this case leaves me no peace, except when I say, "Jesus would have me act the part of a Christian citizen" (Sheldon, 75).[17]

If suffering is the daily experience of Sheldon's Christians, performance of what Maxwell refers to as "Christian citizenship" is their daily role. Sheldon's striving Christians are universally white and middle class. There are no people of color in the book, and the few working class whites represented supply the Christians objects for conversion.[18] These working people are of the lowest class—prostitutes or drunks—and the novel never suggests that they might have their own point of view. Nor for that matter does the novel acknowledge the possibility that a prostitute or an alcoholic might suffer as Christ suffered. In this novel the *imitatio Christi* is the privilege of the already privileged, not the poor.

Generically speaking, *In His Steps* operates more in the realm of the dramatized tract than literary narrative; its characters, for instance, develop piety but not psychological depth, so its considerable cast seems strikingly homogeneous. The novel's moral framework is a series of negative prescriptions. Despite a few initial queries as to how it might be possible to know what Jesus would do in contemporary time and place, the novel quickly abandons any pretense to relativism, its Christians deciding that Jesus would neither drink alcohol nor allow others to drink it, would not have a woman use her voice to sing publicly, would not permit newspapers to report prize fights and other similar sports, and would not tolerate saloons, slum landlords, et cetera, in his town. In order to effect these Christian values, Maxwell and his followers initiate a series of activist purges and lay the foundations for a number of evangelical institutions: they take over newspapers and cleanse them of unchristian matter, they send committed Christians into politics to root out corruption, and they institute settlement houses in cities to uplift the working class. The citizens of the Christian nation envisioned here look, pray, judge, and behave exactly alike, and their mission is to make the rest of the world look, pray, judge, and behave exactly like them. The ideal America Sheldon envisions is white, middle-class, earnest, and utterly devoid of humor.

It's difficult for a non-evangelical to be fair to this novel; its lack of any kind of literary appeal makes it far harder to read than, say, Susan

Warner's bestselling *The Wide, Wide World* (1850), which, although equally evangelical, nevertheless develops real characters; excellent landscape description; and an engaging, if problematical, plot. But the reach of Sheldon's novel was far greater than Warner's; for all its popularity during its time, *The Wide, Wide World* had to be recovered by the Feminist Press in the 1980s and is still rarely encountered outside the academic classroom, whereas *In His Steps* has been in continuous print since its original publication. Its continued mass appeal is reflected in the countless "What Would Jesus Do?" bumper stickers evident across the United States. The point is that this novel has had serious political repercussions over the decades, in large part because it reflects many Americans' basic assumption about who they are and how they should be legislating for each other. And although the novel's events do not move beyond U.S. geopolitical borders, its ultimate goal is the conversion of the world. The discourse within the novel about uplifting the white American poor anticipates the cultural discourse about uplifting the Filipinos that erupted three years after the novel was published. Most interesting are the contradictions inherent in Sheldon's vision of an American citizenry. *In His Steps* assumes a Christian nation obliged to extend itself around the world. At the same time, however, it limits the idea of Christian identity to the white American middle class. It illustrates the contradictory impulses that marked American identity discourse at the turn into the twentieth century.

Part of Sheldon's popularity may rest in the homogeneity of the American demographic landscape in which he believes and the narrow possibilities for success that he envisions. In his novel, differences are of class, not race or ethnicity, and conversion implies economic as well as spiritual salvation. The goal of *In His Steps* is the creation of a middle-class, white Protestant nation; Sheldon's vision reaches no farther. It would be the lot of less evangelically zealous writers to complicate that landscape, tackling the actual diversity of the population and trying to determine how—and if—American identity could be achieved by groups existing outside the magic circle of white Protestantism.

The tension between the desire to uplift and the conviction that non–Anglo-Saxons were incapable of being uplifted becomes most evident when writers move outside U.S. borders. Mary H. Fee's nonfiction memoir *A Woman's Impressions of the Philippines* (1912) traces the adventures of an American teacher among Filipinos living in their own—but American-occupied—country. Fee was among the first wave of Americans sent out by the U.S. government to establish American-style,

English-language schools in the archipelago. In her own words, "I was one of an army of enthusiasts enlisted to instruct our little brown brother, and to pass the torch of Occidental knowledge several degrees east of the international date-line."[19] An intelligent, well-intentioned pedagogue, her memoir illustrates turn-into-the-twentieth-century American educational and racial values. Like her contemporaries, she was initially astounded at the noise and apparent chaos of Filipino schools and she struggled to establish order. Referring to the schoolroom as "the boiler factory," she is keenly attentive to her students. She projects a teacher intent on helping her charges emerge from superstition and ignorance. But Fee ultimately betrays her own belief that in the end, entrenched cultural differences will prevent the Filipinos from competing in the modern world.

What annoys Fee most about the Filipinos is their confidence in their own rectitude. Like Hank Morgan, she finds it hard to believe that the people she is working so hard to uplift don't instantly acknowledge her intellectual superiority. She is irked by the Filipinos' assumption of cultural authority in the face of what she sees as the "narrow experience of the race, and the isolation and the general ignorance of the country" (Fee, 92). Although she was not a missionary, Fee resembles Sheldon's evangelicals in her conviction that the only way to modernity lies in the adoption of middle-class American values. When she realizes the depth of Filipino resistance to losing their cultural identity she decides that they are intellectually inferior—a trait that also explains their affinity for Catholicism. "Roman Catholicism is just what the Filipino needs," she concludes fifteen chapters into the book, in a tone as much piqued as resigned. "[The Filipino] has no zest for morbid introspection, he does not feel the need of bearing testimony to cosmic truth, and in his lack of feeling that need is just as helpless as the man whose system cannot manufacture the necessary amount of digestive juices or red blood corpuscles; he is an invalid, who must be supplied artificially with what his system lacks" (Fee, 204).

Fee believes that the Filipino is constitutionally incapable of developing the spirit of inquiry needed to make an independent people, which she associates with Protestant civilization. Without "the spirit of true Protestantism, which discovers a new light on faith every decade and still is seeking, seeking for the perfect light," Fee's Filipino is content to be told who he is and what his role in life should be. Fee's passion here undercuts her pretension to religious neutrality; the repetition of "seeking," a key word in evangelical discourse, suggests her own understanding of the primacy of Protestant self-questioning in the formation of a self-governing people. One of the Filipinos' constitutional flaws, she suggests, is their contentment with a system that evokes "emotional loyalties" rather than a system that forces individuals to grapple with weighty metaphysical problems. Fee believes the Filipinos are happy with a religion that dictates life patterns and promises salvation because they have never been engaged in religious wars, and never had to justify their religious beliefs in the face of a persistent theological challenge. The Roman Church, Fee concludes, obviates the need to develop the Protestant passion for truth and with it, the intellectual rigor necessary for modern rationality.

Fee also criticizes the Filipinos for accepting their status quo. Comparing American and Filipino schoolchildren, Fee focuses on the Filipinos' national pride and their propensity to question their teacher's own values. Fee's Filipino students think their teacher is poorly informed. "It is sometimes very trying," she complains, "to feel that after long-winded eloquence, after citation and demonstration, you have made no more real impression upon the silent than upon the talkative, and that, indeed, the gentle reserve of some of your auditors is based upon the conviction that your own position is the result of indomitable ignorance" (Fee, 90). Fee's students pass tests on modern science but don't believe its basic premises, they refute her assertions that American oratorical styles are superior, and they have a propensity to over-read praise, taking any favorable comment as evidence that they—and their culture—are "above average for all the world" (Fee, 92).

As one of the first American teachers in the Philippines, Fee arrived in the midst of the American-mandated conversion of the official language from Spanish to English. Linguistically, she was dealing with students who were fluent in one or more native languages but who had limited experience in two Western ones. Although not all Filipinos spoke Spanish, Fee's students seem to be familiar with their former master's tongue. Fee, who spoke some Spanish herself, implies that the Filipinos' Spanish was as inadequate as their English. Apparently unfamiliar with the vibrant Latin American conversation over national variants of the Spanish mother tongue, she insists on the primacy of the northern Spanish form. When a Filipina criticizes her Spanish pronunciation—the Castillian lisp on the letter c for instance—she is outraged by the student's claim that "the Filipinos speak better Spanish than do the Spanish themselves" (Fee, 88). "I imagined some of that young lady's kindred ten years later arguing to prove that the Filipino corruption of th in English words—pronouncing 'thirty' as 'sirty,' and 'thick' as 'sick'—arguing that such English is superior to

English as we speak it" (Fee, 88). Adamantly claiming authenticity in adopting the Castillian lisp for her own Spanish pronunciation, she just as firmly rejects the suggestion that Filipinos might claim a similar lisp for a Filipino variant of the English tongue.

Fee's presentation of her students' linguistic deficiencies suggests that she framed them through the dialect tradition in American writing, an approach that understood linguistic difference in terms of race, ethnicity, and class. *A Woman's Impressions of the Philippines* does not feature much direct representation of native speech. When it does, it almost always "marks" the speech either by orthographic unorthodoxies or by a syntax and vocabulary that make clear that the character is not a skilled English speaker. Fee represents her students' direct speech as a form of dialect, taking care to mark their ethnic difference through their linguistic variations from standard American English. "Good morning, modham," she reports the children "shrieking" as she enters the room, and when she suggests to the native teacher that he leave her in charge of the class, he also responds in dialect, "Yis, all ri'!" (Fee, 81) A helpful child announces the arrival of "one more pupil, letty—dthe girl's mother" (Fee, 83). Throughout, Filipino speech is represented as foreign, and Filipinos generally as incapable of pronouncing standard English.

Mary Fee's indignation about her students' linguistic variations raises the issue of linguistic purity. Fee's fear is that Americans' "pure English" will be corrupted if Filipinos are permitted to sustain their own variants of the official language. For her, linguistic diversity presents a specter of contagion, of being invaded by the foreign. In this, she joins a debate over the linguistic marking of ethnic, regional, and class differences that had been ongoing in the American literary world for at least fifty years. Dialect, especially, had become an art form among American writers, whose fascination with linguistic difference had much in common with the nascent science of ethnography. In American writing of the nineteenth and early twentieth centuries, linguistic purity—the dialect that came to be labeled "standard English"—provides a measure of distance from the center of power. The closer a character stands to the power structure, the more "standard" is his or her speech. Children were taught to speak and write in the standard dialect as a means of transcending their parents' status and obtaining access to powerful communities. But if purity of form represents proximity to power, penetration of the form by linguistic difference represents a threat to the definition of the power itself. In short, Americans attacked the invasion of standard speech by other forms because they saw it as symptomatic of the decline of white Protestant culture and the dilution of Anglo-Saxon purity. And as Senator John W. Daniel's metaphorical use of references to miscegenation made clear (chapter 2), white Americans were morbidly sensitive to the suggestion that purity, whether of language or of blood, might be diluted.

Frank Steward was also interested in language, dialect, and Americans in the Philippines. He was interested in miscegenation as well. A Harvard Law School graduate, he served as an army captain in the archipelago during the Philippine-American conflict. After he returned home he published three short stories in the *Colored American Magazine* between 1902 and 1903. All examine the relationship between American servicemen and Filipinos, especially Filipinas. Most importantly, he shows the effects of the Philippines on the Americans who served there. Steward's stories suggest that Americans should be wary of what they do in the islands because the consequences of their actions might follow them home, like an infection, and spread throughout American culture.

Like Charles Chesnutt in his *Conjure Woman* tales, Steward leaves no textual indication that the author of his stories is black. *Tales of Laguna*, the umbrella title for the three stories published in the CAM, appear to be written from the "default" value of the white American point of view.[20] Racial marking in the stories is reserved for the Filipino characters, and the narrator, like Steward a military officer, speaks from the vantage point of an American whose job it is to monitor the camp and keep order among the men. He has earned the trust of some of the Filipino servants who work for him and appears to be on friendly terms with individuals in the village, although he clearly mistrusts their professions of allegiance. The stories document the ways that the Filipinos, especially the women, use, and are used by, the Americans.

As he documents sexual liaisons between Americans and Filipinas, Steward also documents the commingling of Spanish and Tagalog with English. In these stories miscegenation works on two levels, the sexual and the linguistic, with the linguistic having the farthest-reaching consequences.[21] Even though Stewart's soldiers leave their Filipina paramours behind when they return to the United States, they take home the words and phrases that they have learned in the archipelago, which Stewart perceives as already having begun to corrupt the purity of American English. The soldiers think that they have left the sad Filipinas and their hybrid children behind when they leave the islands—they assume that the Filipinas, not themselves, will suffer the consequences of their actions. But in reality linguistic corruption, a sign of racial corruption, follows them home. Steward's narrator himself exemplifies the process. On the one hand, the narrator refers to the Filipinos' "broken patois" of English, Spanish, and Tagalog as "a gibberish the Army of Occupation has brought about."[22] He reproduces the patois as dialect—a linguistic marker of the racial difference representative of native speakers. "Capitan, esta Enriqueta es (is) mucho starlik," he has one of his female informants report of the protagonist of the story "Starlik."[23] "Pepe was a scribiente at the presidencia and had loved Chata, so the hentes say," he tells us in "Pepe's Anting-Anting" (CAM, vol. 5, no. 5, 359). In sentences like these the mix of English, Spanish, and Tagalog create the "gibberish" to which the narrator refers. The effect of such linguistic mixing is to break down the borders between languages, hybridizing English. The publication of the stories within the United States—as the African American editors of *The Colored American* may have realized—suggests that the worst fear of the Anglo-Saxon majority was being realized; the purity of the race and its language was being undermined by the contact between Americans and the inhabitants of an archipelago 7,000 miles from the Pacific coast.

Tales of Laguna demonstrate how alien the Filipinos appeared to American soldiers and how the men assumed their own racial and cultural superiority. The Americans, including the narrator, refer to older women as "hags," and the rest of the Filipinos as "pickaninnies" and "gugus." The islanders' Catholicism is treated as both exotic and retrograde, from the descriptions of the elaborate black clothes that women wear for church to the toleration the Church appears to have for native fetishes, or talismans. At once exotic and inferior, the Filipinos are too far from the American idea of racial and religious homogeneity to be imaginable within U.S. borders. American soldiers' readiness to cohabit with Filipinas, coupled with their equal readiness to desert them when the soldiers are mustered out, suggests that such unions, and the children that result from them, are outside the boundaries of "real" American identity. Yet the story of Texan soldier Duncan Lane, of "The Men Who Prey," shows the process of both racial and linguistic hybridization. In Texas, we are informed, Lane and his wife are known as the model American couple. This, however, presents no obstacle to Lane's "matrimoning" with a young servant, Jacinta, in the Philippines. The story is not just an indictment of Lane's betrayal of both wife and mistress, however. What to the American Lane is a casual liaison without consequences turns out to be the first step in the undermining of the white purity he and his family represent. Jacinta believes that Lane will take her to the United States, a goal for Filipinas who enter relationships with American soldiers. She dreams of

> a big ship, a long journey, railroad cars swift-running, great cities, wonders and marvels without end in the land of the Americanos, and amid all a large house in the far-off country, numerous servants, and a husband so tall, so loving, so white.[24]

Despite Jacinta's expectations, when Lane's term of service is ended he joyously returns home, carelessly abandoning Jacinta, who is about to deliver his child. Yet, Steward suggests, the model American family will not escape infection by the Philippines. Lane's Texas wife, operating on Lane's written instructions, has unwittingly named their new baby girl after her husband's Filipina paramour. "Jacinta Lane" will grow up as a sign that not only have the Americans left something of themselves in the islands, but that the islands have also begun to transform even the whitest of American families.

Steward's stories resemble Mary Fee's memoir in their illustration of American attitudes toward people whose racial and religious cultures differed radically from the American norm. They also closely examine how those attitudes are played out in a location where the American, himself a stranger, attains colonial power. Steward's Americans are not preparing Filipinos for self-governance; rather, they are unwittingly setting in motion a process that will transform their own country. Perhaps because, as an African American, Steward had a vantage point beyond Fee's, he could see that imperialism would inevitably impact American culture. And in his insight he confirmed the worst fears of those who opposed annexation on racial grounds: acquisition of the Philippines would change the trajectory of American life. As a colonial power, the United States would face the experience of becoming an abusive authority, a position for which it had always criticized other countries. Moreover, in the long run it would also experience the erosion of white hegemony, as the increasing political and economic power of people of color became apparent.

Fee and Steward were both participants in the Philippine-American War and its aftermath. In contrast, Ernest Crosby watched from the comfortable—but considerably more outraged—vantage point of a member of the Anti-Imperialist League. Crosby's 1902 *Captain Jinks, Hero*, a biting antiwar novel illustrated by Dan Beard (who also illustrated *A Connecticut*

Yankee in King Arthur's Court), was the best-known work of anti-imperialist fiction of its day, a dramatic counterpart to Twain's "To the Person Sitting in Darkness." In fact, Crosby's chapter on General Funston is probably what motivated Twain to write his own satiric "Defense of General Funston" (1902).

Like Frank Steward, Ernest Crosby was trained as a lawyer. During the course of his life he served both in the New York State legislature and as a judge in the International Court in Alexandria, Egypt. A disciple of Tolstoy and Henry George, he became one of the most notable reformers and anti-imperialists of the turn into the twentieth century, including a stint as president of the Anti-Imperialist League of New York. He also was a poet, an essayist, a popular speaker, and a prolific writer of letters to editors. He was published in the *New York Times*, the *International Socialist Review*, and *The Social Gospel*, and he was a friend of both Mark Twain and of William Dean Howells. Among Crosby's publications is *Swords and Ploughshares*, a selection of his anti-imperialist poems.

Captain Jinks, Hero follows the life of Sam ("Captain") Jinks, a gentle farm boy whose father makes the mistake of giving him a set of tin soldiers for his sixth birthday. The child, despite his "tenderness of disposition," also had "inherited another still stronger trait, and this was a deep respect for authority," and this becomes the conduit for all his subsequent adventures.[25] Sam is a Candide character who worships authority and believes whatever he is told, which makes him the ideal soldier. The tin soldiers channel the boy's proclivities and he becomes obsessed by everything military. After childhood he attends "East Point," the military academy in the East, where he excels in obedience and adulation for authority, even glorying in his near brush with death from hazing because, he believes, it puts him in *imitatio* of all the great military figures who have experienced the same torture. With his friend, Cleary, a budding journalist, he quits East Point to fight in the war with the "Cubapines," Crosby's fusion of the Cuban and Filipino insurgents.

The young men go to "Havilla," where, as Cleary sends back dispatches glorifying his adventures, Sam makes his name, capturing "Gomaldo," leader of the insurgents (i.e. Emilio Aguinaldo, whom Funston captured). After winning fame in the Cubapines, Sam (and Cleary) go to "Porslania" (China), to take part in the suppression of the "Fencer" (Boxer) rebellion. Sam's reputation soars, putting him in line for the American presidency. However, Sam has a sudden, terrifying realization that for all his military experience and expertise, he will never be the perfect soldier because he cannot imagine killing his fiancé, Marian, if ordered to do so for the good of the state. Sam goes into a decline, returns home, and eventually ends up in a lunatic asylum, playing with tin soldiers.

Captain Jinks, Hero is no more subtle a novel than *In His Steps*. A satire, its characters could be easily transformed into comic book or cartoon figures. Crosby trots gleefully through it, taking aim at targets ranging from the hazing of new cadets at West Point to the transformation of local criminals into military heroes, rural thugs who are decorated for deploying their barn-burning skills to the destruction of ancient Chinese temples. One of Crosby's heaviest barrages targets missionaries who are despoiling China and the Christian rhetoric they use to justify the Western invasion. Like Twain's "To the Person Sitting in Darkness," Crosby argues that the missionaries were in China for worldly wealth rather than for converts. He recounts the story of the missionaries' appropriation of Porsslanese land and their collusion with foreign governments, commenting on their readiness to provide "temporal as well as celestial advantages" in the form of "cheap goods, rum, opium, and fire arms." When the Porsslanese steadfastly resist these "benevolent enterprises," the Great Powers—the "Anglians," the "Musconians," the "Tutonians," the "Franks," and the "Japs"—come to the missionaries' aid by invading and dividing the country among themselves.

Having provided his readers with the outlines of recent Chinese history, Crosby satirizes the rhetoric of benevolence used to legitimize the destruction the Westerners had caused. When Sam arrives in Porslania and travels up the Hai-Po River toward Gin-Sin, the capital, he notices civilian corpses floating in the water, "bodies drifting past, brainless skulls, eyeless sockets, floating along many of them as if they were swimming on their backs" (Crosby, 260). An "Anglian" passenger explains that the occupying armies, particularly the Europeans, shoot civilians and kill the wounded military men as a disciplinary measure. He regards the murders as "really a fine example of the power of civilization." He also reproves the young Americans for their own country's restraint. "You and the Japs have been culpably lenient, if you will permit me to say so," he notes. Instantly on the defensive, Sam protests that the military might of the United States is still developing. "We are only just starting out on our career as a military nation," he explains. "You must not expect too much of us at first. We'll soon get our hand in. As for the Japs, why they' re heathen. They can hardly be expected to behave like Christians" (Crosby, 260).

"Christian behavior" and Christian ideology become Crosby's targets in the "Purslania" section of the novel. A man of the cloth, the "Canon Gleed," delivers the Christian point of view. "'These are great days, Colonel Jinks,'" the missionary begins, "rubbing his hands with a benignant smile."

> Great days, indeed, for foreign missions. What would St. John have said on the island of Patmos if he could have cabled for half-a-dozen armies and half-a-dozen fleets, and got them too? He would have made short work of his jailers. As he looks down upon us to-night, how his soul must rejoice! The Master told us to go into all nations, and we are going to go if it takes a million troops to send us and keep us there (Crosby, 271).

Gleed offers to introduce Sam to "a true saint of the Lord," the "Rev. Dr. Amen"—Crosby's pointed reference to the Reverend William Ament, whose insistence that Chinese peasants pay enormous restitution for missionary deaths so enraged Mark Twain. In Crosby's novel, Amen's reputation precedes him. Seeing valuable Chinese goods being unloaded from carts by American soldiers, Sam and Cleary ask a young lieutenant where the objects came from. "Oh, anywhere," the young man replies.

> Some of it from the houses of foreign residents even. But we don't understand the game as well as old Amen. He's a corker. He's grabbed the house of one of his old native enemies here, an awfully rich chap, and sold him out, and now he's got his converts cleaning out a whole ward. He's collected a big fine for every convert killed and so much extra for every dollar stolen, and he's going to use it all for the propagation of the Gospel.

To which Sam affirms that he is "glad we have such a man to represent our faith" (Crosby, 286). The "our" here is telling. Amen represents American Protestant culture generally. For Sam, Amen is a model for America's Christian mission to the world.

Because the Boxer Rebellion was triggered by missionary activities, it gave Crosby an opportunity to challenge Christian rhetoric as it was used to justify the Western invasion of China. In contrast, the Spanish-American War had been triggered by colonies attempting to free themselves from an imperialist power, and Americans could justify their intervention in terms of their own revolutionary history. In *Captain Jinks*, Crosby's satire aims at the rhetoric of rights as it was actually played out in the islands in the aftermath of war. During a brief stint as Censor in the Cubapines, Sam is brought a set of handbills confiscated from a local printer, which suggest, in Spanish, that "governments are made to preserve liberty, and that they get their only authority from the free will of the people who are ruled by them." Sam labels the sentiments "clearly seditious," and orders the handbills burned and the printer arrested (Crosby, 228). Although he learns that the circulars were copies of the Declaration of Independence that had been translated into Spanish for distribution to the Cubapinos, he reaffirms that "the circular ought to be suppressed anyway. What business have these people to talk about equal rights and the consent of the governed? The men who wrote the Declaration—Jeffries and the rest—were mere civilians and these ideas are purely civilian" (Crosby, 239).

Sam's reference to Thomas Jefferson as "Jeffries" illustrates his tenuous grasp of American history, a potshot at the U.S. educational system. His reference to the Cubapines as "these people" illustrates many Americans' conviction that the rhetoric of rights really only applies to white Americans. And his dismissal of the Founding Fathers as "mere civilians" illustrates the danger posed by a military that feels itself empowered to act beyond the law. Despite steamships and telegraphs, the U.S. military in the Philippines was a long way from home, and the lack of immediate communication with stateside authorities gave rise to systematic transgressions of the rules of warfare. Four years after *Captain Jinks* was published, the Moro Massacre of 1906 would provide the most egregious example of the consequences of military empowerment when the American military systematically killed over 600 Moro civilians—many of them women and children—who had taken shelter in the crater of a dead volcano. Certainly ongoing investigations into reports of torture by the U.S. military throughout 1902 fueled Crosby's anger. Sam's devotion to the military system, his conviction that only the military matters, is Crosby's warning that the conversion of America's republican energies into imperialism and militarism was undermining American freedoms.

In *Captain Jinks, Hero*, the rhetoric of rights, wedded to the rhetoric of Christian mission used to justify the U.S. army as it joined forces with England and Europe to rape and pillage their way through Southeast Asia, provided evidence of the fragility of the American narrative. Within U.S. borders, the rise of lynching, the passage of numerous anti-immigration acts, and the brutal suppression of worker revolts had already proved the narrow application of the narrative of American civil liberties. As Mark Twain noted in "The Secret History of Eddypus, the World Empire," the country's accession to colonial power exposed the national narrative as a fraud. Confronted by peoples they believed incapable of self-government, most Americans could not imagine uplift actually succeeding—morally, economically, or politically. One result of the experiment was that the rhetoric of benevolence quickly evolved into the language of colonial domination. If Hank Morgan's story proved that American Protestant culture could not be exported, Sam Jinks's illustrated the fallacy of using the rhetoric of American rights and Christian outreach to justify imperialism.

FIGURE 1. Albert Beveridge (1862–1927), Library of Congress, Prints and Photographs Division, LC-USZ62-118042.

FIGURE 2. Benjamin Tillman (1847–1918), Library of Congress, Prints and Photographs Division, LC-DIG-ggbain-13454.

FIGURE 3. William McKinley (1843–1901), Library of Congress, Prints and Photographs Division, LC-USZ62-13025.

FIGURE 4. José Martí (1853–1895), Library of Congress, Prints and Photographs Division, LC-USZ62-113376.

FIGURE 5. Rubén Darío (1867–1916), courtesy of National Archives.

FIGURE 6. José Enrique Rodó (1872–1917).

FIGURE 7. José Rizal (1861–1896), Library of Congress Prints and Photographs Division, LC-USZ62-43453.

Emilio Aguinaldo.
National Archives photo no. 111-SC-98358.

FIGURE 8. Emilio Aguinaldo. Courtesy of National Archives (Photo no. 111-SC-98358).

nu at wnose insugauon
friends and fellow-country-
itally shot on the Luneta;
of Americans flocking to a
ven to the visitor, beside
Nozaleda and three other
taries. Had these people
onfidence
d kindly
Ameri-
ight have
hopeful
As it is,
us, and
ese rela-
f a com-
i the old
rulers."
o the un-
at Arch-
id stated
orized to
monastic
; undis-
says:
ias given
emphatic
ite effect
el to the
oitterness
eans. All
support
that the
oposed a
existing
id would
by arms
t such a
y beyond
easonable
American
ange the
io people
w of it.
ready as-
Filipino
with the
the Latin
xon, be-
l and the
Spanish
an ways.
orance of
rident to
utterly
it does
constitute
n much of our consideration
Thousands believe in a pre-
i between the American au-
ie religious bodies against
the Filipino people main-

*" Now we have a querulous, discontented
population of half-castes, who, sooner or later,
will bring about a distracted state of society,
and occupy the whole force of the government
to stamp out the discord."*—Father Pedro

Murillo Velarde, of Manila, in his work on
the Filipinos.

It shall be my endeavor to sketch the Mes-
tizo leaders of the Filipino insurrection, and

islands, piunging them ia
revolution? Who are Pate
Mascardo, Artachio, Pila
Luna? Are they men of
and intelligence, or adventu
And what sort of looking
It was more difficult to
looked t
Filipino
possessi
of the
kept the
They g
tives as
contrab.
lest the
to be h
priso
amigos.
ist offi
that no
graphs
out, for
son tha
that th
shooter
miliar
Howeve
fort and
tograph
known
cured, a
ed. (Se
On C
the ne
Pedro
house.*
section
is there
interest
On the
a life-s
mother,
Paterno
nearly
leaders,
For ye:
controll
That he
was ar
Spain
"Granc
Filipino
nila th
When
tion
mised,
Spain buying out the Fil
Paterno was so well pois
he was able to draw a do
his services. Despite his
Spain, and his public a

SEÑOR APOLINARIO MABINI
Ex-Secretary of State in Aguinaldo's cabinet, as he appeared in 1900 in his invalid chair at the
Anda Street Police Station, Walled City, Manila

FIGURE 9. Apolinario Mabini. Reproduced from *Harper's History of the War in the Philippines*, ed. Marrion Wilcox. New York: Harper & Brothers Publishers, 1900, p. 363. Image provided courtesy of The New York Public Library (Milstein Division).

FIGURE 10. Mark Twain at the top of the steps. Courtesy of Elmira College.

FIGURE 11. "Mauvais Sujet"
"Spain: `Caramba! Amigo Jonathan, your new citizen looks happy!'
Jonathan: `Citizen!" Not much. Guess I'll have to make a subject of him!'"
Punch, or the *London Charivar*, Punch Publications Ltd., London, June 5, 1901,
p. 413. [artist: Bernard Partridge]

FIGURE 12. "The White Man's Burden (Apologies to Kipling)"
Judge, Arkell Publishing Company, New York, 1899. [artist: Victor Gillam]

FIGURE 13. "The Two Great Missioners of Civilization"
Judge, Arkell Publishing Company, New York 1898. [artist: Victor Gillam]

The first step towards lightening

The White Man's Burden

is through teaching the virtues of cleanliness.

Pears' Soap

is a potent factor in brightening the dark corners of the earth as civilization advances, while amongst the cultured of all nations it holds the highest place—it is the ideal toilet soap.

FIGURE 14. Pears' Soap Ad, "The White Man's Burden"
Harper's Weekly, Harper & Brothers, New York circa 1898.

FIGURE 15. "Peace"

Puck, Keppler & Schwarzmann, New York, March 29, 1905. [artist: John S. Pughe]

FIGURE 16. "Can the Missionary Reach This Old Savage?" *Journal* (Minneapolis), also published in *The Literary Digest*, vol. 22, no. 19, May 11, 1901, p. 578. [artist: "Bart" Charles Bartholomew]

Section III

The Eyes of the World

"The White Man's Burden," the Philippines, and the Anglo-American Alliance

The London *Times* published "The White Man's Burden" on February 4, 1899, two days before the Senate debate on annexation. The publication date and the poem's subtitle, "An Address to the United States," suggest its calculated timeliness; Rudyard Kipling, arguably Britain's best-known living poet, was urging the United States to annex the Philippines. Interestingly, Mark Twain seems to have said nothing in regard to the poem, even though it appeared just when he was beginning to understand that U.S. intervention into Spain's struggles with its colonies was a means for the United States to gain territories, not to assist struggling revolutionaries. The amount of attention that Kipling's poem received on both sides of the Atlantic would suggest that Twain, who rarely hesitated to pass judgment on imperialist issues, might have at least commented on the numerous parodies that instantly appeared, but there is no record of his having said a word, or contributed a parody of his own. Nor did he address the poem in any extant speeches or writings, including letters and journal entries, despite his numerous references to many of Kipling's other works. In his excellent examination of Twain and Kipling's literary friendship, Leland Krauth has noted the writers' mutual admiration and Kipling's own literary debts to Twain, especially in learning to utilize the vernacular voice and the "good bad boy" as a protagonist. But he also notes that their paths diverged on the subject of imperialism, with Kipling very much in support of the British program in India, and Twain, especially

FIGURE 5.1: "Hands Across the Sea. John Bull—'Shake, and we will boss the whole world.'" *Judge*, Arkell Publishing Company, New York, June 11, 1898. [artist: Victor Gillam]

after his trip around the world, gradually coming to understand that "benevolent assimilation" was just another name for commercial greed. Late in life Twain would privately comment that Kipling "loves power and authority and Kingship."[1] But he never said anything critical of Kipling publicly, and he remained an avid reader of Kipling's work. In a rare act of self-restraint, he refrained from an attack that might destroy his relationship with a fellow writer.[2]

Mark Twain, however, seems to have been one of the few people *not* to have commented on the poem in one way or another. Perhaps because of its timeliness, perhaps because of Kipling's fame, perhaps because of its bouncy rhyme scheme, "The White Man's Burden" entered popular consciousness in a way that few poems ever do. My focus here is on the conversations out of which the poem sprang and into which it was received, on both sides of the Atlantic. Most of the scholarly conversations about the poem have focused on Kipling's intentions, or on exactly what he meant by "white."[3] In contrast, I am interested in the way the poem was used by his contemporaries, especially in their arguments about annexation. I am also interested in the poem's function as an agent in the

Anglo-American alliance that emerged during the later years of the nineteenth century and was fortified by events at the turn into the twentieth century. The prospect that the United States might enter the circle of imperialist nations was of considerable interest to Britons, and several British periodicals, especially those generally favorable to imperialism, urged the United States to annex. The language of the arguments proffered in these periodicals provided the linguistic source from which the language of Kipling's poem was generated.

The poem found a ready audience as soon as it was published. In England the pro-imperialist periodicals, reading it as encouragement, instantly recycled it to enhance their arguments. It entered into the discussions on the opposite side of the Atlantic as well, although not all readers interpreted it as encouraging imperialism. As we have seen, three days after it was published, anti-imperialist Senator Tillman had it read into the *Congressional Record* as a warning about the dire consequences of a U.S. vote in favor of annexation. Expansionists, on the other hand, heard it as a call to spread Anglo-Saxon civilization around the globe. Clearly, the poem's murky language gave turn-into-the-twentieth-century readers as much trouble as it gives readers today. For our purposes, however, the incorporation of "The White Man's Burden" into the conversation highlights the role that the national narrative of religion and race played in the debates over annexation. If the poem was generated within a British context that celebrated Anglo-Saxons' responsibilities to the peoples they conquered, it was received within a U.S. context that filtered messages through Americans' preoccupation with their destiny as a Christian nation.

The British Context

When Mark Twain talks about the Concert of World Powers in "To the Person Sitting in Darkness," he is referring to the group of European nations holding the most colonies. While U.S. congressmen debated the effect of annexation on their country's moral fiber, this group was watching to see what the young nation would do. Conscious of the wealth and energy already demonstrated by the United States, European nations generally—and the imperialist powers particularly—were both curious about and leery of the American decision. Given its material wealth and power, the United States could prove a formidable contestant in the battle for foreign territory. Beyond Spain, which responded to the loss of the last shreds of its empire by retreating into a national doldrum, no European country was more interested in the Americans' decision than Great Britain, where imperialists looked for ways to contain and control the rising power. The dialogue begun by pro-expansionist British periodicals such as the *Spectator* and the *London Times* during this period shows how the mass media interpreted Britain's imperialist history and urged the United States to model itself on the mother country.[4]

Although many Britons opposed U.S. expansion, a sizeable—and articulate—element supported it. The British periodicals that I am examining here actively encouraged the United States to launch itself upon the global stage. For these papers, American imperialism was a significant factor in the evolving relationship between Great Britain and its former colony. Their steady stream of commentary influenced the Americans' decision to annex and provided the ideas and language from which Kipling's poem was generated. The poem's signal phrases, understood within the framework of racial and national obligations, entered into sentiments on both sides of the Atlantic and provided both the British and the Americans with a shorthand for discussions about the U.S.'s future role in the Philippines and on the global stage generally.

Despite the very different tones and target audiences of the individual papers, the explicit goal of the pro-imperialist press in England was to encourage readers to support British expansion around the world. The papers saw one aspect of their job as creating imperialist ideology and teaching their readers how to understand it. The *Economist*, dedicated to providing financial information to its readers, also employed political writers who supported "principled imperialism," that is, a commitment to imperialist interventions that would benefit both the home country and the colonials themselves. Oriented more toward arts and letters than the *Economist*, in the 1880s and 1890s the *Spectator* bore similar sentiments, in part because some of its political writers also wrote for the *Economist*.[5] The *Times*, generally conservative, joined the *Economist* and the *Spectator* in their views of the course America should take. And a newcomer, the *Daily Mail*, launched in 1896 and aimed at a middle-class readership, was militantly—jingoistically—pro-imperialist from the start.

Interestingly, given that they were staunch supporters of their own country's colonial projects, these periodicals all encouraged the United States to join the imperialist club.[6] All betray a sense of unease with the energetic young country, and they endorse American imperialism as a way to create new alliances between Great Britain and the United States. It is possible to see this as a conscious ploy—rather than actively discouraging the Americans from becoming global competitors, periodicals supporting imperialism urged them to join Great Britain in what they described as an international enterprise to uplift the world. An important corollary to their argument was that the British would mentor the fledgling colonial power in the ways and means of imperial rule. Their encouragement would contain a potentially serious competitor, especially in the rush to control the Far East. The British, who already had substantial merchant houses in the Philippines, knew that the archipelago was the gateway to China. If they could not control it themselves, it would be useful to have a strong ally there. Otherwise, they feared that the islands would fall to one of the other predator nations, particularly Germany.[7]

The papers' commentary played variations on four major themes: Anglo-Saxon unity, the responsibilities inherent in being a colonial power, the need for a well-defined and knowledgeable colonial administration, and the British colonial regime in India as a model for U.S. imperial rule.[8] The emphasis on Anglo-Saxon unity was the most frequently proclaimed: the papers established a racial brotherhood between Americans and Englishmen, alleging a common heritage and pledging support in times of crisis. They also suggested that of all the European nations, England was America's only real friend. Finally, they painted the racial brotherhood in a moral hue, emphasizing that Anglo-Saxon superiority brought with it the duty to bring Anglo-Saxon civilization to those whom Mark Twain labeled "the person[s] sitting in darkness." As we have seen, the call for cultural unity was sounded frequently in the United States, so the British proclamation of Anglo-Saxon brotherhood played nicely into pre-existing American racial ideologies. The emphasis on "responsibility" rendered another rationale for imperialism: according to the "principled imperialism" creed, conquerors should not simply exploit the lands they occupy; rather, they have a responsibility to uplift the subject peoples, bringing them gradually into the light of Western civilization.[9] The papers argued that in contrast to Spain, which shamelessly exploited the archipelago, the United States could improve the Filipinos' lives, an argument that dovetailed admirably with the idea of missionary outreach. The model for all of this, according to the periodicals, should be British rule in India, which had benefited the Indians by instituting an ordered civil government even while preserving most native customs. The papers described the development of the British Civil Service as a model for Americans; Great Britain, they suggested, could teach the Americans how to develop a similar service for their own colonies.

Historians have long noted that in the British narrative, the ideological roots of Anglo-American friendship pointed to a common race and a shared history. For Americans much of the framework for the war had to do with complex racial issues. As the U.S. congressional debates demonstrate, both expansionists and anti-expansionists were anxious to keep the United States "white"—to hold on to the belief that the vast majority of the U.S. population was descended from Anglo-Saxon stock. Although by 1898 this claim had become less and less tenable, the racial narrative so dominated American self-imaging that all arguments, pro or con, had to reflect it. The British papers happily conformed, using American prejudices to further their own ends. The *Daily Mail* may have been the most blatant on this score, though not by far. An article by G. W. Steevens, published early in the U.S.-Spanish conflict, concretely states that even though Americans "are not really Anglo-Saxons at all,"

> it is still true that we are of common stock. Whether that will be true a century hence is a hard riddle; but to deny it now is to mistake a process— the modification of the old English blood by admixture of . . . Teutons and Slavs—for an accomplished fact.
>
> I look down the columns of news, and I find that the men who are leading the States today—McKinley, Long, Miles, Sampson, Dewey— are all as plainly of British stock as were the Lincolns, Lees, Grants, and Shermans of the last generation. Till now
>
> THE ANGLO-SAXON HAS ALWAYS LED
>
> the population of the States; let us wait till Poles and Dagos sit in the White House, and lead American fleets, and begin to cavil then.[10]

Less explicit in their ethnic disdain, the other papers conveyed similar sentiments. For the *Spectator*, racial alliances between Britain and the United States were primary, especially when one of the pair was attacked: "We have no desire to go beyond the acknowledgment of the fact, for fact it is, that if either we or the States ever get our backs to the wall the other Anglo-Saxon will be at his side" (*S*, November 19, 1898: 726), it claimed. Implicit here is the message that on the Continent at least, Great Britain was America's only friend.

Not surprisingly, arguments for taking on the responsibility for governing the Philippines appeared most frequently between the U.S.-Spanish truce declared in August of 1898 and the vote to annex the Philippines in early February 1899. The *Times* made its position clear when it commented on the initial Spanish response to U.S. demands in negotiations over the Treaty of Paris. "This demand for the absolute cession of the Philippines is said to have been received with profound astonishment by the Spanish delegates," the *Times* reported late in 1898.

> It is somewhat difficult to believe that the surprise with which the American demand has been met can be entirely unfeigned. . . . American opinion has gone through some rapid changes since the collapse of the Spanish power. At first there was an extreme unwillingness . . . to assume dominion of distant territories, inhabited by alien races and with a tropical climate. But the manifest inability of the Spanish Government to exercise effective dominion . . . has compelled the Americans to recognize to the fullest extent the *responsibility* involved in the victory.

The *Times* was anxious that readers should know that England was acting disinterestedly. "Great Britain has no other interest in the Philippines except that peace and order should be maintained and that there should be an 'open door' for commerce," the editorial continued.

> We cannot hope that these objects would be secured by leaving the islands either to the defeated and discredited Spaniards or to the semi-civilized followers of Aguinaldo and his rivals, who are crying, "The Philippines for the Filipinos." We can hardly doubt that either an inefficient protectorate or an unstable independence would make these regions the scene of mischievous international conflicts. It is for the Americans, as we have said from the outset, to decide whether or not they will formally take upon themselves the *responsibilities* in which their victories have involved them. (*T*, November 1, 1898: 9; emphasis added)

In emphasizing "responsibility" and urging the United States to position itself as both protector of the archipelago and—not incidentally—guardian of the gateway to trade with the Far East, the *Times* established its advisory position in regard to the Americans' imperial future. Britain wanted to safeguard its interests in the Philippines, which became even more important as its interests in China expanded. If Britain could persuade the Americans to ally themselves with British interests, British power in the East would be considerably augmented. The pro-imperialist papers pressed the issue as hard as possible. "As our readers know, our hope is that America will accept her *responsibilities* in the Philippines, and not leave the islands virtually derelict, or, still worse, allow them still to continue under Spain," the *Spectator* had urged in August of 1897 (*S*, August 13, 1897; emphasis added). A few days later it laid out its own perspective by wrapping the racial argument together with the argument from responsibility:

> We believe that it is the destiny of the United States to obtain possessions oversea peopled by inferior races, who will require for many generations to be governed wisely and humanely rather than to have flung at their heads rights and privileges which, though admirably suited to men of the Anglo-Saxon race, and to those white races which they have absorbed and digested, have no meaning for, and are of no use to, men in a lower stage of social and political development (*S*, August 20, 1897: 232–33).

In other words, the United States, by virtue of its Anglo-Saxon heritage, must assume the responsibility for governing peoples constitutionally incapable of governing themselves.

The British press also capitalized on the fact that U.S. intervention in Spanish affairs had made the Americans unpopular in Europe. As early as May, 1898, the *Economist* suggested that the United States would not receive much support from other European countries. Americans, the *Economist* reported,

> had been, we believe, under a perfectly honest illusion that they were popular on the Continent; that if they had "unfriends" anywhere it was in England, and that France in particular was sure to be on their side. They had not an idea that the Continent has a kind of solidarity, that the attack on Spain was bitterly resented, and that . . . they themselves were cordially disliked by the Governments of the Continent. Their only sincere well-wisher, in fact, was the Government of Great Britain. . . . (*E*, May, 28, 1898: 794–95)

The strategy here is telling—the *Economist* first informs the United States that it is far more isolated than it thinks and then suggests that Great

Britain is its only friend. The *Spectator*, too, notes that whereas the Europeans "are in full cry, especially in Paris, against this insulting and arrogant Power," nevertheless in England "public opinion . . . is quite sound, and strongly, if decorously and prudently, with America" (*S*, April 9, 1898: 530). "I understand that had Britain's attitude not been so extremely pro-American, certain European Powers would have openly sided with Spain before the outbreak of the war," chimed in the *Daily Mail'*s Vienna correspondent. "The United States was never so unpopular in Europe as now, and the 'effete' Continental monarchies would gladly strike a blow at the flourishing Republic across the Atlantic" (*DM*, May 7, 1898: 4).

In suggesting why other European powers might sympathize with Spain rather than with the United States, the correspondent for the *Times* pointed out American hypocrisies and noted that for many Europeans, Spain, for all her faults, merited sympathy from the European family:

> The Americans began by declaring that they were waging a war of principles and enfranchisement. They then confiscated Puertorico [*sic*] as a war indemnity. Next . . . they refused the sovereignty of Cuba, which has a debt of two milliards of francs. Then, repudiating their declaration of disinterestedness, they demand the sovereignty of the Philippine archipelago. . . . These are not hypotheses, but facts, and the most ardent supporters of the United States cannot prevent public opinion in Europe from noting them. Spain, no doubt, has to regret . . . many violent and arbitrary acts, which she is now expiating . . . but this series of faults . . . cannot prevent Europe from perceiving her present misfortune, and from judging equitably the crushing harshness of the conditions she is undergoing (*T*, November 4, 1898: 8).

The papers were not fabricating European antipathy; it existed. Twain, then in Europe, felt it, noting to his sister-in-law that "French sympathy with Spain is outspoken; & by consequence Paris is not an American heaven any more, now."[11] News of the hostility echoed across the Atlantic, as did Great Britain's avowals of friendship. During a speech in the Senate, Colorado senator Edward O. Wolcott, speaking of the British as Americans' "brethren," reminded his colleagues that "Had it not been for England we should not have emerged from the late war with our colours flying so high as they do to-day. We have among the nations of Europe only one friend—Great Britain. The other nations stand with rapacious hate hoping we may encounter some repulse" (*T*, February 6, 1899: 6).

The British pro-imperialists also took it upon themselves to advise the Americans about colonial policies. All agreed that the United States should practice "principled imperialism," governance based on the theory that effective colonial power is exercised for the greater good of the subject colony, not the mother country. In order to put colonial policies in place, they argued, the Americans would have to develop an administrative body for the archipelago. The British, they modestly concluded, should become advisors to the United States because their long experience in colonial governance had taught them all that the Americans would need to know. This would be especially important when it came to racial matters. Both the *Economist* and the *Spectator* insist that the United States should heed her Anglo-Saxon sibling in learning how to manage the people of color whose lives they suddenly controlled. The papers did not hesitate to note that the Americans had a poor track record on the racial front. "Can the nation which can hardly be said to have done justice to its 7 millions of black citizens at home, do justice to 10 millions of black, yellow, and brown men 6,000 miles away?" asked the *Economist* in November (*E*, "The American Elections," November 12, 1898: 1618–19).

The periodicals agreed that Great Britain should tutor the fledgling imperialist in administrative matters, especially in the ways and means of "principled imperialism." They hastened to remind the United States that their new dependents lacked the Anglo-Saxon's talent for self-government. In the scheme they outline, "for their own good" signals "protection" rather than republicanism. The *Spectator* recommended that the United States not attempt to impose republican institutions on the islands: "They must not, because at home they believe in representative government and elective institutions, rush to endow the people of the tropics with similar powers. They must rather consider, not whether voting is good in the abstract, but whether an electoral system is likely or not to be conducive to the prosperity, moral and physical, of the Philippines" (*S*, "America's New Empire," December 3, 1898: 821–22). "A Tagal will need the training of generations before he is made into an American citizen," agreed the *Economist* (*E*, "Some Minor Difficulties in the Way of Americans," July 23, 1898: 1070). "Will [the U.S.] make the first grand failure of the Anglo-Saxon race in the government of inferior races?" asked the *Spectator*, blithely ignoring Britain's own colonial history. The periodical hastened to assure readers that it was acting from disinterest: "Lest our attitude should by chance be misrepresented, let us state clearly that if we thought merely of England's own selfish interests, rather than of those of the race, we should wish America to shrink from, and so miss, the opportunity presented to her."

As 1898 drew to its close, British pressure to ensure that the United States administer the islands on the British model intensified. All four papers insisted that administrative expertise should be exercised in behalf of the subject peoples. For the *Spectator,* "the main, the essential principle which the Americans must pursue in establishing their sway over their new Empire is that in every case the government set up must be for the benefit of the peoples governed." To do otherwise "would be to make a capital error in the Imperial art. What the Americans must consider is what scheme of government will be most productive of happiness to the races governed" (*S,* December 3, 1898: 821–22).

All four publications also worried about American administrative styles, especially in light of well-publicized U.S. antipathies for people of color and American naiveté about what, exactly, exporting "self-rule" might mean. As early as July of 1898 the *Economist* had wondered what the Americans would do should they win all of Spain's colonies. Noting that Cuba alone "contains a million of people, half of them Creole Spaniards, and the other half Hispaniolised half-castes, and neither of them will be found much inclined to become American citizens in feeling and ways of life," the article emphasizes Cubans' animosity toward North Americans. The paper first points out how poorly the United States had handled Hispanic populations in Florida, California, and Texas, and then adds that Puerto Ricans are openly hostile to U.S. intervention and may prove to be "fiercely recalcitrant under foreign domination" (*E,* July 23, 1898: 1070).

For all their bluntness, the *Economist*'s comments on U.S. religious and racial issues were mild compared to the *Spectator*'s. That organ saw the difficulties of annexing the Philippines as confounding. "As the population consists of dark persons," the paper commented tartly,

> Americans will not be much troubled by feeling about their claims to self-government, but still there are nearly as many persons in the islands as in Mexico, most of them brave, with very little tincture of civilization, and accustomed to manage for themselves, very badly, it is true, to an extraordinary degree. The Spaniards . . . did not govern them at all, but left them in some islands to the religious Orders, who provoked them to madness by interference; and in other islands to chiefs, Luzon alone being regularly administered by Spaniards, and that only to a

certain distance from the towns (*S*, "The American Debate on Expansion," January 14, 1899: 43–44).

The *Spectator* did not, however, assume that this history would make the Philippines impossible to administer. At the end of an article remarkable for its raw portrayal of American racial ideologies and political activities, the paper concludes,

> If Americans can constitutionally govern dark races within the union without conceding to them political powers, so they can govern them in distant possessions, and the single thing for them to consider is whether in so governing them they are doing good and not evil. We maintain that they are doing good, that the dark races of both Asia and Africa need a century or two of discipline before their full powers can reveal themselves, and that there are races which can enforce this discipline without tyranny and with a perceptible reduction of the great sum of human misery. We believe the Americans to be one of these, and that fifty years hence under their control the Filipinos, who now retain so many savage instincts, will be orderly, law-abiding persons like our own hindoos. . . .
> (*S*, "The American Debate on Expansion," January 14, 1899: 43–44)

"The authority of the United States will be upheld, and the work of Civilisation inaugurated," the *Daily Mail* piously concurred (*DM*, "The Philippines Puzzle," January 13, 1899: 5). Across the board, the British papers insisted that the United States was responsible for the moral and administrative well-being of the Philippines and the Filipinos and that such well-being could only be brought about through a firm, rationally delivered system of governance that was premised on racial and political inequality.

That the U.S. heard this message is without doubt. *How* Americans heard it is evident in speeches by two U.S. officials. In both, the references to humanitarian intent, duty, and righteousness show how receptive American conceptual frameworks were to British ideas. But they also show how the Americans' frameworks shift the imperialist vision from the relatively secular to the recognizably sacred. On February 10, 1899, shortly after the treaty was ratified, Pennsylvania congressman Marriott Brosius delivered a speech to the House of Representatives. Brosius supported annexation, and his speech begins with the Monroe Doctrine, which he regards as the legal foundation for Manifest Destiny, then segues to the missionary mandate to Christianize the world. The Filipinos are "wards of the civilized and enlightened powers whose duty it is to give them good government and promote their advancement in civilization," he avers: "The United States . . . are in honor and good morals bound to hold control in trust for civilization, and discharge the duties which dominion and responsibility impose."[12] "The eyes of the world are upon us," he warns his colleagues, "and for the character of our conduct and the elevation of our principles we must answer to the deliberate judgment of enlightened Christendom." Brosius then shifts to the language of the British periodicals, arguing that "the problem is not how to escape our responsibilities . . . but how to meet them; not how to use these new possessions for our own benefit, but for their own use and the world's."[13] Like the *Spectator*, he reminds his listeners that "The government of an inferior race is a trust"[14]; unlike the British periodicals, who treat religion as a given but rarely highlight it, he brings Christianity into the foreground, seeing an imperial America as the next stage in God's plan for the world:

> this is the goal toward which the moral forces of this vital, organic, divine universe . . . is certainly tending. He who opposes this progress . . . contends with God. . . . we must not forget that America can only establish the legitimacy of her title to that leadership which belongs to the English-speaking people by so . . . guarding her action that every page of our annals will reveal elevation of mind, rectitude of purpose, integrity of principles, and supremacy of conscience, thus certifying to all the world that we are moving on the everlasting lines of equity, truth, humanity, and liberty, following the foreshadowings of the ethical method of God in human history.[15]

President McKinley also recast the British message into the context of America's Christian mission. Proclaiming that the U.S. flag now flew over "two hemispheres," a "symbol of liberty, law, peace, and progress," McKinley used the British arguments about American responsibility to uplift the Filipinos in his argument for ratification.

> With less *humanity* or less courage on our part, the Spanish flag instead of the Stars and Stripes would still be floating over Cavite, Ponce, and Santiago, and *a chance in the race of life* would be wanting to millions of human beings who to-day *call this nation noble* and who, I trust, will live to *call it blessed*. Thus far we have done *our supreme duty*. Shall we

now . . . when . . . the civilized world applauds and waits in expectation, turn timidly from the *duties* imposed on the country by our own great deeds? . . . May we not go forth rejoicing in the strength which has been employed solely for *humanity* and has always been tempered with *justice and mercy*, confident in our ability to meet the exigencies which await us because we are confident that our course is that of *duty* and our cause that of *right*? (*T*, 1 December 1898: 6; emphasis added)

In bringing words such as *blessed* and key phrases such as "justice and mercy" into play, McKinley's words transformed the British call into a religious duty. For Americans, the words, phrases, and sense of mission most centrally associated with Protestant outreach constituted one major context for reception of the British call for "responsibility." Both men employ phrases resonant in U.S. providential history. Brosius's claim that "the eyes of the world are on us" references a sermon that John Winthrop, first governor of the Massachusetts Bay Colony, delivered on board the ship *Arbella* as it neared New England in 1630. His phrase signaled the Puritans' understanding of their journey as an experiment in self-constitution, as they determined to fashion a society free from the pollutions of the non-Puritan world. But the Puritans were separatists. They believed in a small community of saints, elected by God alone, and although they routinely prayed for the salvation of the rest of the world, they were generally not active proselytizers, believing, as they did, that salvation was a matter of God's grace, not man's efforts. Winthrop claimed that the new colony was to be "as a city on a hill," with "the eyes of the world upon us," but in terms of interacting with that world on an ideological basis, Winthrop's city was essentially passive.

How, then, did Winthrop's words become pro-active? How did the Puritans' self-absorbed separatism become Brosius's racially-inflected imperialism? One path, as we have seen, lay in the general conflation of American identity with Protestant Christian identity. After the Second Great Awakening, which sanctioned evangelicalism as a cultural mode, American Protestantism experienced a mood shift in which it began to see its major mission as outreach rather than isolated sanctity. The concept of the United States as an exemplary nation has resonated in political speeches throughout American history, functioning as a call to action for policies both at home and abroad.[16] American auditors "heard" the speeches through their education in the narrative of American rights, especially as it had evolved over the century in sermons, editorials, and American textbooks from Noah Webster's *History of the United States* and Caleb Bingham's *Columbian Orator* to Aaron Chapin's *First Principles of Political Economy*. We can see the results of the evolution in Brosius's speech, which argues that expansion constituted an opportunity for the United States to "be placed on the foundations of righteousness . . . [to] become the foremost nation to recognize that equity, justice, humanity, are the winning forces of civilization." "Is there not," he asked, "warrant for the assumption that the United States have [*sic*] a mission to guide this force of humanitarian feeling to beneficent ends in the amelioration and civilization of inferior people within the sphere of our influence?"[17]

President McKinley's speech also reflects Winthrop's "Model of Christian Charity." Not only does it evoke the vision of the United States as the cynosure of all nations, McKinley's reference to "justice and mercy" recalls the biblical injunction to "act justly, love mercy, and walk humbly with your God" (Micah 6:8) that was the text on which Winthrop built his sermon. Winthrop justifies inequality as a divine mandate—as God's means of insuring that human beings care for each other across social and economic boundaries. When McKinley speaks of "the strength which has been employed solely for humanity and has always been tempered with justice and mercy," he evokes that part of the narrative that envisions Americans as committed to acts of mercy even while guarding social and economic borders. Both McKinley and Brosius assume that in order for the United States to continue world leadership the country must maintain its unblemished virtue—continue in its role as the holy community—and prove its purity through acts of mercy, which will extend charity from superior to inferior groups. But by the closing years of the nineteenth century neither McKinley nor Brosius assumed that isolation was the only path to communal virtue. Rather, both politicians want the United States to gather the world under its purview and to elevate all peoples to its moral standards. In effect, they transform Winthrop's words into a mandate for evangelical action. At the same time, they reserve American liberties for white Americans alone, never attempting to grant equality of rights or citizenship—membership in the holy community—to the conquered peoples. In this reading "mercy" is the same as "charity," the friendly distribution of goods and services to the unfortunate. It does not mean equality, however. Mercy is the distribution of benevolence across social, economic, and racial divides.

It is within this conundrum that we see the unstable yoking of white America's desire to define American civilization as a white Protestant idea and to argue its obligation to convert the rest of the world to its own social and economic values. Most importantly, Americans "heard" the British call to imperialism within this paradox.

Enter "The White Man's Burden: An Address to the United States." Theodore Roosevelt's judgment of Kipling's intervention into American politics was that it was "rather poor poetry, but good sense from the expansionist point of view." Whether interpreted as supporting expansion or as warning against it, "The White Man's Burden: An Address to the United States" was instantly absorbed into the debates themselves. I am italicizing the most often quoted phrases.

> Take up the *White Man's* burden-
> Send forth the best ye breed-
> Go bind your sons to exile
> To serve your captives' need;
> To wait in heavy harness,
> On fluttered folk and wild-
> Your new-caught, *sullen* peoples,
> *Half-devil and half-child.*

> Take up *the White Man's burden-*
> In patience to abide,
> To veil the threat of terror
> And check the show of pride;
> By open speech and simple,
> An hundred times made plain
> To seek another's profit,
> And work another's gain.

> Take up *the White Man's burden-*
> The savage wars of peace-
> Fill full the mouth of Famine
> And bid the sickness cease;
> And when your goal is nearest
> The end for others sought,
> Watch sloth and heathen Folly
> Bring all your hopes to nought.

> Take up *the White Man's burden-*
> No tawdry rule of kings,
> But toil of serf and sweeper-

The tale of common things.
The ports ye shall not enter,
The roads ye shall not tread,
Go make them with your living,
And mark them with your dead.

Take up *the White Man's burden*—
And *reap his old reward*:
The *blame of those ye better*,
The *hate of those ye guard*—
The cry of hosts ye humour
(Ah, slowly!) toward the light:—
"Why brought ye us from bondage,
Our loved Egyptian night?"

Take up *the White Man's burden*-
Ye dare not stoop to less—
Nor call too loud on Freedom
To cloak your weariness;
By all ye cry or whisper,
By all ye leave or do,
The silent, *sullen* peoples
Shall weigh your gods and you.

Take up *the White Man's burden*—
Have done with childish days—
The lightly proferred laurel,
The easy, ungrudged praise,
Comes now, to search your manhood
Through all the thankless years
Cold, edged with dear-bought wisdom,
The judgment of your peers!

Kipling's poem was first published in the February 4, 1899, issue of the London *Times* and the February 12, 1899 issue of *McClure's* magazine, Kipling's major U.S. venue. Since the *Times* publication appeared two days before the American Senate was scheduled to vote on the Treaty of Paris, it was clear that the poem was an intervention into the debate over the fate of America's new possessions. The poem's brilliance lies in transforming the British arguments into convenient phrases and memorable rhymes. The British papers embraced it, instantly recycling it to emphasize their points: on February 6, the morning of the day the Senate was to vote on the treaty, the *Times* reiterated the benefits American rule would bring to the islands: "The work may be tedious and the sacrifices it entails heavy, but sooner or later it will be accomplished and the Filipinos, greatly to their own benefit, will be brought for the first time under an Administration at once strong, sympathetic, and inflexibly just," it begins, reiterating its previous arguments about responsibility. Noting the outbreak of violence between the Filipino and American troops two days previously, the *Times* asks if the incident will affect the Senate vote: "Will it strengthen [the Senators'] conviction that the Filipinos are unfit for independence and their resolve to civilize them with a firm hand, or will it disgust them with the ungrateful duty they must assume if they hold their conquests at all?" The paper summons Kipling's lines to reinforce its arguments: "We imagine that, in spite of the difficulties, and a little, perhaps, because of the difficulties, that beset the task, the men of Anglo-Saxon blood across the Atlantic will 'take up' '*the White Man's burden*' in the Philippines as they have taken it up in Cuba, and that the incidents of the last couple of days will strengthen their determination to do so without delay" (*T*, February 6, 1899: 9; emphasis added).

Having employed Kipling's signal phrase to stand in for the litany of moral duty, the *Times* sprinkles other key words from the poem throughout its argument that Americans should look to Britain for models of sound colonial administration. Pointing out recent American administrative changes in Cuba, the newspaper first attributes the Americans' progress to the influence of "English Imperial policy," suggesting that the American official who persuaded the Cubans to welcome U.S. intervention had learned his lessons from Great Britain. "If our cousins across the Atlantic can turn out a sufficient number of administrators of this stamp," the *Times* continues, "they will find the business of ruling their '*new-caught sullen peoples*' onerous, no doubt, and sometimes repugnant, but a task, too, which brings its own reward. They will do in the Philippines, more slowly perhaps and with greater effort, what they seem to be now doing in Cuba. They will help on the cause of civilization and hold high the name and credit of their race amongst mankind" (*T*, February 6, 1899: 9; emphasis added).

The *Daily Mail* also recycled Kipling's lines to argue the benefits that U.S. rule would confer on the Filipinos. Whereas the *Times* attempted to mask its racism through dignified language, the *Daily Mail* did not mince its words: "For the Filipinos there is little excuse," it commented on February 6.

If they could only see it—these "*half-taught, sullen children*" —President McKinley and the American expansionists are their best friends. If America withdrew from the islands, these would inevitably be scrambled for by the Powers of Europe, and the Filipinos would discover that they had jumped from the frying pan into the fire. They would not find French or German rule kindlier or juster than American. We trust that the sharp lesson they have received will show them the error of their ways and prove to them that the Anglo-Saxon is not a man with whom it is safe to trifle. (*DM*, The Outlook, "America's Uphill Task," February 6, 1899: 5; emphasis added)

The *Spectator* not only quoted, but also openly acknowledged the ideological significance of "The White Man's Burden." "It is the prerogative of Mr. Rudyard Kipling to embody in ringing verse the latent thought of the English-speaking peoples," it wrote shortly after the poem's publication:

The duty of the white man is to conquer and control, probably for a couple of centuries, all the dark peoples of the world, not for his own good, but theirs . . . We all admit that duty . . . Only we must perform it in the right spirit, taking it up, as Mr. Kipling sings, as "*the white man's burden*" . . . expecting no gratitude from those whom we may help to redeem. If we fail . . . "*the new caught, sullen peoples, half devil and half child*" will curse us . . . if we succeed . . . they will but bid us begone unthanked. . . . Nevertheless, there is our duty clear before us, and Mr. Kipling . . . bids us perform it though we do but "*reap the old reward, the blame of those we better, the hate of those we guard.*" (S, February 11, 1899: 193–4; emphasis added)

In changing Kipling's "you" to "we," the *Spectator* signals how personally it took the poet's call to racial kinship and responsibility. Clearly, the poem spoke to British pro-imperialist sentiments; the papers recognized its value as a vehicle for arguing their case.

The American Reception

If "The White Man's Burden" sprang from and instantly fed back into British conversations about the United States, it also fell into conversations the Americans were having about themselves. And because it fit so well into both the national narrative of divine mission and American racial and religious ideologies, the poem was co-opted by both sides. Teddy Roosevelt may have read it as supporting expansion, but others read it through anti-imperialist lenses, whether racially or religiously inflected. For those opposed to annexation on racial grounds, the poem articulated a dire warning. Benjamin Tillman brought it into the Senate, claiming that it was to his mind "a prophecy"—a portrayal of "our danger and our duty." He read the poem aloud, interpreting it as a lesson about the burden of having "two races side by side that can not mix or mingle without deterioration and injury to both and the ultimate destruction of the civilization of the higher." "We of the South," he continues, "have born this white man's burden of a colored race in our midst since their emancipation and before."[18] For Tillman, both a member of the Anti-Imperialist League and a staunch opponent of African American enfranchisement, Kipling's imagery plays into the postbellum construction of the South as the victim of slavery, a country of honorable Anglo-Saxons desperately holding onto white civilization in the face of a foreign race that had been forced upon them 300 years before and which it was now their duty to manage. He used the poem to argue that the United States did not need yet another assortment of races to endanger its white destiny.

Tillman may have been the only senator to actively read the poem into the Congressional Record, but its sentiments and, often, its vocabulary, spring up in debates across the aisles—and the chambers. The construction of American history as the unfolding of God's plan in human time provided a context into which Kipling's lines played admirably. Taking up the white man's burden becomes a call to fulfill America's divine mandate, converting British calls for "responsibility" into a national religious duty. Even those who recognized the complexities of annexation betray the sense of obligation that simply being an American seemed to incur; for them "The White Man's Burden" spoke precisely to that responsibility. As late as 1900, Brigadier-General Thomas M. Anderson would use Kipling's lines to justify continued occupation when he claimed that "This task, imposed upon us by a combination of circumstances, we must now carry out to its logical and legitimate conclusion. It is part of 'the white man's burden' which we can not now lay down."[19] In this context, the "burden" was read as the duty to bring American values and administrative stability to those "fluttered folk" who are incapable of self-government. Readers such as Anderson filtered the poem through a lens that valorized outreach over—or at least equal to—racial separatism, leading to an often-contradictory ideology claiming that the benefits of the American presence justified forced occupation even while assuming that the people being benefited were racially incapable of rising to the level of American civilization politically, economically, socially, or religiously.

Like Anderson and the British periodicals, many speakers adopted salient words and phrases from Kipling's vocabulary even when they did not cite him directly. The word "sullen," used in reference to the Filipinos and, often, in close proximity to references to children, crops up frequently. On May 22, 1902, in a speech arguing for Philippine independence (and against continued occupation), Massachusetts senator George F. Hoar told his colleagues that "Your practical statesmanship has succeeded in converting a people who three years ago were ready to kiss the hem of the garment of the American and to welcome him as a liberator . . . into *sullen* and irreconcilable enemies, possessed of a hatred which centuries cannot eradicate." And he continued, bitterly, "These people are given to us as *children*, to lead them out of their childhood into manhood. . . . [T]hey needed your kindness and justice, and a respect in them for the rights we claimed for ourselves, and the rights we had declared always were inherent in all mankind. You preferred force to kindness and power to justice, and war to peace, and pride to generosity . . ."[20]

For Hoar, Kipling describes the destruction of what had been a potentially fruitful relationship between the Americans and the Filipinos. A month later Mississippi representative John Sharp Williams referred to the Philippines as a "child" to whom the United States had told a lie, quoted stanzas from "The White Man's Burden" (referring to Kipling as "the poet of jingoism"), and predicted that "'the silent sullen peoples' will judge you by the blood on your sword and by the itching palm." Like the rest of his Southern colleagues, Williams opposed annexation and assimilation on racial grounds, implicitly turning the aftermath of the Civil War into a cautionary tale about the impossibility of cross-racial governance. His speech rejects the doctrine of "benevolent assimilation" in the Philippines because, he argues, "all this world has not shown one instance . . . where two races unequal—one white and the other colored—have ever been able to rule any country, however small, together." In the same breath, however, Williams ignores the racial and religious diversity of the U.S. population in 1900, asserting that the "American people" are "in form of government a constitutional, democratic republic; we are in citizenship equal and free, proud, and civilized, and Christian."

A claim like this—made in the face of patent evidence that not only did the United States contain increasing numbers of non-Christians but that "equality" and "freedom" were contested terms for African Americans, Native Americans, and Asians—suggests not so much that Williams was a hypocrite but that, like the majority of his white compatriots, he was incapable of imagining non-Christians and nonwhites as citizens. Appropriating pre–Civil War abolitionists' insistence that it was morally wrong for Christians to enslave other Christians, Williams argues the injustice of a white Christian nation holding a weaker nation in subjection. Like many of his compatriots, he uses Kipling's words and rhythms to enhance his peroration. Warning that the subjected peoples will "judge your Bible and your Bible's God by you," he concludes that "it is not 'the white man's burden we are bearing,' but the white man's disgrace we are wearing." [21] Williams was so blinded by his own vision of the United States as a nation of white Christians that he could not see that the country already subjected large portions of its own citizens to oppressions similar to those to which they proposed to subject the Filipinos.

Governmental chambers were not the only place where the debates played out. Between 1899, when the Americans first annexed, and 1902, when the first phase of the Philippine-American war came to a close, the archipelago was a hot-button issue throughout the country, subject of commentary in periodicals, pulpits, and other communications media. Here, too, Kipling's lines appear frequently, having become a kind of shorthand for public sentiment over the war. Parodies of the poem itself were legion, serving not only to signal opposition to the war but also to expose the ideological positions that the parodists saw Kipling's lines espousing. [22] Private Louis Dodge, a soldier serving in the Philippines, identified not as the architect of white imperialism but as the "serf and sweeper" who actually carried out imperialism's work. He prefaces his parody by quoting Kipling's own "serf and sweeper" lines, then sarcastically rejoins: "Yea, let the serf and sweeper/Take up the White Man's cross;/ They have no loves nor firesides/To reckon as their loss. /Let those whose right are visions/Set sail across the foam/And bear the White Man's burden— /While *he* remains at home" (emphasis added). Correctly reading the poem as representing a far broader agenda than Kipling's alone, the parodist addresses England through the poet, concluding bitterly, "We need no admonition/From old convention's child;/ And not by rhythmic platitudes/Shall freemen be beguiled. /We do not learn our lessons/From those who chant for kings;/ Our burdens we are bearing:/ A 'serf and sweeper' sings."[23]

If Dodge's parody skewered the poem's class assumptions, H. T. Johnson's skewered its contribution to America's racial divide. Like other African Americans, Johnson understood Kipling's poem from his own position in the racial landscape—reading it as sanctioning continuation of white dominance and injustice to black and brown peoples. "Pile on the Black Man's Burden," his stanzas begin, "His wail with laughter drawn/ You've sealed the Red Man's problem, /and will take up the Brown, /In vain ye seek to end it, /With bullets, blood or death/Better by far defend it/ with honor's holy breath."[24] The poem's racial politics were also engaged in a parody, reprinted anonymously, that admonished the country to "Pile on the brown man's burden/To gratify your greed;/ Go clear away the 'niggers,'/ Who progress would impede;/ Be very stern, for truly/ 'Tis useless to be mild/With new-caught sullen peoples, /Half devil and half child."[25] Another African American parodist used Kipling's pattern to advise the whites not to take the British bait: "Drap dat bundle, white man/Yer burden is too great/I'se speakin' but in kindness, /Wid not one smitch o'hate. /You started down de ages, /To 'dopt another class. /Two hundred years dey served you, /No thanks! But let dat pass . . ."[26]

Although the majority of the parodies tackled the poem's racism, many also read it as denounced the hypocrisy of framing conquest and subjugation as Christian outreach: "Take up the white man's burden— / And send your sons abroad/To prey on other peoples/Who serve another God;/To steal, and starve, and murder/All who oppose his aim— /the Indian and Egyptian— /The men of ancient fame," begins one typical of this group. It concludes: "Take up the white man's burden"— /Have done with charity— /Christ taught commerce, not kindness— /'Twas His mission—don't you see?/The white man has a right to murder— /'Tis part of his commercial creed— /He will slay all other peoples/To satisfy a Christian's greed."[27]

Kipling's poem does not employ religious language, but one sign of Americans' propensity to read public events through a religious filter is that the American parodies of "The White Man's Burden" assume a religious agenda to the imperial mission, and they denounce its hypocrisy. The parody written by Ernest Crosby, President of the New York Anti-Imperialist League and author of *Captain Jinks, Hero*, advises, "Take up the White Man's burden/To you who thus succeed/In civilizing savage hordes, /They owe a debt, indeed;/Concessions, pensions, salaries, /And privileges and right— /With outstretched hands you raised to bless/ Grab everything in sight." Sounding much like the Mark Twain of "To the Person Sitting in Darkness," Crosby concludes: "Take up the White Man's burden/And if you write in verse, /Flatter your nation's vices/And strive to make them worse./Then learn that if with pious words/You ornament each phrase, /In a world of canting hypocrites/This kind of business pays."[28] Finally, George McNeill's "Poor Man's Burden" concludes: "Lift off the Poor Man's Burden— /My Country, grand and great— /The Orient has no treasures/To buy a Christian state, /Our souls brook not oppression;/Our needs—if read aright— /Call not for wide possession, / But Freedom's sacred light."[29] Throughout, the parodies lament America's moral shortcomings, positioning those eager to annex as using the language of special mission to disguise ignoble ends.

In more positive readings of the poem, many papers incorporated references to "The White Man's Burden" into their headlines—proof that it had become shorthand for popular sentiment. Kansas's *Emporia Daily Gazette* reported on a pro-annexation sermon by a local minister under the headline "Preached on 'The White Man's Burden.'"[30] The Memphis, Tennessee, *Commercial Appeal* reported that the Canadian minister of justice had told the United States that "You have entered upon the work begun by the mother of free states a century ago . . . recognizing your high calling, [you] have taken up the white man's burden. . . ."[31] Meanwhile the *Milwaukee Sentinel* headlined: "Whitelaw Reid for Open Door: As Protectionist He Favors that Policy, as Patriotic American Shoulders 'White Man's Burden,'" and quoted Reid's assertion that "The graver the crisis, the plainer our duty." As if the words *responsibility* and *duty* were triggers for the religious frame, Reid concludes: "God give us courage to purify our politics and strengthen our government to meet its new and grave duties."[32]

Whether they embraced or rejected Kipling's sentiments, U.S. periodicals constantly referred to the poem. In the process, its signal phrases became the possession of the entire country. An article in *Harper's Weekly* protested "those who regard it as the right of white men to kill all the savages of the globe in the interest of commerce . . . and who . . . hiding behind the disordered genius of Mr. Kipling, indulge in hypocritical cant about the 'white man's burden.'"[33] A year later the same magazine approvingly commented that Senator Albert Beveridge "long ago maintained his belief that the Anglo-Saxon race owed a duty to the . . . half-civilized countries of the world. He earnestly believes in the white man's burden, and thus early put his strong shoulders . . . to the task."[34] Six months after the poem was published, it was appearing in advertisements: a September, 1899, ad in *Harper's Weekly* featured Admiral Dewey washing his hands and recommended Pear's soap as "the first step in lightening The White Man's Burden."[35] The ad signaled the poem's new status as a cultural icon.

"The White Man's Burden" was written into a global context, speaking *for* Britain *to* the United States, regarding the Philippines. Its eager reception among Americans, especially Southerners, suggests that they embraced the racial ideology that it espoused. As the United States debated the fate of its new possessions, the poem helped shape arguments about annexation and its aftermath. Whether Americans viewed annexation as taking on the "burden" of an irremediably alien people, a divine mandate to export American civilization, or a betrayal of American ideals, they regarded the poem through their own conviction of special mission. Spoken out of a British context that valorized colonial expansion and firm administrative process, it was received into a context that valorized Protestant outreach and national virtue. The poem also contributed to the progressive redrawing of transnational loyalties that would flower during World War I. As the United States stumbled its way toward colonialism, it received the poem, and the British sentiment that produced it, as proof that one of the most powerful imperialist nations stood ready to be America's friend.

Chapter 6

Saxon Eyes and Barbaric Souls

*Responses to the American Annexation of the
Philippines in Europe and Latin America*

Mark Twain remained deeply disturbed by U.S. imperialism throughout the first years of the new century, penning essays, speeches, dramatic
monologues, sketches, and parodies that protested U.S. actions in the
Philippines and elsewhere. One image that he used repeatedly substituted
a skull and crossbones for the stars in the American flag. For Twain as for
other Americans, the flag was the emblem of the country's honor, its claim
to remarkable virtue among the community of nations. The Philippine-
American War, he felt, had destroyed the grounds for the claim. Sometime
during this period Twain read *An Eagle's Flight*, an English adaptation of
José Rizal's *Noli Me Tangere*, originally published in 1886.[1] Rizal, the
Filipino nationalist who had been martyred by the Spanish in 1896, had
written *Noli Me Tangere* as a protest against Spanish misrule in the archipelago; in particular, it attacks the corrupt friars who maintained day-to-day
control over ordinary Filipinos' lives. Rizal's brief introduction, addressed
"To My Country," contends that he is "exposing" the Philippines' diseased
state in order to solicit remedies.

An Eagle's Flight is prefaced by two other documents. One is a poem,
"My Last Thought" ("Mi Ultimo Adiós," literally, "My Last Farewell")
that Rizal wrote on the eve of his execution.[2] The poem is a hymn to the
Philippines; it addresses the archipelago intimately, as "tu," and celebrates
the islands' fecundity. Rizal tells his compatriots that he is honored to take
his place beside other fallen freedom fighters, and he bids readers not to

FIGURE 6.1: "Chorus in Background: Those Pious Yankees Can't Throw Stones at Us Anymore." *Life*, Life Publishing Company, New York, May 22, 1902. [artist: William Bengough]

mourn him because "morir es descansar," to die is to rest. The second, unattributed, prefacing document is a sketch of Rizal's life and accomplishments as a writer, an intellectual, a physician (he was a specialist in eye diseases), and a patriot. This forceful sketch frames the reading of the novel, marking the Filipinos as sophisticated, intelligent people who had been oppressed by the Spanish—especially the religious orders—and who were fully capable of governing themselves.

In 1901 Twain paid Rizal homage by taking the title of Rizal's poem as he had read it in the adaptation and using it for a poem of his own.[3]

Twain's poem names no names—he identifies neither its speaker nor the event about which he speaks—but the U.S. annexation of the Philippines is its implicit backdrop, and its narrator too is a dying man. But whereas Rizal is a martyr speaking to a country he has loved and hoped to guide to freedom, Twain's narrator is an American president speaking to a country he knows he has betrayed. Twain's "My Last Thought" is about the damage annexation has inflicted on America's moral fiber and to its reputation in the world. His speaker blames himself, recognizing that he was inadequate for his responsibilities: "I was only weak, /Not bad. And I was out of place— /A lost & wandering atom in that vast Seat/Which only Lincolns & their like compactly fill."

Like many of Twain's short pieces, the poem is a dramatic monologue. Formally, it is very loose—the lines are written in iambs but the line and stanzas vary in length; there is some interesting internal and slant rhyme but no overall rhyme scheme. Yet, to this reader at least, the poetic mode makes it more effective than many of Twain's other political monologues, such as "King Leopold's Soliloquy." Despite the freedom of the verse, the formal constraints impose a discipline that intensifies the narrator's pathos, his heartfelt regret over his mistakes and their impact on the nation he had led. "I meant my country well," the president begins, and proceeds to rehearse the "loyal service" he had performed, especially in securing Cuban independence. "Pearl of the Antilles, speak!" he beseeches, "I broke your chains, I set you free; I raised/My country's honor to the skies; I won/the Old World's scorn & hate, the New World's/'Well done, thou faithful son!'" For the president, U.S. actions in Cuba showed his "real" intents: "O *then* I was myself," he claims, looking back on the golden moment when, Twain believed, the United States actually carried through on its commitment to help another country to freedom. The president begs his listeners to "Grant me that!" and to "forget the rest." His subsequent misdeeds, he insists, were brought about "through weakness, not intent." Because he had been "Overborne by sordid counsels, /Base ambitions," he laments, "from my head I took/The precious laurel I had earned, & in its place/I set this poor tin glory, now my wear, /Of World-Power, Conquerer of helpless tribes, / Extinguisher of struggling liberties!"

The president's last vision is of the American flag. As Twain had done at the end of "To the Person Sitting in Darkness," here he uses the flag to indicate national dishonor. The speaker first perceives, "upon my fading sight," a "holy vision": "Our Flag of snow & flame far-flashing in the sky!

/And toward it the oppressed of every clime/Uplifting their poor fettered hands/In hope & trust & worship." But the vision fades, to be replaced with another, in which "The Stars are gone, a Skull & Bones/Are in their place; the Red Bars are there, /But soaked with guiltless blood; /The white Bars are Black—and the dying man cries out, 'Hide it from my sight!'" The final stanza returns to the plea for forgiveness; whereas Rizal's last line counseled his countrymen not to mourn him because "to sleep is to rest," Twain's speaker craves sleep as oblivion: "Sleep & forget, sleep and be forgotten— /If that dear boon might be mine!"

The sense of loss in this poem is palpable. The speaker, figuring himself as "an atom" lost in "that vast Seat/Which only Lincolns & their like compactly fill," strikes the note of solitude that marks Twain's late, unfinished manuscripts, many of which feature a solitary consciousness wandering through infinite space. In the poem the space is a "seat," the throne of governance, far too large for the talents of the dying president. As with many of Twain's late protagonists, this speaker's mistaken judgments had precipitated his fall from security to terror, from control to powerlessness. He is acutely aware that his failures had destroyed his country's character. He compares himself to the Revolutionary War traitor Benedict Arnold, but sadly notes that Arnold betrayed only a "garrison," whereas he has "peddled out a Nation & its honor: /And sold them for a song!" His only recourse is to beg forgiveness, and to die.

By 1901, when he wrote this poem, Twain was a sophisticated observer of the world and of America's place within it. He had become one of the most prominent spokesmen for the Anti-Imperialist League in part because his sojourns in Europe and his world travels gave him the authority to judge the United States from the outside. The pathos of "My Last Thought" reflects Twain's perception that the nation had fallen from grace in the eyes of mankind as well as in the eyes of God; the poem reaches beyond internal U.S. protest to evoke the impact the government's actions had made on the country's international reputation. Twain first evokes patriotically charged American icons such as Lincoln and the flag, then accuses the country of betraying the ideals those icons represent. The poem's focus on national dishonor suggests that Twain was attuned to responses to the U.S. annexation of the Philippines from locations beyond the Anglo-American alliance.

The final two chapters of this study look at challenges to the Americans from nations that did not assume that Anglo-American culture was God's gift to the world. After a brief survey of European responses to the

Americans' interference in Spain's struggles to control its colonies, this chapter looks at writings by three Latin American writers—José Martí, Rubén Darío, and José Enrique Rodó—whose ambivalence about the United States help us observe the Americans' activities in a global context. The final chapter examines the responses of Filipino nationalists Emilio Aguinaldo, the president of the short-lived Philippine Republic, and Apolinario Mabini, the author of the Philippine Constitution. Across the globe, observers had listened to the Americans' talk about their special virtue, and they were happy to point out that the country had fallen at the first temptation. The Filipino nationalists especially used the American narrative against their new masters.

Like the Filipinos, writers from other former Spanish colonies called the United States on its hypocrisies. In the writings of José Martí, Rubén Darío, and José Enrique Rodó, we see a critique of North American life and thought that provides a framework for protests about the Philippine-American War from perspectives far distant from most citizens of the United States. Like Mark Twain, these three Spanish American writers critique not just the country's actions, but also the terms within which it identified itself, the national narrative that framed U.S. debates both for and against annexation. And although it is unlikely that Twain knew of Rodó or Darío's writings, and seems to have had little or no relationship with José Martí, all four writers are marked by their deployment of specifically literary genres to communicate their critique.[4] It is as if the very structuring of the story about the United States, with the country's birth in colonial rebellion, its celebrated embrace of equalitarianism, its insistence that its freedoms were rooted in a Protestant worldview, and its iconic documents and figures, encouraged writers to deconstruct the narrative itself, to shatter the self-image of the country they perceived as far too self-confident, far too smug. As we shall see, Mark Twain's opinion that the nation had dishonored itself was a statement with which many commentators largely concurred.

The single most common register among European governments over the Americans' decision to acquire distant territories was discomfort with the idea of an Anglo-American *rapprochement*; many countries had depended on the longstanding enmity between the United States and Britain to secure their own places in the global order, and they were leery of the shifts in balance that such a powerful alliance could facilitate. Beyond that shared wariness, official attitudes varied; Germany and Russia seemed unperturbed, whereas France professed shock and alarm. But governments do not necessarily speak for their people. In their introduction to the collection *European Perceptions of the Spanish-American War of 1898*, Sylvia Hilton and Steven Ickringill note that "Democratic, progressive, and reformist minorities across Europe (and of course in the United States itself) [shared] an ideology suffused by the exaltation and defense of human rights. For them, the United States had represented the world's best hope so far in the on-going anti-militarist, anti-protectionist, anti-colonialist and anti-racist struggle towards international peace, solidarity, cooperation and progress. . . . McKinley's intervention of 1898 was perceived by this handful of ideologues as a betrayal of American traditions and of universal values. For them, the Spanish-American war brought a sense of loss, of innocence irremediably sullied, as the American myth was shattered before their eyes"[5] (33).

Taken across not only European national borders, but also the United States and the Spanish-speaking world, the groups that Hilton and Ickringill characterize as a "handful of ideologues" in fact articulated a pervasive and ongoing protest against U.S. imperialism. In Russia, for instance, the liberal press supported the invasion of Cuba on humanitarian grounds, but evidenced much distress over the annexation of the Philippines, which they saw as a denial of the principles of the Monroe Doctrine and, more significantly, a failure of ideals. In an article in *Vestnik Evropy* refuting American claims to the Philippines, L. Slonimsky commented that "The Americans shifted from philanthropic liberators of Cuba to merciless conquerors of another far-away island, and began to cruelly exterminate the defenders of local freedom." Similarly, the April, 1899, issue of *Vestnik Inostrannoi Literatury* wrote disapprovingly that "the Americans were not able to maintain the loftiness of their political ideal. They were carried away by the example of Europe."[6] If the Russians framed the American seizure of the islands as a fall from democratic grace, the French framed it as outright hypocrisy. Serge Ricard quotes one editorial delivered shortly after McKinley's war message of April 11, 1898, which denounced the United States for its hypocrisy, pointing out that "The sentimental fallacy of Christian and humanitarian motivations, so typically American, was but 'the proclamation of a right of intervention pure and simple.'"[7] French paranoia about the Anglo-American *rapprochement* was if anything more keen than Russian. Quoting Louis Joubert of *Le Correspondant*, Ricard records that

> Two weeks . . . after the declaration of war and Dewey's victory at
> Manila Bay, Joubert . . . (remarked) . . . that John Bull and Brother
> Jonathan, despite their rivalry, were indeed blood kin "when it came to
> grabbing their neighbour's property." They shared the same unscrupu-
> lous, lawless approach to international affairs. Under the pretext of
> freeing Cuba, the United States . . . was now aiming at occupying the
> Philippines and Puerto Rico with London's approval. (Hilton and
> Ickringill, 145)

In addition to boorish diplomacy and faulty etiquette, Washington, the
newspaper *Débats* noted, had confused its duties with its interests (H&I,
148). In August of 1899 the American periodical *The Public* reprinted an
article by the Paris newspaper *Le Figaro*'s special correspondent in Hong
Kong, Jean Hess. In "A French View of the War in the Philippines," Hess
commented that "The American intervention in the struggle engaged in by
the revolutionary Tagals against the Spanish government has turned out
to be nothing but a speculation of 'business men,' and not the generous
effort of a people paying a debt in procuring for others the liberty that it
concedes belongs to all."[8] Hess turns to the Filipino response to the Americans' claim to benevolent intentions:

> The Filipinos also, who now know the Americans pretty well, having seen
> them at this work, smile at their arguments; "You were groaning under the
> Spanish yoke. We have delivered you. But as many of you are yet savages,
> and all of you but big children, you cannot possibly know how to conduct
> your government yourselves. We are going to take upon ourselves as an
> especial charge your prosperity and happiness!" (*The Public*, 15)

Echoing the "savage children" and "responsibility" tropes that gained special
currency after publication of "The White Man's Burden," Hess undermined
U.S. proclamations not only by listening to them through Filipino ears but by
associating them with the discourses of race and duty that Kipling's poem
had come to represent.

Although Europeans generally did not see the Spanish-American conflicts through a religious lens, they were not insensible to its echoes of
earlier Catholic/Protestant conflicts. Like many Americans who regarded
the triumph of Western civilization as the victory of Protestant-inflected
modernity over Catholic feudalism, some Europeans framed the war within
the longstanding enmity between Catholics and Protestants. Nico A. Bootsma

notes that Dutch liberal and socialist papers justified the war as an attack on the corrupt role that the Church had played in the Philippines[9]—an argument that the Filipinos had raised during their struggle against Spain and that was central to Rizal's works, which were well known in Europe. Markus M. Hugo notes one German interpretation as a conflation of racial and religious ideologies, a "Germanic-Latin Duel," in which a Teuton victory was to be celebrated. With this, many German Protestants viewed Spain's distress as a necessary consequence of its Catholicism.[10]

Not surprisingly, the religious reading of the war and its outcome was strongest in Spain itself. *El disastre*, as the Spanish dubbed their defeat by the combined nationalist/U.S. forces, precipitated a period of national introspection during which Spain turned away from global engagements and began an intense reexamination of its own global identity. Within a few years this conversation would give way to *la regeneración*, the artistic, social, and political movement that, until Franco's forces destroyed it, would move Spanish culture toward European modernism. But before *la regeneración* could develop, the Spanish needed time to reimagine themselves; with the exception of Morocco, they were, for the first time in nearly 500 years, a nation without an empire, a status for which they were unprepared. Writing on New Year's Eve of 1899, one correspondent aptly summarized the state of the nation. First laying out the Spanish imperial landscape as it had appeared twelve months previous, he laments, "At the beginning of 1899, what a different picture is sketched!"

> [Spain] has lost a third of its territories; in Puerto Rico, Cuba, and the Philippines the American flag waves, those warships in which we had placed our hopes are buried in the ocean without having the power to fight the enemy; the army sent to Cuba and the Philippines no longer exists; those soldiers who survived the terrible battles with the separatists and the treacherous climate of our colonies have returned home sick and without glory; peace with the Filipinos was smashed by the impudence and bad-faith of the Yankees; in Puerto Rico hitherto loyal Spaniards have committed horrible crimes of treason and ingratitude. This is what is left to us at the beginning of this year—a beginning that catches us in the midst of such great ruin and desolation that those who can still breathe should beg God for good fortune for this unhappy country.

And he closes, "today everyone cries out, lifting their thoughts to heaven, 'God take pity on Spain in the new year!'"[11]

Aware of their readers' despair over their country's loss, Spanish commentators did not extend much sympathy to their former territories, now struggling against new masters. However they were interested in the problems that the United States almost immediately started having with its new subjects. Like other European monarchies, Spain had a popular movement pushing for republican reform, for which the United States had provided a model. Sylvia Hilton notes that late-nineteenth-century Spanish republicans frequently cited the United States as a model of republican ideals. American heroes such as Washington and Jefferson were regarded as models of republican virtue, and American prosperity and energy, though also regarded as materialistic, were evidence that U.S. principles had tangible outcomes.[12] But the Spanish republicans most admired the fact that the United States had no colonies. A running theme in Spanish commentary after the war was the accusation that the Americans had overturned everything in which they professed to believe. "The irony of the thing reveals itself more every day," commented Barcelona's *Diario de Barcelona* on December 30, 1898,

> if one remembers that the United States, a few months past, solemnly declared that it was only in Cuba and the Philippines in order to emancipate the population from the Spanish yoke, so that they could be independent and autonomous. Now it has established a military occupation in Cuba for an indefinite period. It is probable that the Cuban insurgents will resume the guerilla war that they have been fighting for so long with the Spanish. In the Philippines the Americans are also employing force, with the object of repressing the people's hope for autonomy.[13]

Like many groups outside the United States, the Spanish had gained access to the articles and manifestos published by the various U.S. Anti-Imperialist Leagues and were busily translating them into Spanish and including them, in whole or part, in their own reports on the hostilities. For instance, on January 15, 1899, *Diario de Barcelona*'s French correspondent provided a concise summary of one of Senator Hoar's anti-annexation speeches in Congress, noting that Hoar opposed ratification of the treaty based on the argument that the Constitution contained no articles permitting the acquisition or governing of colonies. Annexing the islands, Hoar maintained, would nullify the country's fundamental doctrines.[14] The Spanish also took pleasure in the frustrations being experienced by their former colonists: on February 11, 1899, reporting on General Otis's

January 4 announcement that the United States would maintain sovereignty over the Philippines for the archipelago's protection, the correspondent from Madrid smugly noted that "the document demonstrates little beyond promises of liberty behind which lie an absolute military domination, a thousand times more tyrannical than was ours."[15]

Far more than other European countries, the Spanish perceived their conflict with the Americans as a continuation of the religious struggles of the Reformation. On January 7, 1899, *La Vanguardia* published a front-page article that suggests how keenly the Spanish understood American imperialism as an expression of Americans' faith in their Protestant mission abroad. Reported by the paper's columnist Juan Buscón, the article tells the story of Mathias Heller, a zealous Presbyterian minister in Connecticut who, according to Buscón, told McKinley that it was imperative that the United States establish "the strictest beliefs and practices of the English Reformation" in its new colony. "We must force this unhappy people to eternal salvation," he is reported to have said, "and where the force of the Bible does not persuade, then the force of our guns will do so." And the article somewhat dryly concludes that for Heller, "the best thing [McKinley] can do is to send Mathias Heller to the Governor General of the Archipelago, accompanied by many Protestant preachers and above all, many regiments."[16] To the Spaniards, Heller's zealotry, though comic, nevertheless revealed the Protestant values underlying the Americans' campaign for hearts and minds in their new territories.

Nuestra América

If the Spanish press took a certain pleasure in pointing out that for all their talk about independence, their former possessions had only acquired new masters, Latin Americans were outraged by their northern neighbor's acts. The American Revolution had inspired revolutions in Latin America from the end of the eighteenth century, and like the Spanish reformers, Latin American nationalists hung pictures of George Washington next to portraits of Simón Bolívar. However, the Monroe Doctrine, originally designed to protect some of the smaller and weaker Latin American countries from predatory imperialists by declaring the Americas off-limits to European expansion, in effect gave the United States dominion over the entire hemisphere. After the Americans annexed nearly half of Mexico's territory in 1848 and "Manifest Destiny" became a popular concept, repeated calls by U.S. filibusters for the annexation of Cuba, Nicaragua, and other countries—William Walker's attempted takeover of Nicaragua in the 1850s being the most famous example—continued to keep Latin Americans looking nervously over their shoulders. On the economic and social fronts, U.S. economic success, as manifested by a constantly rising standard of living, stimulated envy at the same time that it inspired accusations that Americans cared more about money than about ideas. A significant portion of the Latin American intelligentsia felt that the United States had sold its soul for prosperity; these intellectuals decried the intellectual and emotional emptiness of American life and values. They also understood the Protestant fervor at the base of the American narrative of freedom and natural rights, a position that they resented, as both Catholics and as nationalists who, they reminded the Yankees, were also "Americans." As a consequence, the Spanish-American War saw many leery of U.S. rhetoric about bringing freedom to oppressed peoples, and the annexation of Puerto Rico and the Philippines confirmed their worst fears.

José Martí, José Enrique Rodó, and Rubén Darío, three Latin American writers who profoundly affected late nineteenth and early twentieth-century Latin American thought, together articulated the ambivalences about the United States expressed by many citizens of Spain's former colonies. Not all of these men commented directly on the Spanish-American War; Martí, for instance, died three years before its inception. But they did all comment on the United States, often with apprehension. Like the Spanish, they tended to see U.S. and Latino cultures as opposites, and also like the Spanish, they tended to frame the struggle in religious terms. Seeking to preserve Latin American culture from the emptiness and materiality that they saw pervading U.S. life, these Americans presented a sharp critique of U.S. ideals that was calculated to counter the white Protestant culture that they feared.

José Martí

José Martí died a martyr in 1895, well before the Spanish-American War. A Cuban nationalist who had been briefly imprisoned for his participation in the first Cuban uprising against the Spanish in 1868, Martí joined General Máximo Gómez during Cuba's third uprising in 1895, only to be killed in battle with Spanish troops. Between his first and his last participation in the resistance, he had lived outside Cuba for most of his life. Fifteen of those years were spent in New York City, where he wrote poetry, provided correspondence for several Latin American newspapers, and contributed numerous letters and articles to U.S. papers. He also served as a nerve center for the Cuban resistance within the United States and as a touchstone for Latin American consciousness in the northern hemisphere. An acute observer, Martí wrote extensively about the United States and its populations, as well as about Cuban-Spanish relations, Latin America generally, and his vision for a Free Cuba.

Like Mark Twain (whose *Connecticut Yankee* Martí compared to *Don Quixote* and which he sent to a friend's son in Mexico shortly after it was published[17]), Martí's relationship with the United States encompassed his own ambivalences. His many years in the country, scrutinizing its peoples and its cultures, gave him far more insight into the American psyche than most European commentators possessed. Although he wrote glowingly of many of the country's institutions, great men, and progressive movements, he also criticized its injustices and its superficialities. From his first days in the United States, the country's size and energies amazed him: in "Impressions of America (By A Very Fresh Spaniard)," written during his first visit to the United States in 1880, he commented with awe on the American proclivity for constant busyness, even in the height of August's heat waves. He also asked whether devoting such energy to business contributed "in the same extent to the development of these high and noble anxieties of soul, that cannot be forgotten by a people who want to escape from unavoidable ruin . . . Material power, as that of Carthage, if it rapidly increases, rapidly falls down. . . . Life wants permanent roots; life is unpleasant without the comforts of intelligence, the pleasures of art and the internal gratification that the goodness of the soul and the exquisiteness of taste produce to us."[18] For Martí—and as we shall see, for writers such as Rubén Darío—U.S. industry and prosperity presented a peculiar challenge: as evidence of the progress that could be made by a former colony they were admirable, a model to the rest of the hemisphere, but as evidence of a materialistic culture eager to extend itself beyond its geopolitical borders they were alien and threatening. To these Catholic Americans, deeply immersed in developing and describing their own very different populations and traditions, U.S. culture, for all its young power, appeared empty, materialistic, soulless.

During his years in the United States, young Martí came to terms with much of the country's culture (he moved, for instance, from lamenting the forwardness of American women to applauding the public speaking skills of Vassar College's graduates), but he maintained his identity as a Cuban revolutionary and the loyalties—and resentments—that identity entailed. Nine years after questioning Americans' spiritual life, he explained Latin American ambivalence about the United States.

> They admire this nation, the greatest ever built by liberty . . . They have made of the heroes of this country their own heroes, and look to the success of the American commonwealth as the crowning glory of mankind; but they cannot . . . believe that excessive individualism, reverence for wealth, and the protracted exultation of a terrible victory are preparing the United States to be the typical nation of liberty, where no opinion is to be based in greed, and no triumph or acquisition reached against charity and justice. We love the country of Lincoln as much as we fear the country of Cutting. ("A Vindication of Cuba," SW, 263–64)

The last line contrasts Abraham Lincoln, the liberator of American slaves, to Francis Cutting, a prominent annexationist who, Martí implies, would enslave Cuba. This long letter to the editor is intended to make the readers of the *New York Evening Post* reevaluate several recent articles that had labeled Cubans effeminate, lazy, morally defective, and unfit for self-government. Martí's goal was to gain Americans' help in the revolutionary cause while making it clear that he was not advocating annexation. Noting that "the political knowledge of the average Cuban compares well with that of the average American citizen," Martí challenges the United States to consider what it would look like if "the nation that was rocked in freedom, and received for three centuries the best blood of liberty-loving men, [employs] the power thus acquired in depriving a less fortunate neighbor of his liberty" (SW, 266). Martí's closing argument accuses the United States of having already proven itself uninterested in extending its own liberties to its neighbors when it refused to assist the Cuban revolutionaries. "A Vindication of Cuba" is the kind of argument that explains why Mark Twain believed that U.S. intervention in Cuba had been a moment of national greatness; we do not know if Twain read Martí's writings, but Martí's ideas provide at least some of the background for the government's decision to invade the island.

Martí's bitterness about U.S. policies toward Cuba and the Cubans did not stop him from continuing to observe the United States and its inhabitants, comparing and contrasting Latin America and its northern neighbor on cultural, intellectual, political, and racial grounds. Writing in *Patria*, the Cuban Revolutionary newspaper that he founded in New York, Martí lays out his understanding of the United States, especially its demographic diversity and its relationship to its Latin neighbors. Unlike U.S. politicians, Martí cautions his fellow Cubans to see the country as a highly diverse, politically fractured population. "Not only have the elements of diverse origin and tendency from which the United States was created failed, in three centuries of shared life and one century of political control, to merge, but their forced coexistence is exacerbating and accentuating their primary differences" ("The Truth About the United States," SW, 330). Painting an increasingly contentious and corrupt U.S. social and political landscape, Martí warns "the American peoples of Spanish descent" not to fall into "servitude to a damaged and alien civilization." He labels the United States' claim to be uplifting its neighbors "a barren and irrational aspiration, the cowardly aspiration of secondary and inadequate people, to seek to achieve the stability of a foreign nation by paths that differ from those that led the envied nation to security and order by its own efforts and by the adaptation of human liberty to the forms required by the particular makeup of the country" (SW, 331).

For Martí, "democracy," "freedom," and "independence" are flexible political goals. "Ideas, like trees, must grow from deep roots," he admonishes, "and must be adapted to the soil in which they are planted in order to grow and prosper." Blind transplantation of institutions from one country to another results in "monsters, . . . not nations" (SW, 331). As he also elaborated in his essay "Our America" ("Nuestra América"), "to govern well, one must attend closely to the reality of the place that is governed" (SW, 290). In "The Truth About the United States" he argues that the Latin countries must probe the depths of their differences from the North Americans and believe in their own surging potential: "the North American character has declined since its independence, and is less humane and virile today, while the Hispanoamerican, from any point of view, is superior today" (SW, 332).

Coming out of well over a decade of close study of the United States and its peoples, and from his fervent belief in a new kind of Latin American civilization, Martí's vision posits a rise and fall of civilizations. The North American civilization, founded in hope and principle, has seen itself fractured by difference and corruption, whereas the Latin republics are now poised to emerge as the new American civilization. In keeping with this, Martí celebrated Latin Catholicism and racial heterogeneity as a contrast to Anglo-Saxon claims to Protestantism and racial unity. "Our feet upon a rosary, our heads white, and our bodies a motley of Indian and criollo we boldly entered the community of nations," he declares of the formation of Latin American republics in "Nuestra América." "Bearing the standard of the Virgin, we went out to conquer our liberty" (SW, 291). And although he decries the faulty paths that Latin republics had taken on their journeys toward realizing that liberty, he also believes that "the real man is being born to America, in these real times" (SW, 293), and that Latin American culture will triumph—at least as long as aggressive forces from the north can be withstood.

Rubén Darío

For José Martí, then, Latin America was the new cradle of yet another New World—a counterweight to the Protestant, materialist, and ideo-logically racist United States. He was joined in that vision by Nicara-gua's Rubén Darío. A decade younger than Martí, Darío was first and foremost a poet, a revolutionary in the arts far more than in politics. Leader of the *modernismo* movement in Latin America, his aesthetic allegiances to Europe, to European Romanticism, and to the Symbolists and Parnassians make him an unlikely candidate to represent Latin American attitudes toward the United States. Yet the Spanish-American War and the annexation of Puerto Rico and the Philippines profoundly affected him, giving rise to at least one stunning poem of resistance and to other writings expressing his own, and his contemporaries', rage. Like Martí, Darío spent years outside of his own country; unlike Martí, most of that time was spent in Europe and other Latin American coun-tries rather than the United States. Like Martí, Darío worked as a jour-nalist, writing in particular for the internationally read *La Nación* of Buenos Aires. Unlike Martí, he also served as a diplomat for his home country, traveling extensively, perhaps obsessively, throughout his life: to Spain, France, Honduras, Argentina, Chile, El Salvador, Panama, Costa Rica, Cuba. Although he visited the United States briefly—in part to meet Martí—the majority of his international experiences took place in Europe and Latin America.

Darío, then, lacked Martí's intimacy with the United States and its inhabitants. However *modernismo*, the artistic movement in which he was deeply engaged, carried with it a commitment to the Hispanic past and faith in the development of Hispanic cultures independent both of Spain and of the United States. Although the critical debates about the history of *modernismo* show that there was—and remains—considerable dispute over the movement's major thrust, at least one element in it emphasized the development of a specifically Latin American identity.[19] Darío's protest against the United States sprang from his commitment to that identity; he feared the influence of North American culture as much as he feared the overt threat of American political control. Like Martí, he was impressed by North American energies but also saw U.S. culture as a vast wasteland. Like most non–Anglo-Saxon Catholics, he resented white American claims to racial superiority and Protestant claims to be practicing the only valid form of Christianity. In response to U.S. arguments that they were uplifting backwards races, he created a counternarrative that celebrated Latin Americans as soulful, passionate, devout, and Catholic. Even more than Martí's "Nuestra América," Darío's writings suggest that the latent power of Hispanic America was ready to burst forth, overpowering the weakened and corrupted North. "From Mexico to Tierra del Fuego, there is an immense continent in which the ancient seed has been sown, and the vital sap, the future greatness of our race, is about to begin once more to run," he declares in "The Triumph of Caliban." "From Europe, from the universe, there comes a vast cosmopolitan wind, which will help to invigorate our jungle."[20] Conscious of the Anglo-American alliance, especially the myth of common blood that the British periodicals employed to convince the Americans of their sibling relationship, Darío posits an identical bond for the Hispanic world: "when the moment comes, and politics and policies and interests of another species rear their heads, our peoples feel the rush of common blood and the rush of common spirit." He makes the enemy explicit:

> Do you not see how the English enjoy the triumph of the United States, locking away in the vault of the Bank of England their old rancors, the memory of past struggles? Do you not see how the democratic, plebeian Yankee throws up his three *hurrahs*! And sings "God Save the Queen" when a ship flying the Union Jack passes by? And together, they think: "The day will come when the United States and England own the world."
>
> And that is why our race must unite, as body and soul unite, at moments of tribulation. We are the sentimental, feeling race, but we have also been masters of power; the sun has not abandoned us, and the renaissance is ours, by ancestral inheritance. (SW, 510–11)

Drawing on a mythic, Native American racial consciousness and wedding it to the inheritance from Spain, Darío suggests that the Latin Americans have more authenticity, a longer history of power, than the blue-eyed Anglo-Saxons of the North. "Ariel"—Darío's symbol for Latin America—will yet triumph over Caliban.

Invested in Latin American potential, Darío was also conscious of impediments to its realization. In "The Threat of Yankee Imperialism," a short section reprinted in the collection *Tantos Vigores Dispersos,* Darío quotes a French commentator on the relations between Hispanic America and the United States and among the Latin countries themselves:

> If Brazil, Argentina, and Chile would abandon their intestinal quarrels and rivalries, achieve political stability, and consecrate themselves to cultivating the marvelous riches of their soil, in a quarter or half a century, they would see power in this region so constitute itself that they would be able to counterbalance Anglo-Saxon America, and render useless the United States' cherished dream of panamerican hegemony.[21]

Hoping that "the thoughtful among us" would listen to these suggestions, Darío feared that if they did not, North American materiality would overcome Latin American spirituality. "The Marvelous Red Gorillas," possibly his most famous essay on the United States, establishes his hostility toward Anglo-Saxon cultures: "No, No I cannot; I do not want to be part of these silver-toothed buffaloes. They are my enemies, they are hated by Latin blood, they are the barbarians."[22] He describes the North American landscape, both physical and spiritual:

> I have seen the Yankees, in their smoky cities of iron and stone, and the hours that I have passed among them have been anxious ones. It seemed to me that I felt a mountainous oppression, I felt like I was breathing in a country of Cyclops, eaters of raw meat, bestial blacksmiths, inhabitants of mastodons' houses. Red, heavy, greasy, they walk along their streets pushing and shoving animatedly, hunting the dollar. The minds of these Calibans are circumscribed by the purse and the factory. They eat, they count, they drink whisky and make millions. . . . [T]hey are enemies of all ideality. . . . They have temples to all the gods and believe in none. They are imitators and counterfeiters in the arts and sciences, these marvelous red gorillas. But all the time in the world will not serve to polish the enormous beast.

No, I do not want to be part of them, I cannot be part of the triumph
of Caliban.[23]

Even in the midst of his anger, however, Darío also expresses the ambivalence, the mixture of admiration with anger, that characterized the
Latin American response to the United States in those days. Darío's primary target was Theodore Roosevelt, who called for honesty between nations but who had personally invaded Cuba and had overseen the annexation
of the Philippines.[24] Darío's most direct attack was motivated by the promulgation of the "Roosevelt Corollary," which interpreted the Monroe
Doctrine to permit the United States to exercise police powers throughout
the Western Hemisphere. His apprehensions were right; over the years, the
corollary would be used to sanction U.S. interventions in Cuba, Nicaragua, Haiti, and the Dominican Republic.[25] "To Roosevelt" (1904), a poem,
compacts Darío's countermythology, his ambivalence about the United
States, and his symbolic use of American figures into vivid, image-laden
verse, brilliant in Spanish and still forceful in its English translation. Sar-
donically addressing Roosevelt as the "Great Hunter," at once "primitive
and modern, simple and complicated . . . arrogant and strong, exemplary
of your race," he figures him as the nation's representative:

> You yourself are the United States.
> You will be a future invader
> Of naïve America, the one with Indian blood
> That still prays to Jesus Christ and still speaks the Spanish tongue.

Having delineated the two Americas, he accuses the United States of assuming that its form of civilization, and the violence it sanctions, makes it
the emblem of progress:

> You think that life is one big fire,
> that progress is just eruption,
> that wherever you put bullets,
> you put the future, too.
>   No.

And with that "No," that flat denial of North American triumph, the
poet launches his counteroffensive. There is a shadow menacing the
United States, the shadow of Latin American potential. Even though

"The U.S. is a country that is powerful and strong. /When the giant yawns and stretches, the earth feels a tremor," nevertheless it is haunted by "our own America . . . America of the great Moctezuma and Inca . . . Catholic America and Spanish America." That Catholic, Spanish, Indian America,

> lives with you, with your Saxon eyes and barbaric souls.
> And dreams. And loves, and vibrates; it's the daughter of the Sun.
> Be careful. Spanish America is alive and well! . . .
> Roosevelt, you'd need to be transfigured by God himself . . .
> To finally capture us in your talons of iron.

According to Darío, the peoples who had arrived before the Anglo-Saxons remain embedded within the United States—both in the Native American communities and in the Hispanic populations of states like Louisiana and California that had been wrested from the Spanish and the Mexicans. These communities stand on the sidelines of the Anglo-Saxon conversation but observe, like Martí, and bide their time. In the face of Anglo-Saxon convictions that America's missions, including Manifest Destiny, are divinely inspired, Darío hurls back Latin America's response: " . . . you think you have it all, but one thing is missing: God!" (SW, 119–21)

In accusing the United States of godlessness, Darío rejects American claims that annexation and other forms of intervention would bring Christianity to benighted peoples. Speaking from inside the subject position that Kipling belittled as a "loved Egyptian night," Darío, by force of his writing, illuminates the darkness, showing its richness and its passions. Like Spain and Catholic Europe, he correctly reads the Spanish-American War as a religious struggle disguised as a battle for the Enlightenment, and this poem, in particular, unmasks the enemy's lies.

Although the precocious Darío had written an anti-clerical essay in his youth, "El jesuita" (1881), Catholicism was in fact one of the frameworks for his writing and, especially, for his construction of Latin American identity. In his homage to José Martí, written after Martí's death, Darío highlights Martí's religious devotion as a way of locating the hero's Latin American roots, a genius, but also "un hombre— . . . a man. More than that," Darío tells us, Martí "was what the true superman should be: grand and virile, possessed of the secret of his excellence, in communion with God and with nature."

In communion with God lived this man of soft yet immense heart . . .
And in communion with God he was, having ascended to God by the
firmest and surest stairway—the stairway of pain. . . . He rose to God by
the path of compassion and by the path of pain. . . . (SW, 447)

Eulogizing Martí as a man of faith, and writing as one himself, Darío also
positions his precursor within the United States, noting that his years in
New York were his most productive. "It was there that one saw Martí the
thinker, Martí the philosopher, Martí the painter, Martí the musician,
Martí the poet . . . With incomparable magic, he portrayed the United
States alive and palpitating, with its sun and its souls" (SW, 449). For
Darío, Martí's identity is rooted in nation and in religion, making him
both a leader for his own peoples and the ideal observer-critic of the North
American scene. Darío reads the Martí of "Nuestra América"—the name
Martí used to designate the America of the Indian, the Catholic, and the
Spaniard—as the counter-figure to what Roosevelt represented. Whereas
the North American leader was aggressive, barbaric, and godless, the
Cuban leader was passionate, religious, and patriotic, using his power
with language to express his love for Hispanic America, his faith in God,
and his desire to free Cuba from domination by others.

José Enrique Rodó

José Martí and Rubén Darío were both native to the Caribbean, a northern hemispheric region that the United States used as a testing ground
for imperialism throughout the nineteenth and twentieth centuries. In
contrast, José Enrique Rodó (1872–1917) was Uruguayan, from a country well below the equator and little known to most North Americans. In
1900, Rodó published an essay, *Ariel*, that remains the most-referenced
formulation of the *modernista* call for an Hispanic culture constructed
in contradistinction to the North Americans. Like Darío, Rodó, taking
his imagery from Shakespeare's *The Tempest*, posited the United States
as Caliban and Latin America as Ariel. The essay's narrative voice is
Rodó, age 29 when he wrote it, in the guise of Prospero, the elder,
teacher, and sage.

Darío and Rodó were not the first writers to take *The Tempest* outside
of its original contexts. One of the major adaptations was Ernest Renan's
Caliban: Suite de "La Tempête," published in 1878. In this French
reading of Shakespeare's play, Caliban, returned to Italy with Prospero,

illustrates Renan's pessimism about the intellectual and cultural advantages of democracy. Like Renan, most Europeans viewed Caliban and the Caribbean island on which the play took place as sites either for white fantasies about the ethnic Other or allegories about European political disputes. However, Darío and Rodó shifted the narrative; in their writings, the island and its characters became a location for rehearsing the story of imperialism and enslavement within the contexts of the Americas. Unlike later postcolonial writers, both Rodó and Darío adopt Shakespeare's dichotomy between the spirit Ariel and the brutish Caliban. They posit the United States as Caliban, emblem of materialism, and the Latin American states as Ariel, emblem of the spiritual. Together Darío and Rodó use the framework of a British play, refracted through a French adaptation, to signal the essential differences between the North Americans and Latin America.

Ariel is a monologue. Prospero, a teacher, sits beside a statue of Ariel, who symbolizes "the noble, soaring aspect of the human spirit."[26] Prospero insists that his students must ground their personal, social, and political lives in spiritual rather than material values. Urging them to "aspire . . . to develop to the fullest possible measure the totality of your being" (A, 41), Prospero inveighs against utilitarianism, a "false and vulgarized concept that conceives of education as totally subordinate to a utilitarian end" (A, 41). The model for the life of the spirit should be Athens, which promulgated "a concept of life based on the total harmony of all human faculties and the mutual agreement that all energies should be directed toward the glory and power of mankind" (A, 43).

If Athens is the exemplum for the virtuous society, the United States represents its antithesis. Rodó carefully posits the United States and the classical world as moral and cultural opposites, redefining New World concepts like "democracy" and pointing out the Americans' mistakes. In contrast to the Americans, Rodó imagines a democracy of the elite, something akin to the "talented tenth" envisioned by the African American activist/intellectual W. E. B. DuBois in his 1903 study of race relations in America, *The Souls of Black Folk*. In *Ariel* Prospero insists that "A democracy, like an aristocracy, will recognize the distinction of quality; but it will favor truly superior qualities—those of virtue, character, and mind" (A, 67). Whereas DuBois argued that the talented tenth would uplift the rest of the community, Rodó rejects the idea that inferior minds can be uplifted. He believes that only a spiritual and intellectual elite can lead Latin America. For Rodó, it is a scientifically proven fact that "hierarchical order is a necessary condition for all progress" (A, 69). For that reason he believes that American democracy has institutionalized "egalitarian mediocrity as a norm for social relationships" (A, 70). Through Prospero, he warns against "*USA-mania*" (A, 71)—the tendency, increasingly pronounced, to emulate the United States socially as well as politically and economically.

Like both Martí and Darío, Rodó sees Protestant and Catholic cultures as producing radically different individuals. Rodó traces U.S. mediocrity to the religious orientation of its founders, who, he claims, balanced a fierce commitment to individualism with an equal commitment to social engagement. "Each [American] marches forward to conquer life in the same way the first Puritans set out to tame the wilderness," Prospero observes. "Persevering devotees of that cult of individual energy that makes each man the author of his own destiny, they have modeled their society on an imaginary assemblage of Crusoes . . . [and yet] they have at the same time created from the spirit of association . . . a plan of research, philanthropy, and industry." Significantly, Rodó understands the power of the American common school system to create new citizens: "[T]hey have made the school the hub of their prosperity, and a child's soul the most valued of all precious commodities" (A, 75). In themselves, these qualities—individualism, a strong communal ethic, and a passion for universal education—are excellent. But they are also limited because they restrict Americans' horizons to the immediate, the material: "their culture is . . . admirably efficient as long as it is directed to the practical goal of realizing an immediate end" (A, 75–76).

For Rodó there is much to be admired about the United States. The Puritan strain encourages morality and a kind of infinite energy. But the celebration of practicality, the "immediate ends" to which the culture is directed, makes a cultural goal of what should be merely a means. The U.S. school system produced "a universal semi-culture, accompanied by the diminution of high culture." He objected to the leveling effect of general education. "To the same degree that basic ignorance has diminished in that gigantic democracy, wisdom and genius have correspondingly disappeared" (A, 82).

The upshot of all this, for Rodó, is that "as an entity," U.S. civilization "creates a singular impression of insufficiency and emptiness" (A, 79). Rather than formulating new ideals, the American genius demonstrates an "eternal preoccupation with material triumphs" (A, 79). Americans have energy, material comforts, and an extraordinary ability to innovate, but they have basically no ideas, much less ideals; in the midst of their plenty, they are spiritually empty, intellectually void; they enjoy wealth but have no sense of beauty, "good taste has eluded [them]" (A, 81). Like Matthew Arnold, who had already critiqued the United States on much the same grounds, Rodó celebrates the spiritual and the intellectual—immaterial qualities—over the practical and tangible.

Prospero's point is that his students should celebrate the spiritual nature of Latin culture rather than yearning for the world's riches. "Everything in *our* contemporary America that is devoted to the dissemination and defense of selfless spiritual idealism—art, science, morality, religious sincerity, a politics of ideas—must emphasize its unswerving faith in the future" (A, 94;. emphasis added). And the Latin American future that he envisions balances spirituality with action, thoughtfulness with enthusiasm. Prospero concludes by asking his students to keep Ariel's image in their hearts as an emblem of their goals. "Once affirmed in the bastion of your inner being, Ariel will go forth in the conquest of souls . . . Often I am transported by the dream that . . . the Andes, soaring high above our America, may be carved to form the pedestal for this statue, the immutable altar for its veneration" (A, 100).

Ariel is a call to resist cultural imperialism. Rodó's prescience lay in his understanding that *U.S.-mania*—the admiration for all things North American—could lead to slavish imitation, which was an open invitation to U.S. corporations to export American material culture. Latin America's spirituality, its sense of communal heritage, would be buried under the weight of North America's goods. This would be as great a threat to Latin American identity as armed interventions. For Rodó, Latin America should choose a developmental process rooted in Spanish and Native cultures, Catholicism, and above all, a commitment to ideality above materiality.

At the turn into the twentieth century, then, Latin American intellectuals, fired by the vision of North American military and cultural imperialism, were formulating a counter ideology to the U.S. narrative. In contrast to the U.S. valuation of individualism, Protestantism, and homogeneity, the Latin American voices valued communalism, Catholicism, and racial diversity. Whether the Latin American countries actually enacted those values was in the end no more relevant than the fact that the idea of a racially and religiously homogeneous United States was a myth. These transnational narratives were intended to unite often squabbling Latin American countries in order to resist an increasing threat from the north. The Latin American counternarrative, however, also provides us with a means of measuring the Filipino response to the American occupation. By 1898, Latin America had had nearly a century to adjust to the Yankees' efforts to annex their neighbors, and their narratives developed out of those repeated experiences. For the Filipinos, annexation came as an unexpected, and unwelcome, surprise.

Chapter 7

Noli Me Tangere

Filipino Responses to Annexation

American Empire

In early 1901, before the Filipino general Emilio Aguinaldo was captured but after U.S. general Arthur MacArthur, then military governor of the Philippines, issued a positive report on the results of the American Occupation, Mark Twain penned "The Philippine Incident," which savages the American government's pretensions to world power. "In General MacArthur's judgment the Philippine incident is closed," he begins.

> In that case we may now take an account of stock, and try and find out how much we have made by the speculation—or lost. The Government went into the speculation on certain definite grounds which it believed, from the viewpoint of statesmanship, to be good and sufficient. To-wit: 1, for the sake of the money supposed to be in it; 2, in order to become a World Power and get a back seat in the Family of Nations. We have scored on No. 2; we have secured the back seat, and the President is sitting on it and trying to enjoy the tacks that are in it. We are a World Power, no one can deny it; a toy one, it is true, still a World Power . . . We have bought some islands from a party who did not own them; with real smartness and a good counterfeit of disinterested friendliness, we coaxed a confiding weak nation into a trap and closed it upon them; we went back on an honored guest of the stars and stripes when we had no further use for him, and chased him to the

FIGURE 7.1 "Save From the Cruel Spaniard." *Chicago Chronicle,* also published in *The Literary Digest*, Vol. XVIII, No. 17, April 29, 1899, p. 484. [artist: Charles Lederer]

mountains . . . we have pacified some thousands of the islanders and buried them; destroyed their fields, burned their villages. . . . Subjugated the remaining ten millions by Benevolent Assimilation which is the pious name of the new musket. . . .

And so, by these Providences of God—the phrase is the Government's, not mine—we are a World Power; and are glad and proud, and have a Back Seat in the Family. With tacks in it. At least we are letting on to be glad and proud, and it is the best way . . . We realize, too late for escape, that we are the kind of World Power . . . that a prairie-dog village is, and . . . it is the duty of our Government to stand sentinel, with solemn mien, and lifted nose, and curved paws, on top of our little World-Power mound, and look out over the wide prairie; and if anything suspicious shows up on the horizon, bark.[1]

For Twain, the American leap into global imperialism exhibited the pettiness of U.S. ambitions and the meanness of Americans' imaginations. The pettiness embarrassed him and the meanness shamed him. And so he began reading what Filipino documents he could access—such as Rizal's *Noli Me Tangere*—and following reports of U.S. military actions in the new territory. In part, he was trying to determine, from afar, how the Filipinos themselves felt about the American Occupation. What he read did not reassure him. In "To the Person Sitting in Darkness," he suggests that the Filipinos felt both baffled and betrayed; that they had assumed the Americans were speaking honestly because to do otherwise appeared "un-American; uncharacteristic; foreign to our established traditions. We . . . had brought back out of exile their leader, their hero, their hope, their Washington—Aguinaldo; we had lent them guns and ammunition . . . fought shoulder to shoulder with them against 'the common enemy' (our own phrase). . . ." Twain concludes that the February 4, 1899, outbreak of shooting between American and Filipino forces, two days before the Senate was scheduled to ratify the Treaty of Paris, had been an American strategy for transforming a joint action between American and Filipino forces against the Spanish into a platform for American occupation of the islands: "What we wanted, in the interest of Progress and Civilization was the Archipelago, unencumbered by patriots struggling for independence. . . . War was what we needed. We clinched our opportunity" (Zwick, 35).

In Twain's eyes, passage of the Philippine Sedition Act proved his case.[2] Enacted on November 4, 1901, the Sedition Act prohibited Filipinos from advocating independence or separation from the United States publicly or privately, in speech or print. Critics pointed out the irony of the act: in bringing the blessings of American civilization to the Philippines the Americans overrode their own Constitutional guarantee of free speech. "If I were in the Philippines I could be imprisoned a year for publicly expressing the opinion that we ought to withdraw and give those people their independence—an opinion which I desire to express now," Twain reported angrily in "Notes on Patriotism." "What is treason in one part of our States . . . is doubtless law everywhere under the flag. . . . On these terms I would rather be a traitor than an archangel" (Zwick, 115).

In this last notation, Twain tackled one of the major issues being debated by both Congress and the general public: just how far *did* American liberties follow the flag? What exactly did the Constitution say not only about acquiring new territories, but about extending American political institutions into those territories? The Sedition Act was not the only legal decision made in 1901 to deny fundamental American rights to Filipinos; that year saw the first of the series of U.S. Supreme Court decisions, known as the *Insular* Cases, that ended in the verdict that the United States did not have to extend Constitutional rights to U.S. possessions deemed "unincorporated"—that is, conquered territories not "incorporated" into the legal structure of the United States. In *Downes v. Bidwell*, the first of the *Insular* cases, the Court declared that Congress had a choice: it could extend full Constitutional rights to new territories, or it could extend partial rights—a finding that took many observers, including legal scholars, by surprise. Kal Raustiala points out that the *Downes* case illustrates Americans' contradictory ambitions during the period: both to remain a nation faithful to American constitutional law and also to join the community of imperialist nations. "The doctrine of incorporation," Raustiala suggests, "facilitated the imperial ambitions of turn-of-the-century America while retaining a veneer of commitment to constitutional self-government." It also reflected the victory of the pro-expansionist Republican platform espoused by McKinley and Roosevelt in the 1900 election.[3] In effect, the *Insular* decisions shifted the interpretation of "territory" from a temporary to a permanent condition, enabling the United States to control its new possessions but to extend to them only fundamental Constitutional rights—which did not necessarily include the right to free speech or to habeas corpus. As Bartholomew H. Sparrow points out, the decisions took the debates over "the meaning and criteria of citizenship" in a very different direction than they had ever gone before (Sparrow, 9). One context for Twain's attack on the Sedition Act, then, was the revised definition of "rights" that the Supreme Court was in the process of promulgating.

Striking Back

> And if the Siren Yankee,
> With a thousand blandishments offers you,
> The advantages of annexation.
> Pay no heed, ignore it
> For it is your undoing.
> What political liberties
> And equality of rights

Are offered with annexation,
Are just hidden plans
Of future domination.
"To Mindanao," by C. de E.M. and A. Za[4]

The Filipino nationalists did not sit silently while the Americans debated their mission and the rest of the world editorialized. Rather, they
actively joined the conversation. Unlike the Latin Americans, turn-into-
the-twentieth-century Filipinos did not have a counter narrative to the
United States, in large part because it had never occurred to them that the
Americans could become a cultural or military threat. However when they
realized that they had been traded from one imperial master to another,
they scrambled to assess the new situation and to determine how to control it. Utilizing skills honed by years of resistance to Spanish rule, they
loudly and incisively critiqued Americans' actions in the archipelago on
legal and moral grounds. Even before the Sedition Act was passed and the
first *Insular* case decided, Filipino nationalists, intellectuals, and artists
not only were listening to American commentators on both sides of the
debates, they also were reading U.S. documents—at first in the hopes of
dissuading the United States from annexing the Philippines, then, after
dissuasion failed, to determine what it might mean to be controlled by a
nation so publicly obsessed with its Anglo-Saxon heritage.

Spain, which had controlled the Philippines since 1561, had been interested in the archipelago for two reasons: as a crossroads for trade with
China, and as a source of souls for the Church. The Spanish government
controlled the political and economic spheres, and Church friars controlled
the educational and religious ones. The majority of Filipinos lived in traditional villages, speaking one or more of the numerous native dialects. The
upper classes, patterning themselves on Spanish society, were educated in
Filipino schools and universities also run by the religious orders. Their
education included Spanish, and the more ambitious traveled to Spain and
to other European countries. They were aware of the United States and
some visited. But the United States was not one of the countries with
which Filipino nationalists believed they had to contend. Their global
horizons looked to Europe, to China, and to the countries—many also
controlled by European powers—that surrounded them: Taiwan, French
Indochina, Borneo, British Hong Kong, the Dutch East Indies.

When the Filipinos thought of the United States at all, it tended to be
as a model for independence. In the late 1880s Rizal himself, in a lengthy

essay speculating on what might happen to the Philippines should they win independence from Spain, dismissed the possibility that the United States might be interested in acquiring them. Rizal believed that even though the United States, as a growing power, was not immune to the "greed and ambition" that are the "vices of the strong," nevertheless the young country would develop itself internally before contemplating so distant a venture as the Philippines. The Panama Canal, then a failing French operation, was far from completion, making it difficult for the eastern United States to access the Pacific. Besides, Rizal suggested, even if the United States did contemplate intervention in the archipelago, "the European powers may not leave the way open to her, as they know very well that appetite is whetted by the first morsels. North America would be a bothersome rival once she enters the field, but colonial expansion is against her traditions."[5] Rizal assumed that the United States did not constitute a threat to an independent Philippines because its traditions rejected overseas expansion, because it had more pressing concerns elsewhere, and because the European powers would not permit a potential rival in the southern Pacific.

Rizal's view of the United States was based on his trip across the continent in 1888, and on his reading, which included Evert A. Duyckink's *Lives of the Presidents of the United States from Washington to Johnson* and Harriet Beecher Stowe's *Uncle Tom's Cabin*. While the reading gave him insight into U.S. political and social histories, his observations of the Americans as he traveled through the country gave him insight into their peculiar bundling of national ideals with racism. "America," he later told a friend, "is the land *par excellence* of freedom, but only for the whites."[6] White Americans' undisguised distaste for brown and black peoples would, in Rizal's view, contribute to their reluctance to engage, either socially or politically, in the Philippines. Events proved him wrong. The United States decided that it wanted the archipelago. "We are of the Anglo-Saxon race," Twain quotes a retired army officer happily announcing, "and *when the Anglo-Saxon wants a thing he just takes it*"(Zwick, 181).

Annexation by the United States found Filipino intellectuals scrambling to understand their new situation. Some welcomed it as a means either for personal aggrandizement or as a shortcut to modernization; Trinidad Pardo de Tavera, an educated and wealthy Filipino, even argued for adoption of the English language in the hope that "through its agency the American spirit may take possession of us and that we may so adopt its principles, its political customs and its peculiar civilization that our redemption may be complete and radical."[7] Pardo de Tavera's words suggest that he accepted the Americans as they had presented themselves; in his reading not only is American civilization exceptional, it is also "redemptive." Rizal himself was no longer alive, having been martyred two years earlier. According to many later critics, Rizal's writings were co-opted by the Americans: the anti-Spanish revolutionary movement for which he was a key figure was appropriated and transformed into an officially sanctioned nationalism that served the Americans' ends.[8]

For many other Filipinos, however, onset of American colonial rule inspired a pressing need to understand the new civilization that was being forced upon them. American media reports about Filipinos rarely reached beyond crude portraiture, painting the Filipinos as savages, peasants, or decadent aristocrats. This meant that most Americans did not know that a well-educated, European-oriented class, many of whom were active in the nationalist movement, had existed for years, rooted in the islands but with strong ties to colleagues in Spain and across Europe. Although the Spanish colonial government had vigorously censored nationalist organizations within the Philippines, Spain itself had been the site where expatriot Filipinos first organized to press for reform. In *The Propaganda Movement, 1880–1895*, a study of the origins of Filipino nationalism, John N. Schumacher notes that a nationalist movement in the Philippines began in the 1880s, in part as a reflection of European nationalism, and that many of its Filipino proponents had studied in Spain.[9] Newspapers, magazines, flyers, and manifestos, all appurtenances of European nationalism, accompanied the formation of nationalist organizations.

One of the most influential of the organizations was La Solidaridad, born among Filipinos at a New Years' Eve banquet in Barcelona in 1888. La Solidaridad developed its own periodical, also titled *La Solidaridad*, the following year (Schumacher, 119). Its first issue, February 15, 1889, contained the organization's *propósitos*, or goals, including the intention "to combat all reaction, to impede all retrogression, to applaud and accept every liberal idea, to defend all progress; in a word [to further] all the ideals of democracy . . . " (Schumacher, 122). Copies were smuggled into the Philippines, where they were received enthusiastically. Leaders of the organization also produced pamphlets, some written in Tagalog, for exportation to the archipelago, a means of conveying information to the many nationalists who could not travel. Schumacher points out that unlike other European colonies, such as India, Egypt, or Vietnam, where nationalist movements struggled to emerge from non-Christian religious frameworks, in the Philippines the majority of the population were followers of a major European religion, making Western ideologies far more accessible to existing cultural mentalities (Schumacher, 272–74). In *Under Three Flags: Anarchism and the Anti-Colonial Imagination*, Benedict Anderson also notes that the folklore movement, popular in Europe and represented in the Philippines through the work of Isobelo de los Reyes, helped Filipinos understand the relationship of local cultures to national political structures.[10] These studies suggest that Filipino nationalists, educated under Spanish authorities and linked to Europe by religion and by language, took recent European histories and European nationalists as their models, giving them confidence that they could construct a viable government once independence from Spain was effected.

Americans refused to recognize the nationalists' competence, treating their leaders as local chieftains and their political aspirations as evidence of their naiveté. The Filipinos were both angry and perplexed. At first they simply tried to determine the Americans' intentions. Once they realized that colonization was the goal, they focused on convincing the young republic that it was a bad idea—for Americans as well as for Filipinos. When that failed, they vigorously protested the imposition of American rule, in part through analyzing American actions in light of American institutions and founding documents, especially the Constitution. Although they may not have constructed a counternarrative in the first years of U.S. occupation, the Filipino intelligentsia did articulate a critical reading of the U.S. Constitution that reviewed both congressional discussions and U.S. foreign policy in the light of U.S. Constitutional law. And they, too, understood the United States in terms of its self-imaging.

As we have seen, Twain's "A Defense of General Funston" attacked Funston for having captured Emilio Aguinaldo, the fugitive president of the Philippine Republic, on slippery moral grounds. In Twain's reading of Funston's adventure, the Americans had employed base means of entrapping Aguinaldo because they had imposed on the revolutionary leader's own honesty and generosity, then let fire. For Aguinaldo himself, capture by the Americans was the beginning of the end of his revolutionary leadership; within a short period he would pledge loyalty to the United States, and over the next half century he would rethink the U.S. enterprise in the Philippines altogether. In the first years of American rule, however, he insisted that the United States had misrepresented its intentions when it volunteered to help the nationalists oust the Spanish and had betrayed its own principles in its policies regarding the Philippines.

Aguinaldo was born in 1869 into a substantial family from the province of Cavite. He attended the Colegio de San Juan de Letran, a Dominican preparatory school in Manila, but did not complete his course of study, returning home and joining the Katipunan, the underground revolutionary movement. Rising quickly through the ranks, he honed his leadership skills through the organization. By 1896 he was being addressed as "General." Because he had a reputation for narrowly escaping death, rumors of his invincibility abounded. On March 22, 1897, he was elected President of the Revolutionary Government, in which position he remained until he was forced to capitulate to the Americans in early 1901.[11] After pledging loyalty to the new colonial power on April 19 of that year, he remained in the Philippines for the rest of his life. He died in 1964.

In the 1950s, the country's evolution into a modern nation convinced Aguinaldo that he should re-evaluate the events of 1899. His attitudes toward the United States at the time of annexation and fifty years later differ radically. In 1899 he was adamantly opposed to the United States; by 1957 he was prepared to concede that the Americans were probably the best of several evils. For this study, Aguinaldo's significance lies in his consistencies rather than his flip-flops; both in 1899 and in 1957 his statements indicate that he understood the United States in terms of its own historical narrative. Whether he was defending his own acts against American perfidy, as he did in 1899, or conceding that the American takeover may have been a good idea, as he claimed in 1957, he measured the United States in terms of its claim to represent freedom and benevolence. Like Twain, it took the nationalists a long time to understand that American liberties were not among the goods the United States planned to export.

Both *True Version of the Philippine Revolution* (1899) and *A Second Look at America* (1957) give Aguinaldo's version of the battle between the Spanish and the Americans and the Filipinos' role in facilitating the Americans' victory. They also both accuse the United States of lying to him about their intentions in the Philippines. According to Aguinaldo, Admiral Dewey, acting for the U.S. government, first sought Aguinaldo's help in defeating the Spanish—in the process promising that the United States would not interfere in the archipelago's internal affairs—and then betrayed his promises. In *True Version*, Aguinaldo cites Dewey's claim that "the United States had come to the Philippines to protect the natives and free them from the yoke of Spain," and he insists that the Admiral had assured him that the Americans did not need any colonies. At the time, Aguinaldo claims, he had responded by expressing his admiration for "the grandeur and beneficence of the American people," especially after Dewey swore that Americans' "word of honor" was "more positive, more irrevocable than any written agreement."[12] At the end of *True Version*, Aguinaldo laments the fate of his country; at the same time, he suggests, he remains confident that Americans will live up to their reputation for fair dealing. In listing his reasons for trusting Dewey he evokes the Americans' Founding Fathers and the U.S. doctrine of liberties. "I trust in the rectitude of the great people of the United States of America," he declares, "where, if there are ambitious Imperialists, there are defenders of the humane doctrine of the immortal Monroe, Franklin, and Washington; unless the race of noble citizens, glorious founders of the present greatness of the North American Republic, have . . . degenerated" (*True Version*, ch. 19).

In his 1899 text, then, Aguinaldo is bitterly opposed to the Americans, but still taken by the story of Americans' respect for other countries' independence. In his 1957 document, he still maintains that Dewey lied to him, but he no longer sees American rule as anathema. Instead, his retrospective narrative casts the American occupation as a viable demonstration of precisely the values that he had earlier accused the expansionists of betraying. *A Second Look at America* reviews Philippine history from the far side of two World Wars, including the Japanese occupation of the islands throughout World War II, and Aguinaldo comes to a very different conclusion about the long-term effects of U.S. colonial rule. In this late rethinking, Aguinaldo concluded that annexation was probably the best of several evils, certainly superior to one of the other possibilities, the partition of the Islands among the world powers. He analyzes McKinley's policies as evidence of the best of American intentions, in line with U.S. constitutional principles. According to Aguinaldo's latter-day reading of Philippine-American history, in 1899 "President McKinley succumbed to the persuasion of Great Britain, the pressure and machinations of the expansionists and the apparent snowballing of the more articulate public and press opinion in favor of Philippine annexation."[13] A year later, according to Aguinaldo, the U.S. president reframed his decision as divine inspiration (*A Second Look*, 65), and shortly after sent the Taft Commission to the Islands with the intent of establishing what the later Aguinaldo considers a viable, and humane, civil government.

The older Aguinaldo represents these events positively; he quotes approvingly from McKinley's "Letter of Instruction" to the Philippine Commission, which established U.S. rule in the archipelago, and is enthusiastic about the decision to expand the school system. He even supports the order to mandate English as the common language, not simply because it would enable the Filipinos to communicate with the wider world but because "education in English opened wide to the Filipinos the doors to the great literature of democracy" (*Second Look*, 135). In Aguinaldo's retrospective glance, adoption of English meant that "Now the younger generations could read . . . the Declaration of Independence and the inspiring pronouncements on freedom of Jefferson, Lincoln and Webster and other great liberty-loving Americans" (*Second Look*, 136). Quoting the final paragraph of McKinley's "Instructions," Aguinaldo comments that its "penitential, ethical, and prophetic tone . . . makes one wonder if McKinley did not after all receive that Divine Inspiration which he said had led him to decide on taking all the Philippines" (*Second Look*, 138)—reference to a passage in the "Instructions" that refers to the U.S. mission to the Philippines as "a high and sacred . . . obligation" and ends with the hope that "all the inhabitants of the Philippine Islands may come to look back with gratitude to the day when God gave victory to American arms at Manila, and set their land under the sovereignty and protection of the people of the United States" (*Second Look*, 138). By 1957 not only was Aguinaldo ready to endorse the occupation, he was also ready to see it in the divinely ordained terms in which the Americans had cast it half a century earlier.

As its title indicates, *A Second Look* is retrospective—and written by a man whose own professed loyalties over the decades suggest that his convictions may have been based more on expedience than on conviction.[14] But Aguinaldo was incorrect in assuming that it took an English-language school system to bring U.S. ideas about freedom and civil liberties to the Philippines. As his own 1899 text suggests, Filipino nationalists writing at the time of the annexation were already well-versed in U.S. history and U.S. Constitutional law. One of the most interesting of these nationalists was Apolinario Mabini, Prime Minister of the Republic of the Philippines under Aguinaldo and crafter of its Constitution.

Apolinario Mabini was born in Batangas Province in 1864, the son of peasants. Often referred to as the "brains of the revolution," he moved quickly from local schooling to the Colegio de San Juan de Letran in Manila. Unlike Aguinaldo, he finished the preparatory course and then entered the University of Santo Tomas, where he completed his law degree in 1894. At the university he became involved with *La Liga Filipina*, a movement begun by Rizal that sought to unite Filipinos in the common cause of social and educational reform. Although members of *La Liga* were not revolutionaries, the Spanish authorities suspected them of subversion, and Spanish prosecutions turned many toward more radical organizations such as the Katipunan. After Rizal's execution, Mabini joined Aguinaldo to form a revolutionary government. Paralyzed from the waist down by polio in 1896, he nevertheless served, albeit briefly, as Aguinaldo's chief advisor and Prime Minister of the Philippine Republic in 1899. He resigned before the year ended, when elements with whom he radically disagreed gained power within the government.[15] In 1901 the Americans exiled him, with other nationalists, to Guam, preventing his return to the Philippines until he took the oath of allegiance in 1903. He died of cholera the same year. Even the Americans he opposed admitted his intelligence; he was arguably the most respected member of the government of the Philippine Republic.[16]

In 1931, the Bureau of Printing in Manila published *La Revolución Filipina (con otros documentos de la época)*, compiled by Teodoro M. Kalaw. This two-volume work contains much of Mabini's writings, from his own recounting of the revolution, through numerous public documents (many signed by Aguinaldo but authored by Mabini). The second volume also features a number of articles written by Mabini, often in response to articles in newspapers published in the British colonies of Singapore and Hong Kong (the latter the residence of a cadre of exiled Filipino nationalists, including Aguinaldo, before Dewey brought him back to Manila). According to the preface, they were written while Mabini was recovering his health after he resigned from the revolutionary government in 1899 but before the Americans took over and exiled him to Guam. Although parts of these volumes have been translated—most notably, the title section, containing Mabini's own version of the story of the revolution—most of the letters and articles have not. Yet these, more than anything beyond the Philippine Constitution itself (which, like those of most new republics in the nineteenth century, was modeled on the U.S. Constitution), show us how steeped Mabini was in American constitutional history and how adept he was at using Americans' descriptions of their own historical trajectory to support his arguments. As we saw with the Europeans and the Latin Americans, the Filipinos had listened while the Americans celebrated their unique traditions of self-determination and civil liberties.

On June 30, 1899, Mabini first summarized, then responded to, articles in the *Singapore Free Press* (May 22) and the *Hong-Kong Telegraph* (May 30) regarding annexation. "The *Singapore Free Press*," he begins, "claims that the government in Washington, not having taken responsibility for its real status in the Philippines, is proceeding very foolishly, having made it evident to the Filipinos that the promises of liberty launched at the beginning of the war have for their object territorial expansion, achieved through the subjugation of races that, because they object to being sold like cattle, must be enforced by military ventures that the U.S. Constitution would reproach and condemn." And he continues: "perhaps a little less exaltation on the part of the military and a bit more appreciation for the words *liberty and rights* might prevent these bloody proceedings, the dirty stains that today we see on the beautiful reputation and humanity of the United States."[17] Like Ernest Crosby in *Captain Jinks*, Mabini demands that Americans admit the degree to which they have allowed militarist enthusiasm to overrule their foundational, and much advertised, respect for liberty and human rights.

Mabini's attack on the United States was relentless. Firmly believing that "it is the intention of the North American Government . . . to rule forcibly over the Philippines," Americans' protestations to benevolence notwithstanding, he predicted that "annexation, whatever form it may take, will result in our eternal slavery by a people . . . different from us in manners and customs, a people who do not want to see a brown people beside them, . . . a people from whom we cannot separate without resorting to armed conflict."[18] His goal is to unmask the racism at the heart of U.S. claims to benevolence and to skewer American policies on constitutional grounds. As with his allusion to "liberty" and "rights," he engages key names from the pantheon of American heroes to force Americans to reflect on their deeds and to encourage Filipinos to know that they are right in resisting American aggression. He reminds his readers that "The great nation of Washington and Lincoln must understand that force, no matter how powerful, cannot annihilate the aspirations of eight million souls who are conscious of their own power, honor, and rights: blood will not drown them, it will only nourish their great ideas, the eternal principles."[19] Here the presidents' names evoke the "eternal principles" that the men had come to represent and suggest that because the people of the United States, by virtue of shared citizenship with Washington and Lincoln, pride themselves on those principles, they should not suffer their country to be dishonored by their breach. The passage also reminds Filipinos that the Americans can be censured on the gap between their words and their deeds.

Like Twain and other anti-imperialists, Mabini does not believe Americans' pretensions to benevolence. "The American government warmly and enthusiastically invokes humanity and liberty, but they only want it for themselves, not others," he alleges.[20] In "The U.S. Government in the Philippines" (intentionally written on Washington's birthday, as was Twain's "In Defense of General Funston") Mabini analyzes the speeches of three Americans deeply implicated in the Philippines: President McKinley, Jacob Gould Schurman (president of Cornell University and head of the First Philippine Commission), and Secretary of War Elihu Root. Root in particular is the focus of Mabini's attack. He summarizes Root's declaration that "the isles ceded [by Spain] had acquired the right to be treated by the United States in conformity with the principles of justice and liberty as declared in the Constitution for the essential security of each individual against the powers of the Government." However, Mabini adds, Root also noted that the Constitution "only prescribes these rights uniformly to the residents of the American continent; the only one the islanders can claim is not to be deprived of life, liberty, or property without due process of law."[21]

Root's words reflect the *Downes* decision, which had held that unincorporated territories need only be extended fundamental constitutional rights. (According to Raustiala, after *Downes* was decided Root had quipped that the Constitution did follow the flag, "but doesn't quite catch up" [Raustiala, 86].) Mabini refuses to accept that the United States could so casually jettison its principles, and he proceeds to explicate the Bill of Rights as part of his protest. Like Twain and the other Americans who challenged the United States on its assumption that it could export the flag without also exporting American liberties, Mabini focuses on the Bill's declaration that all persons born or naturalized in the United States are citizens, fully invested with the rights granted by the Constitution. Mabini suggests that "These . . . rights . . . should be enjoyed by all who are subject to the jurisdiction of the United States." Moreover in regard to Root's claim that the Constitution only applies within the American continent, Mabini tartly rejoins,

> If so, then neither the government nor Congress has power over the Islands; both receive their own powers from the Constitution, and these powers cannot be extended to territories declared outside of the Constitution's reach. Congress can not legislate for the Islands: its power is limited to deciding whether or not to admit them to the Union. If admitted, the Islands must have the status of a State; if not, they must be independent.[22]

This paragraph was written by a mind well acquainted both with U.S. Constitutional law and the debates over annexation as they were being conducted in the United States.[23] As we have seen, political and legal battles over the status of the Philippines continued for years: the Sedition Act was passed shortly after Mabini's death. Mabini anticipates these struggles in his claim that Secretary Root could not simultaneously argue that the Constitution's protection does not extend beyond U.S. geopolitical borders and that the United States had the right to govern the Philippines without the Islands' consent. For Mabini as for Americans who argued against annexation on legal grounds, if the Constitution gives the United States the right to acquire and govern new territories, it also demands that those governments bring Constitutional principals with them. According to this logic, Congress itself exists only by virtue of the Constitution; therefore it cannot act beyond the Constitution, and it cannot limit the rights its own parent document specifies.

Educated through his reading of U.S. founding documents, Mabini understood that Americans saw themselves as integral to their government's actions, and he assumed that they craved consistency between what they perceived as their shared national identity and the national profile that their government's actions implied. Mabini's reasoning that both the president and the Congress derive their powers only from the Constitution shows an acute understanding of American legal history. He was not the only one to argue that if the Constitution did not apply in the territories, then neither the executive nor legislative branches had any power there as well.

Mabini also targeted the Americans' policy of negotiating with despots while refusing to negotiate with a representative government. With the American anti-imperialists, he was outraged by the U.S. policy of negotiating with the Sultan of Joló, the Muslim breakaway region of the Philippines, but refusing to negotiate with Aguinaldo, president of the Philippine Republic. Discussion with the Sultan was one of the items that Secretary of State Root cited in his list of beneficent U.S. actions in the region, but also one that many Americans had loudly protested. In "The Philippine Incident" Twain describes it as the purchase of "the three hundred concubines and other slaves of our business-partner the Sultan," and as the disgrace of having "hoisted our protecting flag over that swag" (Zwick, 58). Mabini accuses the Americans of having chosen expedience over honor in determining their allies:

Filipinos who have voted in a constitution inspired by the most advanced science, those who are struggling to educate themselves and correct their old vices, in order to prepare themselves in friendly relations with all the nations of the world, are fought against by the Americans; meanwhile those [i.e., the Muslim minority] who remain isolated in order to maintain despotism and slavery, enjoy peace and tranquility in the shadow of the Stars and Stripes. Who would have thought the day would come when the Republic of Washington and Lincoln would combat liberty and progress, allying itself with despotism and slavery![24]

Mabini claims that the United States, rather than encouraging Filipinos already advanced in the political arts, had allied itself with the most retrograde element of the Filipino population. Seeking to control the entire archipelago, the United States joined forces with the Sultan of Joló in order to defeat nationalists who would insist on independence.

In his battle to assert Filipino competence for self-rule and to refute American claims to benevolent intentions, Mabini also attacked individual members of Congress who justified annexation as benevolence. Speaking for the Filipinos, Mabini engaged Albert Beveridge, the Progressive, pro-annexationist senator from Indiana. In "Beveridge Ante El Senado" ("Beveridge in the Senate"), dated March 3, 1900, Mabini denounced Beveridge's speech, commonly referred to as "In Support of an American Empire," given on January 9, 1900, and reported on in the *Manila Times* on February 27, 1900. Part call to arms, part sermon, part July 4th oratory, this speech declares that "the Philippines are ours forever," and that "we will not renounce our part in the mission of our race, trustee under God, of the civilization of the world." An outrageous bundle of racist and capitalist statements even for 1900, "In Support of an American Empire" was nevertheless highly effective in swaying the American public. It did not impress Mabini. Characterizing Beveridge as "a young opportunist," Mabini translates key paragraphs of the senator's oratory into Spanish, and then summarizes the rest of the speech. He paraphrases Beveridge's claims that the Filipinos are a barbarous race made even weaker by three centuries of contact with a decadent Spain, and that they are therefore incapable of self-government. He also summarizes Beveridge's argument that the nation, not the Constitution, is "immortal," and that the Constitution must be made to serve the nation rather than the other way around. Mabini reads these lines as Beveridge's assertion that if the Constitution prevents the nation's enlargement, the Constitution should be changed to permit expansion. He also reads Beveridge's rather vague invocation of the "Founders" and "Fathers" of the nation as specifically Washington, Lincoln, and Hamilton.

Mabini was enraged by this speech. He was also baffled by the enthusiasm with which it was received. Dismissing any intrinsic intellectual or literary value, he concludes that Beveridge's success stems from his willingness to lie: "Mr. Beveridge has been quite frank, and said that the best politician is one well versed in the art of deception," he admits. Mabini then lays out the double message that, he claims, the speech offers, the first to the Filipinos and the second to the Americans:

> Mr. Beveridge says to the Filipinos: Do not believe in the promises of humanity, liberty, civilization and progress; the war in the Philippines is rooted in purely mercantile objectives, and in these calculations weigh neither sentiment nor spilled blood, only money and gain.
>
> He says to the Americans: If the principles of divine or natural rights on which our Constitution is based oppose imperialist expansion, let us bypass the Constitution, let us bypass God; the only real God is gold, the only real Constitution is gilded. You must renounce your constitutional liberties and subject yourselves to fortune, because oppressing the Filipinos means that you must first oppress yourselves.[25]

For Mabini, this is utter "impudence." But whence come Beveridge's accolades? According to Mabini, the senator from Indiana "has the skill to play the weakest string of his party, and it has broken." In assuming that Beveridge only appealed to his party's least reputable factions, Mabini was also assuming that most Americans sincerely wanted to practice the principles they professed to honor.

But Mabini was mistaken in his assumption that most Americans wanted to practice American principles in the Philippines. As we have seen, the majority of white Americans feared the prospect of the Philippines becoming part of the United States. Hence the Court's support for an "exceptional" form of colonialism, in which the Islands would be held as an unincorporated territory for an indefinite period of time, but not put into a trajectory for eventual statehood. When he attacked Albert Beveridge for overriding Constitutional principles, Mabini was assuming that Beveridge was appealing to the most degraded elements of American sentiment, the country's "weakest strings." Beveridge's brilliance as an orator, however, was to play *all* his party's strings, knowing that his audience would pay attention only to those they wanted to hear. And Beveridge's auditors heard his call to recreate the world in the image of the United States, not his call to undermine the Constitution. A consummate politician, Beveridge knew that it was far more important to engage the narrative of civil liberties than to enact them. Despite Mabini's understanding of American constitutional law, he only half grasped the power of the American narrative of race, religion, and national destiny within the U.S. context. His chief mistake was to assume that Americans took their founding documents unadulterated; what he missed was the evangelical fervor with which, by 1899, those documents had been imbued. The galleries responded to Beveridge because he assured them that they were appointed to rule the globe: in phrases that compound American mythic history with the sentiments expressed by the British periodicals, Beveridge turns to the Declaration of Independence to sanction the U.S. mission to "do our part in the regeneration of the world," calls for a strong bureaucratic structure to administer the Islands, and claims that "this question . . . is deeper than any question of constitutional power. . . . It is racial."[26] As we have seen, by the time Beveridge gave this speech, Kipling's "The White Man's Burden" already had worked its way into the American language, as one of the "strings" that orators could play. The senator's talent lay in his ability to make all the strings sound in harmony. His words may have seemed extraordinarily "impudent" to Apolinario Mabini, but they were affirmation of national identity to a large portion of the American public. Brilliant as Mabini was, he could not fathom the religious and racial patterns that profoundly affected any discussion of Constitutional principles in the American mind.

Representative Brosius spoke truly: in 1899, the eyes of the world were riveted on the United States. The decision to annex the Philippines, Puerto Rico, Guam, and the other islands far from U.S. borders, signaled U.S. entry onto the global imperialist stage. Using the narrative of American freedoms, already well broadcast around the world, as its calling card, the United States presented itself as the friend of liberty, happy to help struggling peoples obtain independence. It was only after the battles with Spain were over that the struggling peoples realized that the price of freedom from Spain was subjection to the United States. Martí, Darío, and Rodó's dream of a unified Hispanic America was not to be manifested in territories under U.S. purview, and Aguinaldo and Mabini's dreams of an independent Philippines would not be realized for another 50 years. Moreover the U.S. government initiated a pattern that would characterize its foreign engagements throughout the twentieth century and into the twenty-first: to justify intervention in conflicts abroad as bringing U.S. freedoms to oppressed peoples, knowing that such claims would resonate domestically; to have those rationales unmasked by oppositional groups at home and abroad, and then to loose popular domestic support, in part because of widespread media broadcasting of the oppositions' arguments and in part because the conflicts turned out to be long and costly. With the eyes of the world upon them, Americans continued to argue among themselves about who they were and what their role in the world should be. The arguments have not ended.

Epilogue: American Strings: Bush, Obama, Ahmadinejad

Religion remains a key value in American identity politics. Nearly every year sees at least one nationally staged battle between Darwinists and Creationists over the teaching of science, or between professional historians and school board members over the centrality of Protestant culture to U.S. history. The school boards know that the side that controls the textbooks controls the minds of the citizens they produce. Politicians also know that they reach the public most effectively if they sound traditional strings, including references to U.S. founding documents, divine guidance, and unity in a common cause. The rhetorical framing of U.S. ideals in the twenty-first century is not much different from the rhetorical landscape of the turn into the twentieth.

The first decade of the twenty-first century witnessed yet another U.S. intervention into countries far from its own borders as well as the historically significant election of the first African American U.S. president. Both events evoked now-traditional rhetorical fusions of national and religious ideals. For instance, when presidential candidate Barack Obama discovered that his Chicago pastor, the Reverend Jeremiah Wright, had publicly indicted the American government for lies and racism, Obama attempted to deflect the political damage his friend was causing his campaign. The goal of his March 18, 2008, speech on race, "A More Perfect Union," is to bring white and black Americans together by suggesting that they fight their common enemies—corporate greed, exploitative talk-show hosts, dishonest politicians—instead of indulging in old racial antagonisms. Not incidentally, the speech also carefully fuses national and Christian ideals. "A More Perfect Union" situates Obama himself within a Christian context—he praises Wright for having "helped introduce me to my Christian faith"—and implies that his religion and his patriotism operate in tandem. It was even more important for Obama to bring attention to his Christianity than for most American politicians; son of a white Christian American mother and a black African Muslim father, his opponents constantly accused him of being a closet Muslim. Consequently he argues for racial unity from the standpoint of a traditional Protestant-Christian American, speaking of his "firm conviction, a conviction rooted in my faith in God and my faith in the American people—that working together we can move beyond some of our old racial wounds, and that in fact we have no choice if we are to continue on the path of a more perfect union."

Faith and *union* are key words in this speech. The candidate presents himself as a man of faith, both in the body politic and in its divine guidance. References to "union," on the other hand, come freighted with multiple connotations. As calls for unity to defeat the Spanish in 1898 reunited American whites who, forty years before, had battled over the question of slavery, Obama's call for unity in 2008 asks citizens to transcend outmoded feuds, to close ranks and become a tough political wedge to defeat the opposition. Solidarity also will further the national quest for perfection by acknowledging fifty years of progress in race relations. But "unity" in this speech can also imply Obama himself, avatar of a national rebirth. By positioning himself as a Protestant Christian, Obama implicitly rejected his father's religion. However he embraces both parents' racial legacies. Speaking of the black and white communities, Obama positions himself as the synthesis of the nation's most vexed historical binary, claiming that both communities "are a part of me. And they are a part of America, this country that I love." Here Obama's duality becomes transcendence, the embodiment of the "perfect union" toward which national history is striving.

But overcoming the past does not mean forsaking it. National memories are selective. The paradox in Obama's speech, as so often in American political rhetoric, is that overcoming one past depends on a return to the ideals of another. In this case, Obama implies that we can only forget the bitter legacies of slavery and the Civil War by remembering the legacy of the Revolution. And as we have seen, in American political rhetoric, evocations of Revolutionary legacies fuse Enlightenment and Christian values. Here, Obama frames his call for social justice as a religious mandate. "What is called for," Obama insists, "is that we do unto others as we would have them do unto us. Let us be our brother's keeper, Scripture tells us. Let us be our sister's keeper. Let us find that common stake we all have in one another, and let our politics reflect that spirit as well." By the conclusion of the speech, when Obama wraps back to the Declaration of Independence and the journey toward "perfect union" that began at the Declaration's signing, he has fused Christian and national missions. By creating an infrastructure for his speech that rests on key words and phrases from the American narrative, Barack Obama urges the nation to move forward by holding forth the ideals of the past.

Obama's speech shows the persistence of the ideological legacies of the nineteenth century, despite the massive population shifts and technological changes of the last one hundred years. When Obama told his listeners that "a perfect union" was still possible, he assured them that he imagined America as they did—as a place where individuals could be brought together in the pursuit of their common special mission. We see similar ideological legacies in public speeches about foreign affairs. For instance, American responses to 9/11 and its aftermath in many ways echoed the debates of 1898–99.[1] Like the explosion of the American battleship *Maine* in Havana harbor in 1898, the destruction of the World Trade Center by rogue Arab nationalists in 2001 stimulated patriotic frenzy and hyper-masculine vows for revenge. As in 1899, citizens fought over the country's proper response to the current crisis, and the media and the political establishments dove into the archive of cues that would help them persuade Americans to sanction their leaders' strategies. These included invoking the national mythology, especially the legacy of championing freedom from oppression; the binary between good, manifested as Christianity, and evil, manifested as any other powerful ideology; and the image of American troops as the harbingers of modernity to peoples laboring under feudal systems. Like the invasion of the Philippines in the wake of the invasion of Cuba, the 2003 selling of the invasion of Iraq to the American public reflected policy architects' understanding that Americans would sanction intervention abroad only if they could be convinced that they would be welcomed as liberators. The spectacular bombing of Baghdad, the repeated shots of the toppling of the statue of Saddam Hussein, and the apparent welcoming of the American troops by Iraqi Shiites provided visual images affirming those demands.

President George W. Bush's January 29, 2002, State of the Union speech was also designed to sound American strings, setting the stage for positive reception of ongoing American military engagements in the

Middle East. The President's designation of Iran, Iraq, and North Korea as an "axis of evil" played into Americans' demands that their energies be mobilized on the right side in the battle between good and evil.[2] His declaration that the United States "will lead by defending liberty and justice" and his assertion that unlike their enemies, Americans had made a choice for "freedom and the dignity of every life . . . on the day of our founding" cued the narrative of national mission, while a tribute to the power of "free markets and free trade" to "lift lives" across the globe signaled the continuing close association of capitalism with the idea of "free societies." The speech also referenced Americans' role in bringing modernity to benighted peoples; Bush proudly reported that as a consequence of the defeat of the Taliban, Afghani women, domestic prisoners under Taliban rule, were now "free, and part of Afghanistan's new government." For over a century, women's freedom has been a measuring rod for modernity among Western theorists, and media reports of Taliban oppression of women had circulated in the West long before the destruction of the World Trade Center. Like American reports of the progress toward modernity made by Filipinos as soon as the Spanish yoke was removed, Bush's report that the Americans had liberated Afghani women appealed to American voters anxious to help the oppressed.

The final cue in Bush's 2002 State of the Union speech introduced God, not by direct invocation but rather as the citizens' friend, guide, and ultimate comforter. Seeking to quell growing American distrust of his administration's military intentions, Bush summoned Americans' sense of justice, their obligations to others: "Deep in the American character, there is honor," he insisted, "and it is stronger than cynicism." And he linked Americans' resilience to divine guidance: "Many have discovered again that even in tragedy . . . God is near." Godly presence implies heavenly guidance; like the annexation of the Philippines, the post-9/11 military operations in the Middle East were packaged for the American public as the furtherance of a peculiarly American global trajectory, one enacted under the auspices of a divine plan.

If Bush sounded like McKinley, encouraging the American public to think about the global extensions of its divine mandate, the American public of 2003 sounded not unlike the public of 1899, especially in the months following the U.S. invasion of Iraq. As long as the majority of Americans believed that Saddam Hussein was hiding weapons of mass destruction there was tacit assent to the war. As soon as the story was exposed as a fabrication opinion splintered. Those who supported the administration's actions despite the lack of evidence that Iraq posed a threat to the United States accepted the government's claim that "Operation Iraqi Freedom" was a means of rescuing the Iraqi populace from Sunni tyrannies and bringing the Arab world closer to the blessings of Western civilization. Web sites opened for testimonies in support of American military action in both Iraq and Afghanistan, Veterans Associations across the country mobilized to support returning troops, and major news organizations as different as the conservative FOX News and the liberal *New York Times* supported President Bush's policies throughout his first term in office. Those opposing the administration decried the betrayal of American ideals. *Boston Legal*, a popular TV legal drama, succinctly articulated the oppositional view in an episode in which a young woman refuses to pay her federal taxes because, she avers, the government's actions in Iraq have betrayed its founding principles. Citing her grandfather's patriotism across two world wars, she insists on her right to protest by refusing to support an unjust war. In his summing up for the jury, the show's irrepressible defense attorney Alan Schor evokes the Declaration of Independence, especially the right to free speech; reminds the court that civil disobedience has a long history in the United States, and encourages the jury to send a message of protest to the government by finding the defendant not guilty. They refuse.[3] Like Americans at the turn into the twentieth century, citizens in 2003 disagreed over the extent to which their government had the right to intervene in other counties' affairs.

Responses to the American invasion of Iraq from the rest of the world also followed a trajectory similar to global responses in 1899. The Anglo-American alliance, forged in 1899 and tested through two world wars, reappeared in full force, with the United Kingdom supporting the Americans both materially and ideologically, despite opposition from many individual Britons. European governments, on the other hand, split along ideological lines, with Italy and Spain contributing troops but many other countries, most notably Germany and France, refusing to honor the Americans' requests for aid. Other nations, especially former European colonies, opposed the invasion from the beginning, condemning the United States for flouting world opinion and UN rules. Leading religious councils, including the Vatican, spoke in opposition to the war. Arab countries, not surprisingly, saw it as an overt declaration that the United States was targeting Islam and the very essence of Middle Eastern culture. Many Arabs had been educated in the United States, and they understood the American fusion of national and Christian identities. Like the Filipinos, they had read the Declaration of Independence, the Constitution, and the Bill of Rights. Like President Bush, many saw the American invasion in cosmic terms, as the battle between good and evil, Christianity and Islam, civilization and barbarism. Like the Latin American writers at the turn into the twentieth century, Arabs cast the Americans as the barbarians.

Americans have difficulty taking seriously anything said by Mahmoud Ahmadinejad, president of the Islamic Republic of Iran. The American media, with the unwitting collusion of President Ahmadinejad himself, has thoroughly discredited him. By Western standards, he is at best delusional, his rambling speeches difficult for Western sensibilities to grasp and his flat denial of the Holocaust proof either of extreme naiveté or of sympathy with the Nazis. But Ahmadinejad does understand the American narrative. His May 8, 2006, letter to President Bush directly engaged the fusion of American Christianity with Enlightenment ideology, asking Bush how it is possible "to be a follower of Jesus Christ . . . feel obliged to respect human rights, present liberalism as a civilization model" and still "have countries attacked; the lives, reputations and possessions of people destroyed on the slight chance [that criminals may be among them]?"[4] Couched as a meditation from one devout world leader to another, Ahmadinejad's letter not only challenged Bush to live up to his professed religious beliefs, it also tackled Western interpretations of recent world history, including the rationale for displacing millions of Arabs in order to establish the State of Israel, the continued Western exploitation of natural resources in Africa, and the Americans' propensity to effect "regime change" in countries with whose domestic or economic policies they disagree. Throughout, Ahmadinejad founded his critique on the professed values of the man, and country, that he was addressing: "Do such actions," he asked Bush repeatedly, "correspond to the teachings of Christ and the tenets of human rights?"

Officially, Ahmadinejad's letter was dismissed as a ploy to derail negotiations over uranium enrichment currently ongoing in Iran. President Bush, apparently after intense discussion with his advisors, declined to answer it. The Americans, they implied, were interested in tangible results, not philosophical discussion. I suspect they also recognized it as unanswerable. Like Twain's "To the Person Sitting in Darkness," Ahmadinejad's 2006 letter exposes the contradiction between word and deed, the difference between national self-fashioning and international reception.

Like Mabini, however, Ahmadinejad also failed to understand the delicate balance between Christian Protestant and Enlightenment values in the United States. Mabini took the Constitutional text as the ruling idea, missing the religious discourse that offset it. Ahmadinejad took the Christian subtext as the dominant text, missing the constitutional framework that mediates religious and racial battles. It takes a long time for people who do not grow up in the United States to realize that Americans cannot be understood from their written documents alone. Rather, the culture of American discourse about those documents engages Enlightenment, Protestant, and racial legacies in a continuous, and passionate, balancing act.

In *The Idea That Is America, Keeping Faith with Our Values in a Dangerous World*, Anne-Marie Slaughter characterizes Americans as "seekers in a collective quest," and suggests that we "aspire to the *idea* that is America," not its reality (232–33). Slaughter sees the American mission as a process, possibly never ending, toward perfection, with a future dependent on a return to the ideals of the past. Other Americans see their country's identity within a more static framework. They locate values such as "freedom" and "faith" within Christian contexts rather than Enlightenment ones, and they are uncomfortable with the idea that process can be a way of life. These citizens reject the idea that values evolved over time. Rather, for them American identity is synonymous with Christian identity and that Christian identity is a fixed, knowable quality. In 2009, at an Assembly of God church in Berkeley Springs, West Virginia, a parishioner, after enquiring the identity of a *New York Times* reporter researching an article on prayer in America, sent a message to the reporter's readers. "'God bless you,' said the woman. 'Be sure to tell the people up there that this is still a Christian nation.'"[5] For this woman of faith the words *nation* and *Christian* are indissolubly linked. Nor is she alone in that premise. Across the country, representatives to state and national legislatures show the tenacity of religious readings of American identity. Tom Riner, a Democratic representative to the Kentucky legislature, has devoted a career in politics to the erasure of the church/state divide, to him a perversion of the nation's original intention. Perceiving "an attempt to separate America from its history of perceiving itself as a nation under God," Riner believes that "divine providence" is integral to national history: "it's what America is."[6]

"You ask me about what is called imperialism," Twain told a reporter in London, shortly before he returned to the United States in

1900. "Well, I have formed views about that question. I am at the disadvantage of not knowing whether our people are for or against spreading themselves over the face of the globe. I should be sorry if they are, for I don't think that it is wise or a necessary development."[7] After reviewing the Philippine situation, which he labeled "a quagmire from which each fresh step renders the difficulty of extrication immensely greater," Twain adds that he wishes he "could see what we were getting out of it, and all it means to us as a nation" (Scharnhorst, 351).

Quagmire is a word that has been used frequently to describe American military involvements abroad in the last 100 years. And many, perhaps most, Americans would be hard pressed to explain exactly what benefits the engagements have brought the country. Yet we continue to believe that our special history imposes special responsibilities, and our politicians continue to inspire us through references to the past. The sense of national mission that animated Twain and his contemporaries endures: Americans cannot relinquish the conviction that they are God's arbiters, appointed to mediate the destinies of mankind.

Introduction

1. Jim Zwick, *Mark Twain's Weapons of Satire: Anti-Imperialist Writings on the Philippine-American War* (Syracuse, New York: Syracuse University Press, 1992), 5.

2. Books on the Philippine-American War have been appearing since the conflict itself, often in response to later events. Early twentieth-century publications tended to detail battles and politics, mostly from a celebratory viewpoint. The Vietnamese War prompted a number of studies, such as Richard E. Welch, Jr.'s *Response to Imperialism: The United States and the Philippine-American War, 1899–1902* (Chapel Hill: University of North Carolina Press, 1979), that implicitly or explicitly compared that war to 1898–99. There are also a number of anthologies, such as Philip Foner and Richard Winchester's two-volume *The Anti-Imperialist Reader* (New York: Holmes & Meier Publishers, Inc., 1984) and Virginia M. Bouvier's collection of essays *Whose America? The War of 1898 and the Battles to Define the Nation* (Westport, Connecticut: Praeger Publishers, 2001). Starting in the 1990s, most scholarly studies of the conflict, such as Amy Kaplan's *The Anarchy of Empire in the Making of U.S. Culture* (Cambridge, Massachusetts: Harvard University Press, 2002) or Eric. T. Love's *Race Over Empire: Racism & U.S. Imperialism, 1865–1900* (Chapel Hill: University of North Carolina Press, 2004), have focused almost entirely on gender and race. An excellent collection of recent essays is Julian Go and Anne L. Foster, eds., *The American Colonial State in the Philippines: Global Perspectives* (Durham, North Carolina: Duke University Press, 2003). Within that collection, Paul A. Kramer's essay "Empires, Exceptions, and Anglo-Saxons: Race and Rule between the British and U.S. Empires, 1880–1910," establishes many of the points about American exceptionalism and Anglo-American identifications that

I elaborate in this book. David J. Silbey's *A War of Frontier and Empire: The Philippine-American War, 1899–1902* (New York: Hill & Wang, 2007) also gives a clear, straightforward accounting of the events and their consequences. Please see my bibliography for a more complete listing.

3. See Jim Zwick's *Confronting Imperialism: Essays on Mark Twain and the Anti-Imperialist League* (West Conshohocken, Pennsylvania: Infinity Publishing Co., 2007). Zwick's Web site, boondocks.com, may have been one of the primary influences for changing scholarly assessments of Twain's interests in imperialism and related social issues. Although no longer in existence, the site brought together Twain's writings with other materials of the time, including the essays and poems by other imperialists, cartoons, and photographs. The changes are beginning to trickle down into the popular print market as well; the BBC's glossy magazine *Knowledge* featured an article titled "Mark Twain: Did America Let Him Down?" by Twain scholar Peter Messent (April 2010, no. 10, 38–44), and papers on Twain and imperialism have been presented at recent major scholarly conferences, including the Modern Language Association, the American Literature Association, and the 2009 Mark Twain Conference at Elmira College in Elmira, New York.

4. For a primer on nineteenth-century Cuban-U.S. relations see http://xroads. virgina.edu/~hyper/hns/Ostend/Ostend.html.

5. José Martí, *Selected Writings*. Edited and translated by Esther Allen (New York: Penguin Books, 2002), 267. Abbreviated SW.

6. As quoted in Michael Kazin, *A Godly Hero: The Life of William Jennings Bryan* (New York: Alfred Knopf, 2006), 86.

7. Mark Twain to Chatto and Windus, May 6 and 13, 1898. Mark Twain Papers, University of California, Berkeley.

8. See Silbey, *A War of Frontier and Empire: The Philippine-American War, 1899–1902*, for a short, clear reprise of these events. For in-depth information, especially about Roosevelt's role and its repercussions, see Evan Thomas's *The War Lovers: Roosevelt, Lodge, Hearst, and the Rush to Empire, 1898* (New York: Little, Brown, 2010), and James Bradley, *The Imperial Cruise: A Secret History of Empire and War* (New York: Little, Brown, 2010).

9. Jackson Lears gives a good overview of the U.S. betrayal of the Filipinos in *Rebirth of a Nation: The Making of Modern America, 1877–1920* (New York: Harper-Collins Publishers, 2009), 207–21.

10. Aguinaldo (who later swore loyalty to the Americans) claimed that Admiral Dewey had assured him that the United States would recognize Philippine independence. See chapter 3, "Negotiations," in *True Version of the Philippine Revolution*, by Don Emilio Aguinaldo y Famy (Tarlak, Philippines: Imprenta Nacional, 1899). Originally published under the title *Reseña veridical de la Revolución Filipina*. An electronic version is available at www.authorama.com. Aguinaldo published another book, *A Second Look at America* (New York: Robert Speller & Sons), in 1957.

11. General James Rusling, "Interview with President William McKinley," *The Christian Advocate*, January 22, 1903, 17. Reprinted in Schirmer and Shalom, eds., *The Philippines Reader: A History of Colonialism, Neocolonialism, Dictatorship, and Resistance* (Boston: South End Press, 1987), 22–23. See also http://historymatters. gmu.edu/d/5575/. There is some dispute about this quotation; Rusling "remembered"

McKinley's words some four years after the event, and there seems to be no separate documentation. However, McKinley did have a penchant for bringing in Providence when he needed to justify action.

12. The Philippine-American War officially ended in July, 1902, but sporadic fighting continued for at least a decade.

13. A substantial Muslim population, commonly referred to as Moros, dominated the southern islands of the archipelago. Under U.S. rule, these islands were administered separately.

14. Matthew Frye Jacobson, *Barbarian Virtues: The United States Encounters Foreign Peoples at Home and Abroad, 1876–1917* (New York: Hill and Wang, 2000), 228–29.

15. In his introduction to *The American Colonial State in the Philippines: Global Perspectives*, Julian Go distinguishes between "settler" and "administrative" colonialism, noting that previous U.S. annexations of other countries' territories had been performed under the "settler" model. There, Americans had occupied the new lands in great numbers, driving out the older inhabitants and establishing American culture in the new locale. Annexation of the Philippines, however, entailed an "administrative" form of colonialism, where the United States retained political control of the islands, but comparatively few Americans moved into the territories and there was little or no displacement of Filipinos themselves. See introduction, 6–7.

16. For histories of American immigration laws regarding the Chinese see Sucheng Chan, ed., *Entry Denied: Exclusion and the Chinese Community in America, 1882–1943* (Philadelphia: Temple University Press, 1991); Erika Lee, *At America's Gates: Chinese Immigration During the Exclusion Era, 1882–1882* (Chapel Hill: University of North Carolina Press, 2003); and Jean Pfaelzer, *Driven Out: The Forgotten War Against Chinese Americans* (Berkeley: University of California Press, 2007).

17. Twain never visited China, and references to the Chinese in his early letters are as unreflectingly racist as are those of most of his contemporaries. His play *Ah Sin* (1877), written in collaboration with Bret Harte, portrays the Chinese through common stereotypes. However, in the 1860s and 1870s he also defended Chinese residents in San Francisco, who were often abused by local roughs. His growing sympathy for the country and its people were one reason for his disgust over American complicity in the suppression of the Boxer Rebellion. See Twain's "What Have the Police Been Doing" (1866), "Disgraceful Persecution of a Boy" (1870), "John Chinaman in New York" (1870), and "Goldsmith's Friend Abroad Again" (1870–71). These can be found in Budd, ed., *Mark Twain: Collected Tales, Sketches, Speeches, & Essays, 1852–1890 and 1891–1910* (New York: The Library of America, 1992). In 1868 Twain wrote a lengthy critique of the recent U.S. treaty with China. See Mark Twain, "The Treaty with China: Its Provisions Explained," *Journal of Transnational American Studies* 2(1). The journal is an electronic resource. The article can be retrieved from: http://escholarship.org/uc/item/2r87m203. See also Martin Zehr's article "Mark Twain, 'The Treaty with China,' and the Chinese Connection," in the *Journal of Transnational American Studies* 2(1), http://escholarship.org/uc/item/5t02n321. For an account of American treatment of Chinese immigrants, see Jean Pfaelzer's *Driven Out: The Forgotten War Against Chinese Americans*.

18. Thomas Bailey Aldrich, *Unguarded Gates and Other Poems* (Boston: Houghton, Mifflin, 1895), 13–17.

19. Go's introduction to *The American Colonial State in the Philippines: Global Perspectives* also notes the strong element of "exceptionalism" in American discourse about the Philippines. One of the goals of this excellent collection of essays is to move beyond that discourse to see the Philippines-American conflict within the framework of global imperialism at the turn into the twentieth century. Consequently Go discusses the existence of exceptionalist discourse in order to transcend it. I, on the other hand, am interested in the discourse itself; how it evolved, how it circulated, and what it accomplished.

20. Mark A. Noll, *America's God: From Jonathan Edwards to Abraham Lincoln* (New York: Oxford University Press, 2002), 11.

21. Rubén Darío, *Tantos Vigores Dispersos (Ideas Sociales y Políticas)*. Selected and edited by Jorge Eduardo Arellano (Managua, Nicaragua: Consejo Nacional de Cultura, 1983), 82, my translation.

22. Richard H. Collin concludes that the conflict between Cuban, American, Spanish, and Filipino nationalism made the war of 1898 "more of a religious war than a conflict for expansion." *Theodore Roosevelt, Culture, Diplomacy, and Expansion: A New View of American Imperialism* (Baton Rouge: Louisiana State University Press, 1985), 117.

23. William E. Phipps, *Mark Twain's Religion* (Macon, Georgia: Mercer University Press, 2003), 27. On Twain's Christianity, see also Harold K. Bush, Jr., *Mark Twain and the Spiritual Crisis of His Age* (Tuscaloosa: The University of Alabama Press, 2007); Joe B. Fulton, *The Reverend Mark Twain: Theological Burlesque, Form, and Content* (Columbus: The Ohio State University Press, 2006); and Peter Messent, *Mark Twain and Male Friendship: The Twichell, Howells, & Rogers Friendships* (New York: Oxford University Press, 2009).

24. For the Twain-Twichell friendship, see also Leah A. Strong's *Joseph Twichell: Mark Twain's Friend and Pastor* (Athens: University of Georgia Press, 1966) and, more recently, Peter Messent and Steve Courtney, eds., *The Civil War Letters of Joseph Hopkins Twichell: A Chaplain's Story* (Athens: University of Georgia Press, 2006).

25. I will be discussing Anglo-Saxonism and American racial identity more fully in chapter four, but want to note here that Paul Kramer's essay "Empires, Exceptions, and Anglo-Saxons: Race and Rule between the British and U.S. Empires, 1880–1910" (in Go and Foster, *The American Colonial State in the Philippines: Global Perspectives*, 43–85) notes the fusion of Anglo-Saxon and Protestant identities in Great Britain and its transmission to the United States, including the association of Anglo-Saxonism, Protestantism, and the idea of civil liberties. This article provides an excellent overview of the ideology of "Anglo-Saxonism" first, in the changing relationship between Britain and the United States at the end of the nineteenth century, and second, in American discussions of national mission. See especially pages 48–49.

26. Horace Davis to Edward Ordway, February 5, 1904, Ordway Papers, New York Public Library Rare Books and Manuscripts Division.

27. Felix Adler to Edward Ordway, January 2, 1900, Ordway Papers, New York Public Library Rare Books and Manuscripts Division.

28. 56th Congress, 1st session. Recorded in 33 Cong. Rec. Part 1, Tuesday, January 9, 1900, p. 711.

29. As noted earlier, territorial expansion was not a new topic in American politics. For a clear and engaging overview of U.S. expansion into Indian territory see Joseph J. Ellis, *American Creation: Triumphs and Tragedies at the Founding of the Republic* (New York: Vintage Books, 2007), especially chapters 4, "The Treaty," on Indian Removal, and 6, "The Purchase," on the Louisiana Purchase. For another take on the push for annexation overseas, see Amy Greenberg's *Manifest Manhood and the Antebellum American Empire*, (New York: Cambridge University Press, 2005), which explores the role of gender in the late-nineteenth-century filibuster movement to annex Cuba and Nicaragua. The best book I've read on American territorial law is Kal Raustiala's *Does the Constitution Follow the Flag?: The Evolution of Territoriality in American Law* (New York: Oxford University Press, 2009).

30. 56th Congress, 1st session. Recorded in 33 Cong. Rec. Part 1, Tuesday, January 9, 1900, p. 711.

31. As quoted in Pratt, *Expansionists of 1898: The Acquisition of Hawaii and The Spanish Islands*, (Gloucester, Massachusetts: Peter Smith, 1959), 27.

32. Kramer notes that an underlying assumption of the ideology of Anglo-Saxonism is that "only Anglo-Saxon bodies could carry the germs of liberty across space and time." See "Empires, Exceptions, and Anglo-Saxons: Race and Rule between the British and U.S. Empires, 1880–1910" (in Go and Foster, *The American Colonial State in the Philippines*, 49).

33. 55th Congress, 3rd session. Recorded in 32 Cong. Rec. Part 2, Tuesday, February 7, 1899, p. 1532.

34. 55th Congress, 3rd session. Recorded in 32 Cong. Rec. Part 2, Tuesday, February 7, 1899, p. 1532.

35. Stuart Creighton Miller, *"Benevolent Assimilation": The American Conquest of the Philippines, 1899–1900* (New Haven: Yale University Press, 1982), 17.

36. Wallace Radcliffe, "Presbyterian Imperialism," *The Assembly Herald*, vol. 1, no. 7 (January, 1899), 5–6.

37. See especially Kenton Clymer's *Protestant Missionaries in the Philippines, 1898–1916: An Inquiry into the American Colonial Mentality* (Urbana: University of Illinois Press, 1986), and his "Protestant Missionaries and American Colonialism in the Philippines, 1899–1916: Attitudes, Perceptions, Involvement," in Peter W. Stanley, ed., *Reappraising an Empire: New Perspectives on Philippines-American History* (Cambridge, Massachusetts: Harvard University Press, 1984), 143–70.

38. In *Rebirth of a Nation*, Jackson Lears situates Americans' "longing for rebirth" in the Protestant Reformation, and notes that throughout U.S. history the "language of rebirth remained largely Protestant" (1–10).

39. The Reverend Newell Dwight Hillis, D.D. Pastor of Plymouth Church, Brooklyn. "The Self-Propagating Power of Christianity," Annual Sermon before the American Board of Commissioners for Foreign Missions, delivered at Oberlin, Ohio, October 14, 1902 (Boston: American Board of Commissioners for Foreign Missions, 1902), 4.

40. Henry Cabot Lodge, "The United States Soldier Championed Against Unjust Attacks," p. 22. In *The United States and the Philippine Islands: Speeches in the*

United States Senate by Henry Cabot Lodge, George F. Hoar, Joseph L. Rawlins, and John C. Spooner. The Brooklyn Eagle Library, no. 68. Vol. 17, no. 9 (June 1902).

41. According to the Library of Congress Web site, more than 4,200 U.S. soldiers, 20,000 Filipino soldiers, and 200,000 Filipino civilians died during the three years of the Philippine-American War (1899–1902), either as a direct result of the fighting or indirectly, from disease or famine. Sporadic fighting continued for at least 15 more years. "The World of 1898: Chronology," Library of Congress Web site: http://www.loc.gov/rr/hispanic/1898/chronology.html.

42. Jim Zwick, *Mark Twain's Weapons of Satire*, 111.

43. See Sacvan Bercovitch, *The American Jeremiad* (Madison: University of Wisconsin Press, 1978) for a classic study of the work of the jeremiad form in American life and letters.

Chapter 1

1. Jim Zwick, *Mark Twain's Weapons of Satire: Anti-Imperialist Writings on the Philippine-American War* (Syracuse, New York: Syracuse University Press, 1992), 43.

2. On October 19–20, 1865, the young Mark Twain wrote to his brother, Orion, and Orion's wife, Mollie, claiming that "I never had but two powerful ambitions in my life. One was to be a pilot, & the other a preacher of the gospel. I accomplished the one & failed in the other, because I could not supply myself with the necessary stock in trade—i.e. religion. I have given it up forever. I never had a 'call' in that direction, anyhow, & my aspirations were the very ecstasy of presumption." Yet, he adds, "I *have* had a 'call' to literature, of a low order—i.e. humorous. It is nothing to be proud of, but it is my strongest suit, and if I were to listen to that maxim of stern *duty* which says that to do right you *must* multiply the one or the two or the three talents which the Almighty entrusts to your keeping, I would long ago have ceased to meddle with things for which I was by nature unfitted and turned my attention to seriously scribbling to excite the *laughter* of God's creatures." Edgar M. Branch, Michael B. Frank, and Kenneth M. Sanderson, eds., *Mark Twain's Letters*, vol. I, 1855–66 (Berkeley: University of California Press, 1988), 322–23.

3. Martin E. Marty, *A Nation of Behavers* (Chicago: University of Chicago Press, 1976), 45. See also Salazar, *Bodies of Reform: The Rhetoric of Character in Gilded Age America.* (New York: New York University Press, 2010). This latter appeared as *God's Arbiters* was going through press; had I read it earlier, Salazar's excellent discussion of "character" would have played a larger role in my own framework.

4. Aaron L. Chapin, *First Principles of Political Economy* (New York: Sheldon and Company, 1880), 5.

5. See, for instance, "Protection and the Public Revenue," a campaign speech delivered by McKinley at Cleveland, Ohio, October 5, 1889. In *Life and Speeches of William McKinley*, ed. J. S. Ogilvie, with an introduction by the Honorable Steward L. Woodford (New York: J. A. Ogilvie Publishing Company, 1896), 33–52.

6. The scholarly conversation about the relationship between Protestant culture and capitalism also began with the advent of the twentieth century. Two signal early

texts are Max Weber's *The Protestant Ethic and the Spirit of Capitalism* (1904–05) and R. H. Tawney's *Religion and the Rise of Capitalism* (1926).

7. Samuel B. Capen, "The Next Ten Years." *Address at the Centennial Meeting of the American Board*, Boston, MA, October 11, 1910 (Boston: American Board of Commissioners for Foreign Missions, n.d.), 14.

8. Edward J. Blum, *Reforging the White Republic: Race, Religion, and American Nationalism, 1865–1898* (Baton Rouge: Louisiana State University Press, 2005), 212, 221, original italics. See also Julian Go's introduction to *The American Colonial State in the Philippines: Global Perspectives*, 11–12.

9. Clymer, *Protestant Missionaries in the Philippines, 1898–1916 : An Inquiry into the American Colonial Mentality* (Urbana: University of Illinois Press, 1986), 84. Clymer does not give a citation for this quotation.

10. 56th Congress, 1st session. Reported in 33 Cong. Rec. Part 1, Tuesday, January 9, 1900, pp. 704 and 705.

11. For Horace Mann, a common set of values was central to the project of nation-building from a diverse population. See Cremin's discussion of Horace Mann's educational philosophy in Lawrence A. Cremin, *The Transformation of the School: Progressivism in American Education, 1876–1957* (New York: Alfred A. Knopf, 1961), 9–12.

12. Arthur Bird, *Looking Forward: A Dream of the United States of the Americas in 1999* (New York: Arno Press, 1977 [c1899]). As quoted in McKnight, *Schooling, the Puritan Imperative, and the Molding of an American National Identity: Education's "Errand Into the Wilderness"* (Mahwah, New Jersey: Lawrence Erlbaum, 2003), 97.

13. Button and Provenzo, Jr., note Mann's focus on "the primacy of moral education over intellectual training," as foundational for nation-building. See Button and Provenzo, Jr., *History of Education and Culture in America* (Englewood Cliffs, New Jersey: Prentice-Hall Inc., 1983), 102. In Cremin's reading, William Torrey Harris, United States Commissioner of Education, 1889–1906, reinforced Mann's ideas by stressing moral education and relegating religious education to the home (18). Both educators, however, envisioned "morals" as inseparable from Protestant values; for them "nonsectarian" referred to the Protestant world only, not to other points of view. Even Mann sanctioned Bible reading in class (Cremin, 10). Sidney Ahlstrom also notes the religious element in Mann's background, citing him as a prime example of the "evangelical conscience" at work in the world and noting that for Mann, "education, however nonsectarian, must instill the historic Protestant virtues." Ahlstrom sees the McGuffey *Readers*, the "Peter Parley," "Rollo," and "Marco Paul" books—central children's texts of the period—as all reflecting Mann's outlook. See Sidney E. Ahlstrom, *A Religious History of the American People* (New Haven: Yale University Press, 1972), 641–42.

14. Mark Noll discusses "the moral calculus of republicanism" in the early republic, which, he claims, "held that religion could and should contribute to the morality that was necessary for the virtuous citizen, without which a republic could not survive," and notes that in 1833 Supreme Court Justice Joseph Story encapsulated the prevailing understanding of the relationship between Christianity and republicanism when he declared that "in a republic, there would seem to be a peculiar

propriety in viewing the Christian religion, as the great basis, on which it must rest for its support and permanence, if it be . . . the religion of liberty." See Mark A. Noll, *America's God: From Jonathan Edwards to Abraham Lincoln* (New York: Oxford University Press, 2002), 203–04.

15. Patricia Crain, speaking of the way that the process of learning the alphabet hard-wires culture into students' psyches, quotes Bourdieu, who argues that "if all societies . . . that seek to produce a new man through a process of 'deculturation' and 'reculturation' set such store on the seemingly most insignificant details of *dress, bearing*, physical and verbal *manners*, the reason is that, treating the body as a memory, they entrust to it in abbreviated and practical, i.e., mnemonic, form the fundamental principles of the arbitrary content of the culture." See Patricia Crain, *The Story of A: The Alphabetization of America from* The New England Primer *to* The Scarlet Letter (Stanford, California: Stanford University Press, 2000), 62.

16. Herman Daggett, *The American Reader: Consisting of Familiar, Instructive, and Entertaining Stories. Selected for the Use of Schools*, (Poughkeepsie, New York: Paraclete Potter, 1818), 4.

17. In *The Story of A*, Crain notes that "Schooling was . . . presented as a way to help those not born into the ways of the errand to pull themselves out of their 'lesser' moral nature. In 1900, this notion of uplifting the 'weaker members of society' was to include not only the abstract moral principles of the Protestant culture but also the Puritan obsession with the body, for many immigrants were perceived as dirty. Immigrants became objects by which to differentiate desirable and undesirable attributes. Purity meant not only that of the soul but of the body. Cleanliness had now become a sign of the near perfection to which American civilization had risen" (94).

18. Noah Webster, *History of the United States* (New Haven: Durrie & Peck, 1832), 6. In *The Story of A*, Patricia Crain notes that with Benjamin Rush, Webster was one of the strongest voices for "an American paideia in the early republic." *Paideia*, a word from the Greeks, signals a pedagogical environment through which culture is communicated from one generation to the next. For Webster and Rush, the American *paideia* was, or should be, "homogeneous, regulated, disciplined, Christian, and republican" (72–74).

19. In *Guardians of Tradition: American Schoolbooks of the Nineteenth Century* (Lincoln: University of Nebraska Press, 1964), an engaged and engaging survey of nineteenth-century common-school texts, Ruth Miller Elson notes that nineteenth-century U.S. textbooks limited true religion to Protestants, associated virtue only with Christianity, and assumed that only Christian nations could be progressive. Although American education in the nineteenth century has been well treated by historians, very few mention the evangelical thrust of common-school education other than in passing. Most frequently, the subject arises only when the historian is discussing the development of Catholic education, which began in Catholic parents' recognition that "secular education" in fact meant indoctrination in Protestant viewpoints and rituals, including mandatory daily readings from the New Testament. See for instance Button and Provenzo, Jr.'s *History of Education and Culture in America*, which develops the history of the common schools without mentioning religion until the chapter on Catholic schooling, where the authors note that "Catholics were . . . fearful of the corruption of their children's faith by Protestant educators and their

schools"—in part because of the use of the King James version of the Bible. Only here do the authors note that "The inclusion of 'Christian' material in the curricula of the common schools had been suggested by nearly all of the early leaders of . . . the movement, including Horace Mann" (130). Cremin's *The Transformation of the School*, still a standard in the field, notes that early progressivism, as represented by Horace Mann, combined "elements of Jeffersonian republicanism, Christian moralism, and Emersonian idealism," but the body of the book pays little attention to the Christian elements of nineteenth-century education (9). More recently, Joseph Moreau's *Schoolbook Nation: Conflicts over American History Textbooks from the Civil War to the Present* (Ann Arbor: The University of Michigan Press, 2003), which examines ideological battles over the shaping of American history in textbooks from the Republican period well into the twentieth century, gives most attention to the Protestant bias of common school texts when discussing the development of "Catholic American history," as a countermeasure (92–136). All mention the influence of Noah Webster without mentioning the centrality of the Protestant worldview to his understanding. My sense of the histories I have read is that most historians simply assume the fusion of Protestant teleologies and nationalism in these texts without questioning how the associations actually produced American citizens.

20. Leland Krauth suggests that Twain "stages" "To the Person Sitting in Darkness" as "a sentimental melodrama" (44). Krauth also notes that Twain's sentimentalist modes strengthen in direct proportion to the growth of his moralism (45), a proposition that makes me realize that we need a deeper discussion of Twain and sentimentalism (and moralism) than we have had so far. See *Mark Twain and Company: Six Literary Relations* (Athens, Georgia: University of Georgia Press, 2003), 44, 45.

21. In an earlier study, *Proper Mark Twain* (Athens, Georgia: University of Georgia Press, 1999), Krauth notes that even in *Following the Equator*, the book in which we see Twain beginning to rethink Western imperialism, Twain uses Western values to critique Western colonialism (229).

22. 57th Congress, 1st session and Special Session of the Senate. Reported in 35 Cong. Rec. Part 3, Monday, February 24, pp. 1902, 2103.

23. For an excellent discussion of the doctrine of American exceptionalism in the arguments over the Philippines, see Paul A. Kramer's "Empires, Exceptions, and Anglo-Saxons: Race and Rule between the British and U.S. Empires, 1880–1910," in Go and Foster, eds., *The American Colonial State in the Philippines: Global Perspectives*, 43–91.

24. Frances Bartlett, "Descendants." *Liberty Poems: Inspired by the Crisis of 1898–1900* (Boston: James H. West Co., 1900), 99. I want to note that I originally found this and many of the other poems quoted here on Jim Zwick's wonderful, and now defunct Web site, *Anti-Imperialism in the United States, 1898–1935* (boondocksnet). Its disappearance—and the subsequent death of Jim Zwick—has created a sad loss in turn-into-the-twentieth-century studies.

25. Caroline H. Pemberton, "Arming Heathens Against Christians." First published in *City and State* 6 (June 15, 1899). Jim Zwick, ed., *Anti-Imperialism in the United States, 1898–1935* (boondocksnet).

26. Katharine Lee Bates, "Pigeon Post." *America the Beautiful and Other Poems* (New York: Thomas Y. Crowell Co., 1911), 28–29.

27. Michael Kazin, *A Godly Hero: The Life of William Jennings Bryan* (New York: Alfred Knopf, 2006), 92–93.

28. Aella Greene, "Them Fillerpeans." *Liberty Poems: Inspired by the Crisis of 1898–1900*, 44–46. First published in the *Springfield Republican*, December 2, 1898.

29. The Rev. Herbert S. Bigelow, August 22, 1900, Philip S. Foner and Richard C. Winchester, eds. *The Anti-Imperialist Reader, a Documentary History of Anti-Imperialism in the United States. Vol. I: From the Mexican War to the Election of 1900* (New York: Holmes & Meier Publishers, Inc., 1984), 268.

30. Quoted in Kristin L. Hoganson, *Fighting for American Manhood: How Gender Politics Provoked the Spanish-American and Philippine-American Wars* (New Haven: Yale University Press, 1998), 75.

31. Foner and Winchester, *The Anti-Imperialist Reader*, 96.

32. *United States Criticisms from the Congressional Record Concerning the Philippine Islands*. 57 Cong. 1 Session. 1901–02. Technically, this is a scrapbook. It contains pages of congressional speeches, cut from the Congressional Record. The pages from the Record are not pasted onto blank paper; rather, they are cut out of the Congressional Record and bound. Each page has the date and a page number printed at the top, but no Congressional number. The volume was presented to the New York Public Library by Elihu Root, former Secretary of War, on March 9, 1907. The prefatory pages are typed, but there is no publication data, suggesting that this is the only copy in existence. See also 57th Congress. 1st session and Special Session of the Senate. 35 Cong. Rec. Part 2, Monday, February 3, 1902, p. 1240.

Chapter 2

1. In recent years, the critical conversation about the Philippines has focused on race almost to the exclusion of other issues. In the process many excellent books and articles have expanded our understanding of the racial issues involved, and I am indebted to them all. Among those I found most useful are Edward J. Blum, *Reforging the White Republic: Race, Religion, and American Nationalism, 1865–1898* (Baton Rouge: Louisiana State University Press, 2005); Matthew Frye Jacobson, *Barbarian Virtues: The United States Encounters Foreign Peoples at Home and Abroad, 1876–1917* (New York: Hill and Wang, 2000); Amy Kaplan, *The Anarchy of Empire in the Making of U.S. Culture* (Cambridge, Massachusetts: Harvard University Press, 2002), and her essay "Nation, Region, Empire," in Emory Elliott, ed., *The Columbia History of the American Novel* (New York: Columbia University Press, 1991), 240–266; Eric. T. Love, *Race Over Empire: Racism & U.S. Imperialism, 1865–1900* (Chapel Hill: University of North Carolina Press, 2004); Vicente L. Rafael, *The Promise of the Foreign: Nationalism and the Technics of Translation in the Spanish Philippines* (Durham, N.C.: Duke University Press, 2005); David J. Silbey, *A War of Frontier and Empire: The Philippine-American War, 1899–1902* (New York: Hill and Wang, 2007).

2. United States Criticisms from the Congressional Record Concerning the Philippine Islands. 57 Cong. 1st Session. 1901–02, 1927. Donated to the New York Public Library by Elihu Root. See note 29, chapter 1, for details.

3. John T. Morgan, "What Shall We Do With the Conquered Islands?" *The North American Review*, vol. 166, issue 499 (June 1898), 645.

4. R. B. Lemus, "The Negro and the Philippines," *The Colored American Magazine*, vol. 6, no. 2 (February, 1903), 314–18.

5. Joseph O. Baylen and John Hammond Moore, "Senator John Tyler Morgan and Negro Colonization in the Philippines, 1901–1902," *Phylon*, vol. 29, no. 1 (1st Quarter, 1968), 65–75.

6. 55th Congress, 3rd session. Reported in 32 Cong. Rec. Part 2, Tuesday, February 7, 1899, p. 1532.

7. 55th Congress, 3rd session. Reported in 32 Cong. Rec. Part 2, February 3, 1899, p. 1421.

8. In "Signs Taken for Wonders," Homi Bhabha notes the dilemma of colonization for the colonizer as well as for the colonized: the very act of incorporating the Other into its political imaginary threatens the colonizer's sense of cultural unity. See Homi Bhabha, "Signs Taken for Wonders: Questions of Ambivalence and Authority Under a Tree Outside Delhi, May 1817," in *The Location of Culture* (London & N.Y.: Routledge, 1994), 145–74.

9. 55th Congress, 3rd session. Reported in 32 Cong. Rec. Part 2, Tuesday, February 7, 1899, p. 1532.

10. Edward Channing and Albert Bushnell Hart, *Guide to the Study of American History* (Boston: Ginn & Co., 1896), 1. In *Barbarian Virtues*, Jacobson quotes from John Fisk's 1907 *A History of the United States for Schools*, which asks students to rank both races and civilizations (139). Joseph Moreau also suggests that the construction of American history as white and Protestant reflects the composition of the American Historical Association, which, founded in 1884, was populated by white male Protestants (50).

11. As quoted in Oscar M. Alfonso, *Theodore Roosevelt and the Philippines, 1897–1909* (Quezon City: University of the Philippines Press, 1970), 48.

12. As quoted in Thomas G. Dyer, *Theodore Roosevelt and the Idea of Race* (Baton Rouge: Louisiana State University Press, 1980), 140.

13. Mark Twain, *Following the Equator: A Journey Around the World* (New York: Dover Publications, Inc. 1989), 321. The context in which Twain says this is a discussion of the difference between "patriotism" and "fanaticism," a difference, Twain concludes, that only has to do with point of view.

14. Interrogation methods during the American-Iraqi conflict, particularly the one referred to as "waterboarding," have been compared to the water cure.

15. John C. Spooner, "A Plea for Civil Government in the Philippine Islands," May 29 and 31, 1902. *The United States and the Philippine Islands: Speeches in the United States Senate by Henry Cabot Lodge, George F. Hoar, Joseph L. Rawlins, and John C. Spooner* (The Brooklyn Eagle Library: no. 68, vol. 17. June 9, 1902), 29–53, 38. Published by the *Brooklyn Daily Eagle*.

16. In the *Eagle* reprint of Spooner's speech, the senator refers to Colquhoun as "Colquin." Either this is a misprint in the *Eagle* reprints, or Spooner himself misspelled, perhaps phonetically, the name of this author. *The Mastery of the Pacific* was written by an Englishman, Archibald Ross Colquhoun, and published by Macmillan & Co., Ltd., 1902. The passage Spooner cites is on page 122, followed by Colquhoun's comment that the Filipino Malay "is never honest . . . never truthful, and never industrious or persevering."

17. Thomas Bender, *A Nation among Nations: America's Place in World History* (New York: Hill and Wang), 2006, Introduction and throughout.

18. Amy Kaplan, *The Anarchy of Empire*. For a gendered reading, see Kristin L. Hoganson, *Fighting for American Manhood: How Gender Politics Provoked the Spanish-American and Philippine-American Wars* (New Haven: Yale University Press, 1998).

19. 55th Congress, 3rd session. Reported in 32 Cong. Rec. Part 2, Friday, February 3, 1899, p. 1420.

20. 57th Congress, 1st session and Special Session of the Senate. Reported in 35 Cong. Rec. Part 2, Tuesday, February 18, 1902, p. 1854.

21. 55th Congress, 3rd session. Reported in 32 Cong. Rec. Part 2, Friday, February 3, 1899, p. 1423.

22. 55th Congress, 3rd session. 32 Cong. Rec. Part 2, Friday, February 3, 1899, p. 1424.

23. 55th Congress, 3rd session. Reported in 32 Cong. Rec. Part 2, Friday, February 3, 1899, p. 1422. Emphasis added.

24. Judith Butler, "Bodily Inscriptions, Performative Subversions," in *The Judith Butler Reader*, ed. Sara Salih with Judith Butler (Oxford: Blackwell Publishing, 2004), 115.

25. Although turn-into-the-twentieth-century speakers tended to use the term as if everyone knew what it denoted, in fact "Anglo-Saxon" can mean a variety of groups, from the Germanic peoples who invaded Britain in the fifth and sixth centuries, to anyone of white English descent.

26. James B. Salazar, *Bodies of Reform: The Rhetoric of Character in Gilded Age America* (New York: New York University Press, 2010), 13.

27. 55th Congress, 3rd session. 32 Cong. Rec. Part 2 Monday, February 6, 1899, p. 1486.

28. 55th Congress, 3rd session. Reported in 32 Cong. Rec. Part 2, Tuesday, February 7, 1899, p. 1532.

29. 56th Congress, 1st session. Reported in 33 Cong. Rec. Part 1, Tuesday, January 9, 1900, p. 708.

30. 57th Congress, 1st session and Special Session of the Senate. Reported in 35 Cong. Rec. Part 6, Monday, June 2, 1902, p. 6161.

31. See Bartholomew H. Sparrow, *The Insular Cases and the Emergence of American Empire* (Lawrence: University Press of Kansas, 2006) and Kal Raustiala, *Does the Constitution Follow the Flag: The Evolution of Territoriality in American Law* (New York: Oxford University Press, 2009), for a thorough discussion of the legal decisions about the political status of the U.S.'s post-1898 possessions. According to the Court, "unincorporated" territories could be accorded only partial constitutional protections, whereas "incorporated" territories were accorded full protection (Sparrow, 5). In other words, Congress had the right to discriminate between territories, deciding which would be granted full constitutional protections, and which would not (Raustiala, 82–84). The last of the Insular Cases was decided in 1922, but Raustiala demonstrates their significance as precedents for the extension of American legal influence around the globe throughout the twentieth century and into the twenty-first. This latter study

clearly and cogently traces American territorial law from the eighteenth century to the present.

32. 57th Congress, 1st session and Special Session of the Senate. Reported in 35 Cong. Rec. Part 1, Tuesday, December 17, 1901, p. 335.

33. 57th Congress, 1st session and Special Session of the Senate. Reported in 35 Cong. Rec. Part 7, Saturday, June 21, 1902, p. 7185. Emphasis added.

34. As quoted in Oscar M. Alfonso, *Theodore Roosevelt and the Philippines, 1897–1909* (Quezon City: University of the Philippines Press, 1970), 44.

35. Jim Zwick, *Mark Twain's Weapons of Satire: Anti-Imperialist Writings on the Philippine-American War* (Syracuse, New York: Syracuse University Press, 1992), 84.

Chapter 3

1. Hank Morgan has proved a slippery character over the years, and scholars, including me, tend to view him through the lens of their own time and social concerns. For instance, on the labor front, Louis J. Budd, in *Mark Twain: Social Philosopher* (Bloomington: Indiana University Press, 1962), saw it as embodying Twain's "temporary shift from sympathy with employers to sympathy with labor" (113), while Henry Nash Smith, in *Mark Twain's Fable of Progress: Political and Economic Ideas in ACYKAC* (New Brunswick, New Jersey: Rutgers University Press, 1964), contended that Twain was "asking himself whether the American Adam, who began as a representative of a pre-industrial order, could make the transition to urban industrialism and enter upon a new phase of his existence by becoming a capitalist hero" (69). Echoes of World War II appear in Allen Guttman's "Mark Twain's Connecticut Yankee: Affirmation of a Vernacular Tradition?," where Guttman claims that Hank's "technological utopia becomes a holocaust," and that Hank "exults over the strewn dead" (*New England Quarterly* 33 [June, 1960], 232–37). Similarly, in "The Once and Future Boss: Mark Twain's Yankee" *(Nineteenth Century Fiction* 28 [June 1973]: 62–73), Chadwick Hansen reads twentieth-century theories of the authoritarian personality back into Twain's work, seeing Hank as a dictator who might "celebrate the people in the abstract . . . and yet respond to actual persons with contempt, hatred, and . . . distrust," and in a footnote, comparing him to Adolf Hitler. More recently, Amy Kaplan has described the novel as representing "a collective national identity to those outside America's borders and subject to its power." See "Nation, Region, and Empire," in Emory Elliott, ed., *The Columbia History of the American Novel* (New York: Columbia University Press, 1991), 256. Additionally, John Carlos Rowe has discussed the novel as a way for Twain to intellectually process contemporary imperialism, especially Britain's Charles George Gordon's death in Egypt at the hands of natives whom he had sought to uplift and reform. In the course of his discussion, Rowe notes that Twain's writing had long contained anti-imperialist moments, and that in *Connecticut Yankee* in particular, Twain "anticipates [his later] indictment of imperialism by showing how despotism secures its power by controlling people's attitudes and values" ("Mark Twain's Rediscovery of America in *A Connecticut Yankee in King Arthur's Court*," in *Literary Culture and U.S. Imperialism: From the Revolution to World War II* (New York: Oxford University Press,

2000), 2000, 121–39, 126). I first noted my own discomfort with Hank's imperialist designs in *Mark Twain's Escape from Time: A Study of Patterns and Images* (Columbia, Missouri: University of Missouri Press, 1982). For an annotated, alphabetical list of Mark Twain's reading, with commentary on his marginalia, see Alan Gribben's two-volume *Mark Twain's Library: A Reconstruction*. For an in-depth analysis of Twain's marginalia in Lecky, Carlyle, and other texts that influenced the writing of *A Connecticut Yankee*, see Joe B. Fulton, *Mark Twain in the Margins: The Quarry Farm Marginalia and A Connecticut Yankee in King Arthur's Court* (Tuscaloosa: The University of Alabama Press, 2000).

2. Tom Quirk, *Mark Twain and Human Nature* (Columbia: University of Missouri Press, 2007), 184.

3. See Rowe, "Mark Twain's Rediscovery of America in *A Connecticut Yankee in King Arthur's Court*," for an interesting discussion of Twain, Free Trade, communications technologies, and principled (or informal) imperialism. My sense is that Rowe sees Twain as more critical of Hank's methods—and principles—than I read him to be, but Rowe's argument cogently sets out the trajectory of Twain's growing anti-imperialism. See also Quirk, *Mark Twain and Human Nature*, 171.

4. Mark Twain, *A Connecticut Yankee in King Arthur's Court*, The Mark Twain Project edition, Bernard L. Stein, ed. (Los Angeles: University of California Press, 1984), 81.

5. Joe B. Fulton, *The Reverend Mark Twain: Theological Burlesque, Form, and Content* (Columbus: The Ohio State University Press, 2006), 24.

6. On Britain's policies in her colonies see, among others, P. J. Cain and A. G. Hopkins, *British Imperialism, 1688–2000* (Harlow, England: Pearson Education Ltd., 1993, 2001); Bernard Porter, *The Absent-Minded Imperialists: Empire, Society, and Culture in Britain* Oxford: Oxford University Press, 2004) Homi Bhabha, *The Location of Culture* (London: Routledge, 1994); Edward W. Said, *Orientalism* (New York: Vintage Books, 1978).

7. Evergisto Bazaco, an educational historian, contends that under Spanish rule the Philippine school system could be "placed side by side with those of most of the civilized nations . . .," but few seem to have agreed with him. See Evergisto Bazaco, *History of Education in the Philippines, Spanish Period, 1565–1898* (Manila: University of Santo Tomas Press, 1953), vi.

8. In *A History of Publishing in the Philippines* (Philippines: Rex Book Store, Inc., 1998), Dominador D. Buhain notes that the Thomasites, the first post-annexation group of Americans to enter the Philippines specifically to educate the Filipinos, brought with them American textbooks replete with pictures of blonde Johns and Marys. Later, a handful of American publishing companies, including Ginn and Co. and D. Appleton, produced texts specifically geared to Filipino students, even encouraging some Filipinos to write textbooks of their own. These later texts featured dark-haired Juans and Marias, and some did pay attention to Filipino forms of family structure, but the concessions to cultural difference were largely cosmetic. On the topic of American means of educating Filipinos see also Alexander A. Calata, "The Role of Education in Americanizing Filipinos," in McFerson, *Mixed Blessing: The Impact of the American Colonial Experience on Politics and Society in the Philippines* (Westport, Connecticut: Greenwood Press, 2002), 89–97.

9. Frederick S. Marquardt, "Life with the Early American Teachers," in Mary Racelis and Judy Celine Ick, eds., *Bearers of Benevolence: The Thomasites and Public Education in the Philippines* (Pasig City: Anvil Publishing, 2001), 23–27. Many of the early American teachers to reach the Philippines were Protestant missionaries, and the records they left of their battles to combat disorganization, ignorance, and dirt give a good indication of the general American mentality. Many confessed an antipathy to the reigning Catholicism, and like Hank, they harnessed the combined power of scientific education with Protestant organization.

10. See Bhabha, *The Location of Culture*, for Bhabha's discussion of mimicry and British colonialism.

11. Fee, *A Woman's Impressions of the Philippines* (Chicago: A. C. McClurg & Co., 1912), chapter 8, "An Analysis of Filipino Character," 95–96.

12. May, *Social Engineering in the Philippines: The Aims, Execution, and Impact of American Colonial Policy, 1900–1913* (Westport, Connecticut: Greenwood Press, 1980), 17.

13. According to Clymer, American Protestant missionaries were especially eager to use the schoolroom to inculcate values that they equated with both Protestantism and Americanism, such as frugality and social equality. In general, Protestant missionaries strongly supported expansion because they saw the extension of American civilization as equal to the Providential mandate to evangelize the world. See Clymer, "Protestant Missionaries and American Colonialism in the Philippines, 1899–1916: Attitudes, Perceptions, Involvement," in Peter W. Stanley, ed., *Reappraising an Empire: New Perspectives on Philippines-American History* (Cambridge, Massachusetts: Harvard University Press, 1984), 146–47.

14. Cathy Boeckmann, *A Question of Character: Scientific Racism and the Genres of American Fiction, 1892–1912* (Tuscaloosa: University of Alabama Press, 2000), 38.

15. James B. Salazar, *Bodies of Reform: The Rhetoric of Character in Gilded Age America* (New York: New York University Press, 2010), 13.

16. A variant of Bhabha's "mimicry," this was a step toward creating a class competent to mediate between the American administration and the native population—itself a move at odds with the administration's goal to uplift all the Filipinos, not just one class.

17. Harry Couch Theobold, *The Filipino Teacher's Manual* (New York and Manila: World Book Company, 1907), 2.

18. Progressive educators especially saw American education playing a crucial role in the Americanization of immigrants and the "civilizing" of freedmen. Sentiments later coded as the "Melting Pot" theory of American education sought to unify an increasingly diverse population by homogenizing them. However as in past attempts at unification through common ideology, patent differences in religion and race remained in tension with the dominant ideology. Lawrence Cremin notes that "by 1909, when the United States Immigration Commission made its massive study, 57.8 per cent of the nation's largest cities were of foreign-born parentage" (72). See Lawrence A. Cremin, *The Transformation of the School; Progressivism in American Education, 1876–1957* (New York: Alfred A. Knopf, 1961), 66–75.

19. For a discussion of the Protestant missionaries' responses to this order, see Kenton J. Clymer, *Protestant Missionaries in the Philippines, 1898–1916: An Inquiry into the American Colonial Mentality* (Urbana: University of Illinois Press, 1986), 162–64. Catholic parents also objected, because under the Spanish, religious instruction had been part of the curriculum.

20. Jim Zwick, *Mark Twain's Weapons of Satire; Anti-Imperialist Writings on the Philippine-American War* (Syracuse, New York: Syracuse University Press, 1992), 84.

Chapter 4

1. For a fuller treatment of nineteenth-century schoolbooks and the creation of American identity see Susan K. Harris, "At Home and Abroad: Nineteenth-Century Textbooks and the Creation of Christian Citizenship in the U.S. and the Philippines," in the special issue on "Teaching Nation" of *Transformations: The Journal of Inclusive Scholarship and Pedagogy*, vol. 20, no. 2 (Fall, 2009/Winter 2010), 90–112.

2. Noah Webster, *History of the United States*, (New Haven: Durrie & Peck, 1832), 300.

3. Much has been written on the deployment of white solidarity as a means of overcoming sectional hostilities, especially during the Spanish-American and Philippine-American wars. For example, see Edward J. Blum, *Reforging the White Republic; Race, Religion, and American Nationalism, 1865–1898* (Baton Rouge: Louisiana State University Press, 2005), and Amy Kaplan, *The Anarchy of Empire in the Making of U.S. Culture* (Cambridge, Massachusetts: Harvard University Press, 2002).

4. K. J. Stewart, *A Geography for Beginners* (Richmond, Virginia: J. W. Randolph, 1864), 1.

5. When her mistress discovered Mary's interests, she helped the young woman become more literate. After emancipation, Mary Lynch became the first black public school teacher in Halifax County, North Carolina. Profile of Mary Prior Lynch, "Here and There" section, *The Colored American Magazine*, vol. 5, no. 1 (May, 1902), 62–65.

6. William E. Phipps, *Mark Twain's Religion* (Macon, Georgia: Mercer University Press, 2003), 27.

7. In *America Revised: History Schoolbooks in the Twentieth Century* (Boston: Little, Brown and Company, 1979). Frances FitzGerald succinctly and articulately lays out the textbook battles of the first seven decades of the twentieth century, showing how ideological battles influenced American history texts from decade to decade. Her chapter on "Past Masters" briefly surveys nineteenth-century texts, but she does not seem acquainted with Webster's *History* (though she mentions his *Dictionary*), and her survey of the century's textbooks is cursory. On the basis of the books she examined she concludes that nineteenth-century school historians did not know how to construct a coherent historical narrative (48–49). My own researches suggest otherwise; not only do I see a coherent narrative, I see a widely accepted one. FitzGerald also credits the Progressives with a radical turn in the development of the American narrative, whereas I suggest that they secularized the rhetoric but did not otherwise change the trajectory of the exceptionalist idea.

8. Patricia Crain, *The Story of A: The Alphabetization of America from* The New England Primer *to* The Scarlet Letter. (Stanford, California: Stanford University Press, 2000), 7, 62.

9. Thomas Dilworth, *A New Guide to the English Tongue: In Five Parts*, 1793. Webster himself was taught from this text, whose Dedication page celebrates Protestantism, and especially the Church of England, as "the best constituted church" and whose Preface notes the obligation of "every Protestant" . . . "to promote Christian Knowledge." All the literature appearing in this book focuses on the relation of the child to God and to Christian morality. Lesson one, after teaching letters and single syllables, opens with the lines "No Man may put off the Law of God. The Way of God is no Ill Way. My Joy is in God all the Day. A Bad Man is a Foe of God." Later lessons include short moral tales, such as "the boy who cried wolf" followed by "interpretations." The volume closes with a series of daily prayers.

10. A typical lesson in the *Spelling Book* uses a biblical text for a lesson on the elements of reading; for instance, "Vir-tue ex-alt-eth a na-tion; but sin is a re-proach to a-ny peo-ple." See Noah Webster, *The American Spelling Book* (Philadelphia: Johnson & Warner, 1816), 64.

11. Arnold Dodell, *Moses or Darwin? A School Problem for All Friends of Truth and Progress.* Trans., with Preface for the American edition, by Frederick W. Dodell. (New York: The Truth Seeker Company, 1891), 23. The original text, by Arnold Dodell, featured a series of lectures delivered in Zurich and St. Gall, Switzerland, attacking European schools for privileging religious interpretations of the earth's creation. In the preface to his American edition, Frederick Dodell extends the attack to American common-schools. I want to thank Nate Williams for bringing this book to my attention.

12. Edward Deering Mansfield, *American Education: Its Principles and Elements. Dedicated to the teachers of the United States* (New York: A. S. Barnes, 1877), 1.

13. Henrietta Christian Wright, *Children's Stories in American Literature, 1660–1860* (New York: Charles Scribner's Sons, 1896), 7.

14. Caleb Bingham, *The Columbian Orator: Containing a Variety of Original and Selected Pieces, Together with the Rules; Calculated to Improve Youth and Others in the Ornamental and Useful Art of Eloquence* (Troy, New York: William S. Parker, 1821).

15. Increase Cooke, *The American Orator* (Charleston, South Carolina: Sidney's Press, 1819).

16. Gregory S. Jackson, "'What Would Jesus Do?': Practical Christianity, Social Gospel Realism, and the Homiletic Novel." In *PMLA*, vol. 121, no. 3 (May 2006), 644. In this very clear and useful article, Jackson discusses a set of evangelical novels that, emerging from the formal design of seventeenth-century Protestant sermons, encouraged readers to understand their everyday lives within religious frameworks. "Uplift" of the poor becomes one of the key cultural concepts valorized in these texts.

17. Charles M. Sheldon, *In His Steps: "What Would Jesus Do?"* (Chicago, Illinois: The Advance Publishing Company, 1897), 75.

18. Jackson notes that in his life and in some of his other writings, Sheldon did important work to integrate black and white congregations in Topeka, Kansas,

his home town (653). *In His Steps*, however, operates within an entirely white and middle-class centered world.

19. Mary H. Fee, *A Woman's Impressions of the Philippines* (Chicago: A. C. McClurg & Co., 1912), 11.

20. I want to thank John Gruesser for bringing these stories to my attention and both Professor Gruesser and Gretchen Murphy for allowing me to quote from the stories in advance of the edition they have prepared, forthcoming in the Modern Language Association's Little-Known Documents series.

21. In an article on black dialect in the work of George Washington Cable, Gavin Jones has shown how linguistic hybridity inspired fear of racial hybridity among Louisianans of the late nineteenth century. White creoles clung to their belief in their own cultural purity, taking any suggestion that the penetration of linguistic and musical traditions by African-American modes was an imputation of racial miscegenation. The "politics of hybridity," as Jones calls it, insisted on maintaining the myth of white purity in the face of palpable evidence of racial mixing. See Gavin Jones, "Signifying Songs: The Double Meaning of Black Dialect in the World of George Washington Cable," in *American Literary History*, vol. 9, no. 2 (Summer 1997), 244–67. Louisianan Creoles were not the only white American group to associate linguistic and racial purity.

22. Frank R. Steward, "Pepe's Anting-Anting. A Tale of Laguna." *The Colored American Magazine*, Vol. V, no. 5 (September, 1902), 360. Reprinted in *The Black Experience in America, Negro Periodicals in the United States, 1840–1960* (New York: Negro Universities Press, 1969), 358–62.

23. Frank R. Steward, "Starlik: A Tale of Laguna." *The Colored American Magazine*, Vol. VI, no. 3 (March, 1903), 388. Reprinted in *The Black Experience in America, Negro Periodicals in the United States, 1840–1960*, 387–91.

24. Frank R. Steward, "The Men Who Prey." *The Colored American Magazine*, Vol. VI, no. 10 (October, 1903), 723. Reprinted in *The Black Experience in America, Negro Periodicals in the United States, 1840–1960*, 720–24.

25. Ernest Crosby, *Captain Jinks, Hero* (Upper Saddle River, New Jersey: The Gregg Press, 1968), 4. This edition is a reprint of the original 1902 publication by Funk & Wagnalls Company.

Chapter 5

1. Leland Krauth, *Mark Twain and Company: Six Literary Relations* (Athens, Georgia: University of Georgia Press, 2003), 248.

2. In "In the Mirror of the Imagination: Mark Twain's Kipling," Gregg Camfield argues that Kipling intended the poem ironically, as a warning against imperialism, and that Twain would have understood it in those terms. Camfield points out that Kipling's own experience in the United States, coupled with what he saw as U.S. hysteria over the Venezuela incident of 1895, made him mistrustful of U.S. intentions and abilities for administrative rule. And he notes that Kipling and Twain shared a mistrust for human nature. In the end, though, Camfield also notes that Twain did not say or write anything directly about the poem, possibly because he didn't know

himself how he felt about it. In *Arizona Quarterly Special Issue: Mark Twain at the Turn-of-the-Century, 1890–1910*. Vol. 61, no. 1, Spring 2005, 85–108.

3. What exactly Kipling meant when he differentiated between white men and others has been a question that critics have hotly debated. For instance, in *The Long Recessional: The Imperial Life of Rudyard Kipling* (New York: Farrar, Straus and Giroux, 2002), David Gilmour suggests that when Kipling said "white" he was referring to cultural factors more than racial ones: "'white' here plainly refers to civilization and character more than to the colour of men's skins," he avers, although he also concedes that "The White Man's Burden" is profoundly racist. More radically, Camfield, in "In the Mirror of the Imagination: Mark Twain's Kipling," cited above, has pointed out the poem's ambiguities and argued that Kipling's references to white men are ironic, conveying a critique of American colonial policies rather than support of them. For others, such as Eric Love, in *Race Over Empire: Racism & U.S. Imperialism, 1890–1910* (Chapel Hill: University of North Carolina Press, 2004), not only Kipling but the entire Anglo-American alliance defined "white" as very narrowly Anglo-Saxon. Kipling's own letters indicate that while "white" certainly encompasses cultural issues, for him the word represented a specific, racial, genotype whose level of civilization was part and parcel of its racial composition. "The white man [in Johannesburg] is a slave to the Boer," he told James Conland in a letter from South Africa in 1898, "and the state of things turned me sick" (Thomas Pinney, ed. *The Letters of Rudyard Kipling, Vol. 2: 1890–99*. Iowa City: University of Iowa Press, 2002). Here "white" clearly refers to white South Africans of British descent (i.e., Anglo-Saxons), whereas "Boer" designates those of Dutch descent (i.e., mere Caucasians). But as Gilmour observes, to be "white" in Kipling's mind is also synonymous with being organized, having the innate ability to cut and chop alien cultures into sectors comprehensible to the English mentality and to reshape them into bureaucratically manageable social organisms. The white man's work, Kipling told George Cram Cook in reference to the American invasion of Cuba, is "the business of introducing a sane and orderly administration into the dark places of the earth that lie to your hand" (346). See also Robert MacDonald, *The Language of Empire: Myths and Metaphors of Popular Imperialism, 1880–1918* (Manchester: Manchester University Press, 1994), for a discussion of the slippery significations of "whiteness" in imperialist discourse of the time.

4. The influence exerted by British periodicals—or, at least, the influence they attempted to exert—has been noted often, although not often in conjunction with Kipling's poem. Geoffrey Seed, writing in the *Political Science Quarterly* in 1958, divided British sympathizers into three categories: the rational (based on "historical" factors such as Manifest Destiny, an ideology that the British bought—surprisingly, given expansionists' repeated calls to annex Canada), the emotional (especially as manifested in a mystic racial—i.e. Anglo-Saxon—kinship), and the practical (which included political and economic factors such as the value of an American stronghold so near China and the probability that other European powers would annex the Philippines if the Americans didn't). Noting that British enthusiasm for American expansionism waned after the turn into the twentieth century, Seed concluded that nevertheless the pattern established maintained itself throughout subsequent years,

re-invigorating the British/U.S. sense of a primal tie. See Geoffrey Seed, "British Reactions to American Imperialism Reflected in Journals of Opinion 1898–1900," in *Political Science Quarterly*, vol. 73, no. 2 (June 1958), 254–72. One of the most recent essays to review the topic is Paul A. Kramer's "Empires, Exceptions, and Anglo-Saxons: Race and Rule between the British and U.S. Empires, 1880–1910," in Julian Go and Anne L. Foster, eds. *The American Colonial State in the Philippines: Global Perspectives* (Durham, North Carolina: Duke University Press, 2003), 43–91.

5. Ruth Dudley Edwards, *The Pursuit of Reason: The Economist 1843–1993* (London: Hamish Hamilton, 1993), 412, 423–24.

6. The British periodical context is elaborated more fully in my article "Kipling's 'The White Man's Burden' and the British Periodical Context, 1898–99." (*Comparative American Studies*, Fall 2007, 243–64). I wish to thank the editors and publishers of CAL for permission to republish parts of that article here.

7. According to Paul A. Kramer, in "Empires, Exceptions, and Anglo-Saxons: Race and Rule between the British and U.S. Empires, 1880–1910," the British ran three major Filipino banks, and were heavily invested in commerce and building in the archipelago. See page 57 of Go and Foster, *The American Colonial State in the Philippines: Global Perspectives*. Rafael notes that the merchant houses provided banking services for the colony and funded local farmers who provided them with crops for export. See Vicente L. Rafael, *The Promise of the Foreign: Nationalism and the Tecnics of Translation in the Spanish Philippines* (Durham, North Carolina: Duke University Press, 2005), 7.

8. Kramer's "Empires, Exceptions, and Anglo-Saxons: Race and Rule between the British and U.S. Empires, 1880–1910," also notes the British emphasis on Anglo-Saxon blood ties and British colonial experience as a strategy for overcoming American prejudice against Britain. My investigation into the periodicals here highlights Kramer's more general analysis.

9. Historian Ruth Dudley Edwards sees the focus on benevolence as one of the linchpins of the British argument for "principled imperialism." See *The Pursuit of Reason: The Economist 1843–199*, 415.

10. *Daily Mail*, May 10, 1898, 4. Throughout this chapter, abbreviations for British periodicals are as follows: DM: the *Daily Mail*; S: the *Spectator*; E: *The Economist*; T: *The London Times*. Please note: both the *Spectator* and *The Economist* were published weekly; the page numbers cited refer to the pagination furnished in the bound volumes I consulted in the British Library.

11. Mark Twain to Mary E. (Mollie) Clemens, May 16, 1898, Vienna, Austria. MTP ms: IaCrM, #11916.

12. 55th Congress, 3rd session. Recorded in 32 Cong. Rec. Part 2, Friday, February 10, 1899, 1695.

13. 55th Congress, 3rd session. Recorded in 32 Cong. Rec. Part 2, Friday, February 10, 1899. 1696.

14. Ibid.

15. Ibid.

16. For a still-resonant reading of the rhetorical legacies of the Puritan experiment in American political life, see Sacvan Bercovitch, *The Puritan Origins of the American Self*. (New Haven: Yale University Press, 1975).

17. 55th Congress, 3rd session. Recorded in 32 Cong. Rec. Part 2, Tuesday, February 7, 1899, 1532.

18. 55th Congress, 3rd Session. Recorded in 32 Cong. Rec. Part 2, February 10, 1899, 1694.

19. Brigadier-General Thomas M. Anderson, "Our Rule in the Philippines." In *North American Review*, Vol. 170, Issue 519, 283.

20. 57th Congress, 1st session and Special Session of the Senate. Recorded in 35 Cong. Rec. Part 6, Thursday, May 22, 1902, 5792. I originally found this speech in the scrapbook of congressional speeches donated to the New York Public Library by Elihu Root, cited in chapter 1, note 30.

21. 57th Congress, 1st session and Special Session of the Senate. Recorded in 35 Cong. Rec. June 24, 1902, 7331–33.

22. Philip Foner published a number of parodies of "the White Man's Burden" in his anthology of anti-imperialist writings, *The Anti-Imperialist Reader; A Documentary History of Anti-Imperialism in the United States* (New York: Holmes & Meier Publishers, Inc., 1984), but many more appeared in newspapers around the country.

23. Private Louis Dodge, 23rd U.S. Infantry. Printed in *Arkansas Democrat*, June 2, 1899.

24. H. T. Johnson, "The Black Man's Burden," *Voice of Missions*, VII, Atlanta: April 1899, 1. Reprinted in Willard B. Gatewood, Jr., *Black Americans and the White Man's Burden, 1898–1903* (Urbana: University of Illinois Press), 1975, 183–84.

25. Albert E. McKay, "Parodies on 'The White Man's Burden,'" *New York Times Saturday Review of Books and Art*, May 27, 1899, p. BR351.

26. Quoted in Roger Lane's *William Dorsey's Philadelphia and Ours: On the Past and Future of the Black City in America* (Oxford: Oxford University Press, 1991), 26.

27. E.E.W. (only initials are provided), Atchison, Kansas, *Daily Globe*, February 11, 1899. Newspapers that printed the parodies generally sided with their sentiments. For some, the target was simply English arrogance in presuming to tell Americans what to do. The Atchison, Kansas, paper that published this last parody commented that

> Rudyard Kipling recently printed a lot of poetical rot entitled "Take up the White Man's Burden." We see the statement made that Mr. Kipling intends to advise the Americans to assume the burden of civilizing and educating the Filipinos. This is the trouble with poetry: people do not agree as to its meaning. We have read Mr. Kipling's poem, at the expense of a headache, and *we* say he advises the *Filipinos* to take up the white man's burden: that is, they should quit lying around in the shade like dogs, and go to work, and worry, and die of dyspepsia, and go to hell, like white men.

Moving on, the paper asks, "What attention should the people of this country pay to the good advice of a poet? If you wanted to engage in any venture, would you consult a poet as to the advisability of it?" And it concludes: "In addition to being a poet, and a poor one at that, Kipling is a foreigner. There never will come a time when American should accept the advice of foreigners." (Atchison *Daily Globe*, Friday, February 10, 1899, p. 4; my italics). Quirky, grouchy, populist (a true Kansas paper), the Atchison *Daily Globe* was less interested in the poem's sentiments than in its presumption that the old world could give advice to the new.

28. Ernest Crosby, *Swords and Ploughshares* (New York: Funk & Wagnalls Company, 1902), 32–35.

29. George McNeill, "The Poor Man's Burden," *American Federationist*, March, 1899.

30. "Preached on the White Man's Burden," *The Emporia Daily Gazette*, February 13, 1899, Column A.

31. "'The White Man's Burden': Canadian Minister Mills Congratulates the U.S. Upon Taking It Up," Memphis, Tennessee, *Commercial Appeal*, February 26, 1899, p. 8, Column C.

32. "Whitelaw Reid for Open Door: As Protectionist He Favors that Policy, as Patriotic American Shoulders 'White Man's Burden,'" *Milwaukee Sentinel*, February 12, 1899, Column D.

33. "Our Duty in Asia," *Harper's Weekly*, February 12, 1899, p. 158.

34. "Senator Beveridge: Republican Leader of the Senate," *Harper's Weekly*, April 14, 1900, p. 349.

35. Advertisement, *Harper's Weekly*, September 30, 1899, p. 968.

Chapter 6

1. "Noli me tangere" is Latin for "touch me not." In St. John's narrative of Christ's death and resurrection, Jesus says these words to Mary Magdalene when she encounters him, newly risen, at the mouth to the sepulcher where his body had been laid the previous night. See St. John 20:17, in the Vulgate (Latin) or the King James (English) bibles. My warm thanks to my colleague Stanley F. Lombardo for his kind assistance here.

2. José Rizal, *An Eagle's Flight: A Filipino Novel Adapted from Noli Me Tangere* (New York: McClure, Phillips & Co., 1901).

3. In *Mark Twain's Library: A Reconstruction* (Boston: G. K. Hall & Co., 1980), Alan Gribben quotes Isabel Lyon's diary entry of 1906, recording that Twain had read her both Rizal's poem and his own. Twain's version was dated May 1901, from New York City, and he originally laid it loose in his copy of *An Eagle's Flight*. In 1966, Arthur Scott reprinted the poem in *On the Poetry of Mark Twain* (Urbana: University of Illinois Press), now long out of print. My sincere thanks to Kevin Bochynski, who provided me with an electronic copy of the poem and of Scott's commentary.

4. Martí knew and admired Twain's writings, but there is no evidence that Twain was aware of the Cuban journalist, even though they frequented the same scenes in New York City, including, if Justin Kaplan is correct, sitting on the stage together at Madison Square Garden on April 14, 1887, when Walt Whitman gave a lecture on the 22nd anniversary of Lincoln's assassination. See Justin Kaplan, *Walt*

Whitman: A Life (New York: Simon & Schuster, 1980), 29. My thanks to David H. Fears for bringing this to my attention.

5. Sylvia L. Hilton and Steve J. S. Ickringill, eds., *European Perceptions of the Spanish-American War of 1898* (Berne: Peter Lang, 1999), 33. Abbreviated H&I.

6. L. Slominsky, *Vestnik Evropy*, April 1898, p. 825, and *Vestnik Inostrannoi Literatury*, 252–53, as quoted in H&I, 130.

7. Serge Ricard, "The French Press and Brother Jonathan: Editorializing the Spanish-American Conflict," H&I, 144.

8. Hess was *Le Figaro*'s correspondent in Hong Kong. "A French View of the War in the Philippines," dated Hong Kong June 20, 1899, published in *Le Figaro* July 28, 1899; reprinted in *The Public*, no. 72 (Vol.2), August 19, 1899, 13–16, this excerpt p. 13.

9. Nico A. Bootsma, "Reactions to the Spanish-American War in the Netherlands and in the Dutch East Indies," H& I, 35–52.

10. Markus M. Hugo, "'Uncle Sam I Cannot Stand, for Spain I Have No Sympathy': An Analysis of Discourse about the Spanish-American War in Imperial Germany, 1898–1899," H& I, 70–93.

11. Al empezar el año de 1899 ¡cuán distinto es el cuadro trazado! Especialmente ha perdido una tercera parte de su territorio; en Puerto Rico, Cuba, y Filipinas ondea el pabellón norte-americáno; aquellos buques de guerra, en los que tantas esperanzes cifrábamos, se hundieron en la mar sin poder combatir con los barcos enemigos; aquellos ejércitos enviados á Cuba y Filipinas no existen; han regresado á la patria enfermos y sin gloria aquellos soldados que sobrevivieron en la terrible lucha sostenida con los separatistas y con el clima traidor de nuestras colonias; la paz de Filipinas fue rota por la impudicia y mala fe yankee; en Puerto Rico los hasta entonces leals españoles cometieron con la patria el horrendo crímen de la traición y de la ingratitude. Esto es lo que nos deja el año que acaba, y el que mañana empieza nos sorprende en medio de tanta ruina y desolación tan grande, que apenas si quedan alientos para pedir de nuevo á Dios venturas para este infortunado país. . . . En fin, todo el mundo grita hoy, llevando al cielo su pensamiento; ¡Dios tenga piedad de España en el año nuevo!—C. De C. "Correspondencias Particulares de Diario de Barcelona," *Diario de Barcelona*, 2 enero, 1899, 76–77 (my trans.).

12. Sylvia Hilton, in H&I, *62*.

13. "La ironía de las cosas se advierte mas á cada dia que transcurre, si se recuerda que los Estados Unidos, hace pocos meses, declaraban solemnemente que en Cuba y en Filipinas solo trataban de emancipar las poblaciones del yugo español, para que pudiesen ser independientes y autónomos. Ahora se procede a la ocupación militar de Cuba por un período indefinido. Es probable que los insurrectos cubanos acabarán por hacerles la misma guerra de guerrillas con la cual han combatido por tanto tiempo á los españoles. En las Filipinas emplearán tambien la fuerza los americanos al objeto de reprimir las aspiraciones autónomas de la población." *Diario de Barcelona*, December 30, 1898, 140 (my trans.).

14. En el Senado Americano M. Hoar abrió la campaña contra la política anexionista del gobierno en materia de territorios extranjeros. M. Hoar combatió la ratificacion del tratado de paz Hispano-Americano, apoyándose en que la Constitucion americana no contiene ningun artículo que permita la adquisición y el gobierno de una dependencia que no se encuentra en condiciones de ser admitida como Estado

ó como territorio de la Union americana. Hizo observar el orador que el gobierno no tenia derecho de adquirir ningun territorio extranjero, ni de governarlo sin su consentimiento. La adquisición de territorios como las Filipinas situados á miles de kilómetros de distancia de los Estados Unidos y habitados por razas inferiores, incapaces de ejercer derechos políticos, viene á anular la doctrinas y el pueblo americano se hallan embriagados por la conquista y no dispuestos á escuchar los consejos de la prudencia, es muy probable que mas adelante recuerden las advertencias de los que deseaban impedir que su país se metiese en aventuras peligrosas y siempre costosísimas. *Diario de Barcelona*, 15 enero, 1899, 569 (my trans.).

15. . . . el documento no acusa mas que muchas promesas de libertad tras un dominio militar absoluto, mas tiránico cien mil veces que el tan criticado nuestro. . . . *Diario de Barcelona*, 11 de febrero, 1899, 1737–39 (my trans.).

16. Y si hoy hemos sacado á colación el nombre y las ideas del piadoso pastor, ha sido por encontrar en una hoja extranjera un singular ex-abrupto del mismo. Mathias Héller, que á pesar de todos los vicios y defectos inherentes á la raza yankee, cree en la absoluta superioridad de ésta sobre todas las demás razas del globo, es partidario decidido de la política llamada imperialista. Aplaude la anexión de Puerto Rico; aplaude la anexión del Archipiélago filipino, y "espera" que Cuba quedará definitivamente anexionada á la Unión. Pero esa serie de conquistas no las abona el por motivos de lucro colonial; no. Lo que él exije imperiosamente, en una especie de memorial dirigido á Mac-Kinley, es que éste imponga á los habitantes recientemente anexionados, las creencias y las prácticas más severas de la Inglesia reformada. Singularmente en Filipinas. "Hay que obligar á esos infelices indios—dice—a la salvación eterna y donde no llegue la fuerza persuasiva de la Biblia, llegue la fuerza convincente de las carabinas." Lo mejor que puede hacer, por lo tanto el Jefe de la Unión, es enviar de gobernador general al Archipiélago a Mathias Héller, acompañado por supuesto de muchos predicadores protestantes y sobre todo de muchos regimientos. *La Vanguardia*, "Busca, Buscando," 7 enero, 1899, 1 (my trans.).

17. See José Martí's *Obras Completas* (La Habana, Cuba: Editorial de Ciencias Sociales, 1975), 144, 363. In the second letter, Martí notes the vernacular nature of Hank Morgan's language and the novel's "moving and profound idea." My warmest thanks to Laura Lomas, author of *Translating Empire: José Martí, Migrant Latino Subjects, and American Modernities* (Duke University Press, 2008), for this reference. Shelley Fisher Fishkin has edited an anthology of writings about Mark Twain, which includes a full translation, by Edward M. Test, of two of Marti's letters to Latin American newspapers, contributed under the general title "Escenas Norteamericanas: 1884" ("North American Scenes: 1884"). Both letters focus on Twain's writings, the first discussing them generally and the second praising *A Connecticut Yankee in King Arthur's Court* particularly. Martí reads *CY* as a document in the struggle for recognition of the common man. These translations are a wonderful addition to the conversation about Mark Twain's international impact. See Shelley Fisher Fishkin, ed., *The Mark Twain Anthology: Great Writers on His Life and Work* (New York: The Library of America, 2010).

18. José Martí, *Selected Writings*. Edited and translated by Esther Allen (New York: Penguin Books, 2002), 33.

19. Gerard Aching notes that there is little consensus about the actual work that *modernismo* performed. Commentators tend to fall into three camps: seeing the movement purely as an art form, seeing it as a means of forming alliances with Europe, and seeing it as a means of creating cohesiveness among the Latin American intelligencia. See *The Politics of Spanish American modernismo: By exquisite design* (New York: Cambridge University Press, 1997), 7.

20. Rubén Darío, *Selected Writings*. Translated by Andrew Hurley, Grez Simon, and Steven F. White. Edited and introduced by Ilan Stavans (New York: Penguin Books, 2005), 511.

21. "Si Brasil, Argentina y Chile, abandonaran sus querellas intestinas y sus rivalidades, hallasen la estabilidad política y se consagrasen a cultivar las riquezas maravillosas de su suelo, se podría ver en un cuarto de siglo, o en medio siglo, constituirse en esa región naciones potentes, capaces de contrapesar a la América anglosajona, y de hacer en lo de adelante vano el sueño de hegemonía panamericana acariciado por los Estados Unidos" (*Tantos Vigores Dispersos*, 82, my trans.) *Tantos Vigores Dispersos*, the title a line from one of Darío's poems, is a collection of his short writings. See *Tantos Vigores Dispersos (Ideas Sociales y Políticas)*, Selected and Edited by Jorge Eduardo Arellano (Managua, Nicaragua Libre: Consejo Nacional de Cultura, 1983). Abbreviated TVD.

22. NO, NO PUEDO, no quiero estar de parte de esos búfalos de dientes de plata. Son enemigos míos, son los aborrecedores de la sangre latina, son los Bárbaros (TVD, 83, my trans.).

23. Y los he visto a esos yankees, en sus abrumadoras ciudades de hierro y piedra, y las horas que entre ellos he vivido las he pasado con una vaga angustia. Apréciame sentir la opresión de una montaña, sentía respirar en un país de cíclopes, comedores de carne cruda, herreros bestiales, habitadores de casas de mastodontes. Colorados, pesados, grasosos, van por sus calles empujandose y rozandose animadamente, a la caza del dollar. El ideal de esos calibanes está circunscrito a la bolsa y a la fábrica. Comen, calculan, beben whisky y hacen millones . . . Enemigos de toda idealidad. . . . Tienen templos para todos los dioses y no creen en ninguno . . . En el arte, en la ciencia, todo lo imitan y lo contrahacen, los estupendos gorilas colorados. Más todas las rachas de los siglos no podrán pulir la enorme Bestia.

No, no puedo estar de parte de ellos, no puedo estar por el triunfo de Calibán (TVD, 84, my trans.).

24. In "Mr. Roosevelt, a Marvelous Gorilla," originally published in 1910, Darío cites Roosevelt's philosophy that the principle requirements for good citizenship should be energy and honesty, then quotes Roosevelt's own words: "I have never believed that a nation should treat other nations differently than an honest man should treat other men." According to the endnote in *Tantos Vigores Dispersos*, "Mr. Roosevelt" was originally published, in French, in the *Paris Journal*, May 27, 1910, under the title "The Words and Acts of Mr. Roosevelt." It was also collected and republished by Margarita Gómez Espinosa in *Rubén Darío, Patriot* (Madrid: Ediciones Triana, 1966, 320–24).

25. See the U.S. Department of State Web site "Diplomacy in Action: Roosevelt Corollary to the Monroe Doctrine, 1903." www.state.gov/r/pa/ho/time/lp/17660 htm.

26. José Enrique Rodó, *Ariel*. Translated by F. J. Stimson (Boston: Houghton Mifflin Company, 1922), 31. In his prologue to this edition, Carlos Fuentes notes that the oratorical structure of the essay reflects Rodó's own roots in classical oratory, and that the essay often functions as a peroration.

Chapter 7

1. Jim Zwick, *Mark Twain's Weapons of Satire: Anti-Imperialist Writings on the Philippine-American War* (Syracuse, New York: Syracuse University Press, 1992), 57–58.

2. For the Philippine Treason Act, see *Annual Reports of the War Department for the Fiscal Year Ended June 30, 1902*, vol. 11, *Acts of the Philippine Commission* (Washington: Government Printing Office, 1902), 51–54. See also Dominador D. Buhain, *A History of Publishing in the Philippines* (Philippines: Rex Book Store, Inc., 1998), 28.

3. See Kal Raustiala, *Does the Constitution Follow the Flag?: The Evolution of Territoriality in American Law* (New York: Oxford University Press, 2009), 86, and Bartholomew H. Sparrow, *The Insular Cases and the Emergence of American Empire* (Lawrence, Kansas: University Press of Kansas, 2006).

4. C. de E. M. and A. Za., "A Mindanao" (To Mindanao), *Ang Bayang hapis* (August 31, 1899): PIR Newspaper No. 1. As translated and included in Maria Serena I. Diokno's "'Benevolent Assimilation' and Filipino Responses," in Hazel M. McFerson, ed., *Mixed Blessing: The Impact of the American Colonial Experience on Politics and Society in the Philippines* (Westport, Connecticut: Greenwood Press, 2002), 75–88. Diokno does not provide information about these poets, and I have been unable to find out exactly who they were, or their full names.

5. José Rizal, "Reflections on the Philippines and the Filipinos," Part 2: "The Philippines Within a Century" (ca. 1889), pp. 145–83 in Teodoro A. Agoncillo, ed., *Filipino Nationalism, 1872–1970* (Quezon City: R.P. Garcia Publishing Co., 1974), 181. For a slightly different translation see the Rizal essay under the title "The Philippines a Century Hence," pp. 242–63 of Gregorio F. Zaide, *José Rizal: Life, Works, and Writings* (Manila: Villanueva Book Store, 1957). The paragraph on the United States is on p. 262.

6. As quoted in Zaide, 116. Zaide's own reference is to Jose Alejandrino, *The Price of Freedom (La Senda del Sacrificio)*, 7. No further citation materials are given for Alejadrino's book.

7. As quoted in Maria Serena I. Diokno's "'Benevolent Assimilation' and Filipino Responses," in *Mixed Blessing*, 84. De Tavera also wrote a short history of the Philippines from its discovery by the Spanish to 1903. In it he lays out the governance system established by the Americans but makes very few judgments, possibly because the book was authorized by the Philippine Commission—i.e., subject to the Sedition Act. See *Reseña Histórica de Filipinas Desde Su Descubrimiento Hasta 1903*, by Trinidad Hermengildo Pardo de Tavera (Manila: Bureau of Printing, 1906).

8. See Florio C. Quibuyen's *A Nation Aborted: Rizal, American Hegemony, and Philippine Nationalism* (Manila: Atenio de Manila University Press, 1999), 3–4.

9. John N. Schumacher, *The Propaganda Movement, 1880–1895: The Creators of a Filipino Consciousness, the Makers of Revolution* (Manila: Solidaridad Publishing House, 1973), especially chapter 2, "Early Filipino Student Activities in Spain, 1880–1882 (pp. 17–35) and throughout. For a social history of the period, with Rizal at the center, see also Benedict Anderson's *Under Three Flags*.

10. Benedict Anderson, *Under Three Flags: Anarchism and the Anti-Colonial Imagination* (London: Verso, 2005), 23.

11. See Agoncillo, *Filipino Nationalism, 1872–1970*, and Carlos Quirino, *The Young Aguinaldo* (Manila: Regal Printing Company, 1969).

12. See *True Version of the Philippine Revolution*, by Don Emilio Aguinaldo y Famy. www.authorama.com/true-version-of-the-philippine-revolution-1.html. Chapter 3. Originally published as *Reseña veridical de la revolución Filipina, por Emilio Aguinaldo y Famy* (Tarlak: Imprenta Nacional, 1899).

13. Emilio Aguinaldo, with Vicente Albano Pacis, *A Second Look at America* (New York: Robert Speller & Sons), 1957, 61.

14. Aguinaldo was a revolutionary against the Spanish and the Americans, declaring himself President of the Philippine nation and leading what the Americans called an "insurrection" against the United States until he was captured by General Funston in 1901. Shortly after, he recognized U.S. sovereignty. For the next few decades, he alternated between private life and public positions, including an unsuccessful bid for the presidency. However he cooperated with the Japanese during World War II, even though a subsequent trial absolved him of voluntary collaboration.

15. Usha Mahajani, *Philippine Nationalism: External Challenge and Filipino Response, 1565–1946* (St. Lucia, Queensland: Queensland University Press, 1971), 176.

16. During this time, Americans acknowledged Mabini's formidable intelligence even while opposing his political demands. In "'Benevolent Assimilation' and Filipino Responses," Marian Serena I. Diokno quotes James Le Roy, who in volume 2 of his *The Americans in the Philippines* (Boston: Houghton Mifflin, 1914), noted that Mabini not only was possessed of a rare theoretical intelligence, but that he also spoke for a sizeable portion of his fellows. See Diokno, in *Mixed Blessing*, 82.

17. "El Singapore Free Press de 23 de mayo, a su vez, afirma que el gobierno de Washington, no habiéndose hecho cargo de su verdadera posición en Filipinas, procedió muy neciamente, haciendo comprender a los filipinos que las promesas de libertad lanzadas al principio de la Guerra tienen por objeto la expansión territorial por medio de la subyagación de razas que no quieren ser vendidas como vacunos, y metiéndose en aventuras militares que reprocha y condena la Constitución de los Estados Unidos; y, después de haber dudado de la sinceridad de los Comisionados americanos en las negociaciones de arreglo que están gestionando con los filipinos, reflexiona que un poco menos de exaltación de parte del militarismo y un poco más de aprecio a las palabras *libertad* y *derecho* hubieran evitado ese proceder sanguinario, la mancha sucia que hoy se vé en la hermosa fama y humanidad de los Estados Unidos. "América en Filipinas," in Apolinario Mabini, *La Revolución Filipina (con otros documentos de la época)*. Tomo segundo. Manila: Bureau of Printing, 1931, 10–11, original italics; my trans. Unless otherwise noted, all the Mabini documents reproduced below are from this volume. For the sake of brevity, I have edited the translated quotations. I provide the full quotations in these endnotes.

18. Apolinario Mabini, "The Struggle for Freedom (1899)," in Teodoro A. Agoncillo, ed. *Filipino Nationalism, 1872–1970*, 236–37, 239.

19. Tenga entendido el gran pueblo de Washington y Lincoln que la fuerzo, por grande que sea, no es capaz de aniquilar las aspiraciones de ocho millones de almas que tienen conciencia plena de su fuerza, honor y derechos: la sangre no ahoga, sino abona las grandes ideas, los eternos principios "Al Pueblo de Los Estados Unidos," 11 de Julio, 1899, *La Revolución Filipina (con otros documentos de la época)*, 38, my transl.

20. "El Gobierno americano invoca con calor y entusiasmo la humanidad y las liberatades; pues las quiere solo para sí y no para otros." "Gobierno de los EE.UU. en Filipinas," 22 febrero de 1900, *La Revolución Filipina (con otros documentos de la época)*, 158, my trans.

21. Mr. Root empieza diciendo que el pueblo de las islas cedidas ha adquirido el derecho de ser tratado por los Estados Unidos conforme los principios de justicia y libertad, declarados en la Constitución para la salvaguardia esencial de cada individuo contra los poderes del Gobierno; pero hace notar que la Constitución sólo prescribe la uniformidad de derechos entre los pobladores del Continente americano: de aquí el que los isleños sólo pueden exigir que no sean privados de la vida, libertad o propiedad sin el debido proceso legal; que no proceda a la expropiación de la propiedad privada sin compensación; que no se decrete ley alguna, menoscabando la obligación proveniente de los contratos, etc., porque los Estados Unidos han declarado que estos derechos son inherentes a todo hombre y la observación de los mismos es una parte de la naturaliza del Gobierno de los Estados Unidos. Ignoramos si Mr. Root se ha olvidado o de intento no ha hecho mentón, por impertinentes, de los artículos adicionales de la Constitución, que prescriben lo siguiente: no se podrá dictar ley alguna que establezca una religión o impida el libre ejercicio de ninguna de ellas . . . todas las personas nacidas o naturalizadas en los Estados Unidos y sujetas a su jurisdicción, son ciudadanos de los Estados Unidos y del Estado en que residen, y no se les podrá coartar los privilegios e inmunidades de los ciudadanos de los Estados Unidos. El derecho de los ciudadanos de los Estados Unidos para votar no podrá ser negado o coartado por los Estados Unidos o por cualquier Estado, por razón de raza, color o anterior estado de servidumbre. "Gobierno de los EE.UU. en Filipinas," *La Revolución Filipina (con otros documentos de la época)*, 163–64, my trans.

22. Los enumerados son también derechos inherentes a todo hombre, que deben disfrutar todos los que están sujetos a la jurisdicción de los Estados Unidos. Que la Constitución sólo rige dentro del Continente americano? Entonces ni el Gobierno ni el Congreso tienen poder alguno sobre las Islas: uno y otro reciben sus poderes de la Constitución, y estos poderes no pueden extenderse a los Territorios declarados fuera de la misma. El Congreso no podría de ninguna manera legislar para los Islas: su poder debe limitarse a declarar si admite o no a las Islas dentro de la Unión. Si las admite, las Islas deben ser consideradas como Estado; si no, deben ser independientes. "Gobierno de los EE.UU. en Filipinas," *La Revolución Filipina (con otros documentos de la época)*, 165, my trans.

23. Raustiala notes that Justice Harlan later came to a similar conclusion about the relationship of Congress to the Constitution in *Hawaii v. Mankichi*. See Raustiala, 85 and 267.

24. Los filipinos que han votado una Constitución inspirada en los adelantos de la ciencia, los que se afanan por instruirse y corregir sus antiguos vicios, para ponerse en contacto y relación amistosa con todas las naciones del mundo, son combatidos por los americanos; al paso que los que se mantienen aislados para conservar el despotismo y la esclavitud, disfrutan de la paz y tranquilidad a la sombra de la bandera estrellada de los Estados Unidos. Quién dijera que llegaría el día en que la República de Washington y Lincoln combata la libertad y el progreso, aliándose con el despotismo y la esclavitud! "Gobierno de los EE.UU. en Filipinas," *La Revolución Filipina (con otros documentos de la época)*, 166, my trans.

25. Será probablemente su valor o alcance político? Tampoco lo vemos, porque Mr. Beveridge ha sido demasiado franco, y dicen que el mejor político es el más instruído en el arte de engañar. Mr. Beveridge dice a los Filipinos: "No crean Uds. en las promesas de humanidad, libertad, civilización y progreso; la guerra en Filipinas obedece a puros cálculos mercantiles, y en todo cálculo mercantil no pesan esos sentimentalismos ni la sangre que se ha de derramar, sino única y simplemente el lucro o ganancia. No puede darse una propaganda revolucionaria más enérgica y eficaz." Dice a los americanos: "Si los principios de derecho natural o divino que informan nuestra Constitución se oponen a la expansión imperialista, se pasas por encima de esa Constitución, se pasa por encima de Dios; el verdadero y único dios es el oro, la verdadera Constitución, la Constitución dorada. Debéis renunciar a vuestras libertades constitucionales a favor de los favorecidos por la fortuna, porque, para oprimir a los filipinos tenemos que oprimir primero a vosotros." No puede darse mayor impudencia.

Pero, dónde está el origen de los aplausos? Mr. Beveridge ha tenido la habilidad de tocar la cuerda más floja de su partido, y se ha roto. La codicia rompe el saco, como suele decirse. "Beveridge Ante El Senado," *La Revolución Filipina (con otros documentos de la época)*, 172, my trans.

26. 56th Congress, 1st Session. Reported in 33 Cong. Rec. Part 1, Tuesday, January 9, 1900, p. 711.

Epilogue

1. As with the Vietnam War, the Iraq War has triggered memories of the Philippine-American War. Paul Kramer's article "The Water Cure" rediscovered American methods of torture in the wake of Abu Ghraib (*The New Yorker*, February 25, 2008, 38–43). Bush himself drew analogies between the American invasion of Manila and the invasion of Baghdad (Shankar Vedantam, "History Teaches Lessons in Forced Democracy," *Lawrence Journal World*, September 19, 2007). And Anne-Marie Slaughter, Dean of the Woodrow Wilson School at Princeton, published *The Idea That Is America: Keeping Faith with Our Values in a Dangerous World* (New York: Basic Books, 2007), a book opening with the premise that "We have lost our way in the world" and asking "what role should America play in the world?" The table of contents includes chapters entitled "Liberty," "Democracy," "Equality," "Justice," "Tolerance," "Humility," and "Faith." The entire structure and vocabulary of the book illustrate the author and publisher's assumption that the general readers for whom it is intended will respond to verbal cues that call on their identity as citizens of a highly principled nation.

2. President George W. Bush, State of the Union Address, January 29, 2002. http://archives.cnn.com/2002/ALLPOLITICS/01/29/bush.speech.txt/.

3. See ABC's *Boston Legal*, Season 2, Disk 5, Episode 19, Episode title, "Stick It."

4. "Ahmadinejad's Letter to President Bush," the *Washington Post*, Tuesday, May 9. washingtonpost.com. Reuters 14:40 05–05–06.

5. Zev Chafets, "Is There a Right Way to Pray?" *New York Times Magazine*, September 20, 2009, 42–47.

6. "Lawmaker in Kentucky Mixes Piety and Politics," *New York Times*, Sunday, January 4, 2009, p. 12.

7. "Mark Twain, the Greatest American Humorist, Returning Home, Talks at Length to *The World*," *New York World*, October 14, 1900, 3. In Gary Scharnhorst, ed., *Mark Twain: The Complete Interviews* (Tuscaloosa: The University of Alabama Press, 2006), 346–52.

Abaya, Doroteo, and Bernard Karganilla. *Miguel Malvar and the Philippine Revolution: a Biography*. Philippines: Miguel Malvar (MM) Productions, Inc., 1998.

Acereda, Alberto. "La hispanidad amenazada: Ruben Dario y la Guerra del 98." In *The Legacy of the Mexican and Spanish-American Wars: Legal, Literary, and Historical Perspectives*. Ed. Gary D. Keller and Cordelia Candelaria. Tempe, Arizona: Bilingual Review/Press, 2000, 99–110.

Addams, Jane. *Newer Ideals of Peace*. New York: The Macmillan Company, 1911 (1907).

Adler, Felix. "The Philippines War: Two Ethical Questions." In *Ethical Addresses* 9:10 (June 1902). www.Boondocksnet.com/ai/ailtexts/adler02.html.

Agoncillo, Teodoro A. *Filipino Nationalism, 1872–1970*. Quezon City: R. P. Garcia Publishing Co., 1974.

Aguinaldo, Emilio. *True Version of the Philippine Revolution*, by Don Emilio Aguinaldo y Famy, President of the Philippine Republic. Farlak (Philippine Islands), September 23, 1899 (microfilm).

Alfonso, Oscar M. *Theodore Roosevelt and the Philippines, 1897–1909*. Quezon City: University of the Philippines Press, 1970.

Althusser, Louis. "Ideology and Ideological State Apparatuses (Notes towards an Investigation)." In *Lenin and Philosophy and Other Essays*. London: Monthly Review Press, 1971, 127–86.

Anderson, Benedict. *Imagined Communities: Reflections on the Origin and Spread of Nationalism*. Revised ed. London: Verso, 1983, 1991.

———. *Under Three Flags: Anarchism and the Anti-Colonial Imagination*. London: Verso, 2005.

Anderson, Brigadier-General Thomas M. "Our Rule in the Philippines." In *North American Review*, Vol. 170, Issue 519, 272–283.

Angelis, Angelo T. "For God and Country: Crafting Memory and Meaning from War and Independence." Review Essay in *Reviews in American History* 31.3 (2003), 356–363.

Annual Meeting of the Anti-Imperialist League. "Address by the President, The Hon. George S. Boutwell." November 25, 1899.

Bain, David Haward. *Sitting in Darkness: Americans in the Philippines.* Boston: Houghton Mifflin Co., 1984.

Balfour, Sebastian. *The End of the Spanish Empire, 1898–1923.* Oxford: Oxford University Press, 1997.

Bazaco, Evergisto. *History of Education in the Philippines, Spanish Period, 1565–1898.* Manila: University of Santo Tomas Press, 1953.

Bender, Thomas. *A Nation among Nations: America's Place in World History.* New York: Hill and Wang, 2006.

Bercovitch, Sacvan. *The Puritan Origins of the American Self.* New Haven: Yale University Press, 1975.

Bhabha, Homi. *The Location of Culture.* London: Routledge, 1994.

Bingham, Caleb. *The Columbian Orator: Containing a Variety of Original and Selected Pieces, Together with the Rules; Calculated to Improve Youth and Others in the Ornamental and Useful Art of Eloquence.* Troy, New York: William S. Parker, 1821.

Blum, Edward J. *Reforging the White Republic: Race, Religion, and American Nationalism, 1865–1898.* Baton Rouge: Louisiana State University Press, 2005.

Bouvier, Virginia M. *Whose America? The War of 1898 and the Battles to Define the Nation.* Westport, Connecticut: Praeger Publishers, 2001.

Brainard, Cecilia Manguerra and Edmundo F. Litton, eds. *Journey of 100 Years: Reflections on the Centennial of Philippine Independence.* Pasig City: Anvil Publishing, Inc., 1999.

Branch, Edgar M., Michael B. Frank, Kenneth M. Sanderson, eds. *Mark Twain's Letters*, vol. I, 1855–66. Berkeley: University of California Press, 1988.

Bremer, Francis J. "Faith and Society: The Making of a Christian America." Review Essay in *Reviews in American History* 32.1 (2004), 7–13.

Brooklyn Eagle Library, eds. *The United States and the Philippine Islands: Speeches in the United States Senate by Henry Cabot Lodge, George F. Hoar, Joseph L. Rawlins, and John C. Spooner.* The Brooklyn Eagle Library: No. 68, Vol. XVII. No. 9, June 1902. Published by the *Brooklyn Daily Eagle*.

Brown, Reverend Charles R. "Palm Sunday Sermon." First Congregational Church, Oakland, California, 1899. San Francisco: Press of The Hicks-Judd Company (Microfilm, NYPL, Z-Bff).

———. *Mark Twain: Collected Tales, Sketches, Speeches, & Essays, 1891–1910.* New York: The Library of America, 1992.

Buhain, Dominador D. *A History of Publishing in the Philippines.* Philippines: Rex Book Store, Inc., 1998.

Bureau of Education. *English Composition: A Manual for Use in Philippine Public Schools.* Manila: Bureau of Printing, 1916.

Bush, Harold K., Jr. *Mark Twain and the Spiritual Crisis of His Age.* Tuscaloosa: The University of Alabama Press, 2007.

Butler, Frederick. *A Modern Atlas, to accompany the system of geography and history combined, in a catechetical form*. Wethersfield, Connecticut: Deming & Frances, 1825.

Butler, Judith, and Sara Salih, eds. *The Judith Butler Reader*. Oxford: Blackwell Publishing, 2004.

Button, H. Warren, and Eugene F. Provenzo, Jr. *History of Education and Culture in America*. Englewood Cliffs, New Jersey: Prentice-Hall Inc., 1983.

Cain, P. J., and A. G. Hopkins. *British Imperialism, 1688–2000*. Harlow, England: Pearson Education Ltd., 1993, 2001.

Camfield, Gregg. "In the Mirror of the Imagination: Mark Twain's Kipling." In *Arizona Quarterly Special Issue: Mark Twain at the Turn-of-the-Century, 1890–1910*. Vol. 61, no. 1, Spring 2005, 85–108.

Capen, Samuel B. "The Next Ten Years." *Address at the Centennial Meeting of the American Board*, Boston, MA, October 11, 1910. Boston: American Board of Commissioners for Foreign Missions, n.d.

Carr, Jean Fersuon, with Stephen L. Carr and Lucille M. Schultze. *Archives of Instruction: Nineteenth-Century Rhetorics, Readers, and Composition Books in the United States*. Carbondale: Southern Illinois University Press, 2005.

Channing, Edward, and Albert Bushnell Hart. *Guide to the Study of American History*. Boston: Ginn & Co., Publishers, 1896.

Chapin, Aaron L. *First Principles of Political Economy*. New York: Sheldon and Company, 1880.

Chaudhuri, Nupur, and Margaret Strobel, eds. *Western Women and Imperialism: Complicity and Resistance*. Bloomington: Indiana University Press, 1992.

Clymer, Kenton J. *Protestant Missionaries in the Philippines, 1898–1916: An Inquiry into the American Colonial Mentality*. Urbana: University of Illinois Press, 1986.

———. "Protestant Missionaries and American Colonialism in the Philippines, 1899–1916: Attitudes, Perceptions, Involvement," in Peter W. Stanley, ed., *Reappraising an Empire: New Perspectives on Philippine-American History*. Cambridge, Massachusetts: Harvard University Press, 1984, 143–170.

Coates, Tim., ed. *The Siege of the Peking Embassy, 1900. Sir Claude Macdonald's Report on the Boxer Rebellion*. London: The Stationery Office, 2000.

Collin, Richard H. *Theodore Roosevelt, Culture, Diplomacy, and Expansion: A New View of American Imperialism*. Baton Rouge: Louisiana State University Press, 1985.

Cooke, Increase. *The American Orator; or, Elegant Extracts in Prose and Poetry; Comprehending a Diversity of Oratorical Specimens, of the Eloquence of Popular Assemblies, of the Bar, of the Pulpit, &c. Principally Intended for the Use of Schools and Academies. To which Are Prefixed a Dissertation on Oratorical Delivery and the Outlines of Gesture*. Charleston, South Carolina: Sidney's Press, 1819.

Craig, Austin. *The Filipinos' Fight for Freedom: True History of the Filipino People During Their 400 Years' Struggle, Told After the Manner of Jose Rizal*. Manila: Oriental Commercial Company, 1933. Republished by AMS Press, New York, 1973.

Crain, Patricia. *The Story of A: The Alphabetization of America from* The New England Primer *to* The Scarlet Letter. Stanford, California: Stanford University Press, 2000.

Crapol, Edward P., ed. *Women and American Foreign Policy: Lobbyists, Critics, and Insiders.* Westport, Connecticut: Greenwood Press, 1987.

Cremin, Lawrence A. *The Transformation of the School: Progressivism in American Education, 1876–1957.* New York: Alfred A. Knopf, 1961.

Crosby, Ernest. 1902. *Captain Jinks, Hero.* Upper Saddle River, New Jersey: The Gregg Press, 1968 (reprint).

Crossley, Nick, and John Michael Roberts, eds. *After Habermas: New Perspectives on the Public Sphere.* Oxford: Blackwell Publishing /The Sociological Review, 2004.

Daggett, Herman. *The American Reader: Consisting of Familiar, Instructive, and Entertaining Stories. Selected for the Use of Schools.* Poughkeepsie, New York: Paraclete Potter, 1818.

Dane, G. Ezra, ed. *Letters from the Sandwich Islands, Written for the Sacramento Union by Mark Twain.* New York: Haskell House Publishers, Ltd., 1972.

Darío, Rubén. *Selected Writings.* Translated by Andrew Hurley, Grez Simon, and Steven F. White. Edited and introduced by Ilan Stavans. New York: Penguin Books, 2005.

———. *Tantos Vigores Dispersos (Ideas Sociales y Políticas).* Selected and edited by Jorge Eduardo Arellano. Managua, Nicaragua: Consejo Nacional de Cultura, 1983.

Daydi-Tolson, Santiago. "La influencia del 'Poeta de America' en el nacionalismo puertorriqueno." In *The Legacy of the Mexican and Spanish-American Wars: Legal, Literary, and Historical Perspectives.* Ed. Gary D. Keller and Cordelia Candelaria. Tempe, Arizona: Bilingual Review/Press, 2000, 87–92.

Davis, J. Merle. *Davis—Soldier Missionary: A Biography of Reverend Jerome D. Davis.* Boston: The Pilgrim Press, 1916.

Delgado, Rafael Perez. *1898: El Ano del Desastre.* Madrid: Ediciones Giner, 1976.

Dementyev, I. P. *USA: Imperialists and Anti-Imperialists (The Great Foreign Policy Debate at the turn of the Century).* Trans. David Skvirsky. Moscow: Progress Publishers, 1979.

Diggs, Annie L. "Little Brown Brothers." In *The Public, and City and State* 73, August 26, 1899, 13.

Dodell, Arnold. *Moses or Darwin? A School Problem for All Friends of Truth and Progress.* Trans., with Preface for the American edition, by Frederick W. Dodell. New York: The Truth Seeker Company, 1891.

Dyer, Thomas G. *Theodore Roosevelt and the Idea of Race.* Baton Rouge: Louisiana State University Press, 1980.

Easton, Edward D., Rev. "Missions and the Modern Evidences of Christianity." Annual Sermon before the American Board of Commisioners for Foreign Missions. Delivered at Hartford, Connecticut, October 8, 1901.

Edwards, Ruth Dudley. *The Pursuit of Reason: The Economist 1843–1993.* London: Hamish Hamilton, 1993.

Eggleston, Edward. *A History of the United States and its People: For the Use of Schools*. New York: D. Appleton and Company, 1888.

Ellis, Joseph J. *American Creation: Triumphs and Tragedies at the Founding of the Republic*. New York: Vintage Books, 2007.

Elson, Ruth Miller. *Guardians of Tradition: American Schoolbooks of the Nineteenth Century*. Lincoln: University of Nebraska Press, 1964.

Fee, Mary H. *A Woman's Impressions of the Philippines*. Chicago: A. C. McClurg & Co., 1912.

Fetterley, Judith. *The Resisting Reader: A Feminist Approach to American Fiction*. Bloomington: Indiana University Press, 1978.

Fishkin, Shelley Fisher, ed. *The Mark Twain Anthology: Great Writers on His Life and Work*. New York: The Library of America, 2010.

FitzGerald, Frances. *America Revised: History Schoolbooks in the Twentieth Century*. Boston: Little, Brown and Company, 1979.

Foner, Philip S., and Richard C. Winchester, eds. *The Anti-Imperialist Reader, A Documentary History of Anti-Imperialism in the United States. Vol. I: From the Mexican War to the Election of 1900*. New York: Holmes & Meier Publishers, Inc., 1984.

Foner, Philip S., ed. *The Anti-Imperialist Reader, A Documentary History of Anti-Imperialism in the United States. Vol. II: The Literary Anti-Imperialists*. New York: Holmes & Meier Publishers, Inc., 1984.

Foster, Francis Smith, ed. *A Brighter Day Coming: A Frances Ellen Watkins Harper Reader*. New York: The Feminist Press, 1990.

———. "African-Americans, Literature, and the Nineteenth-Century Afro-Protestant Press." In *Reciprocal Influences: Literary Production, Distribution, and Consumption in America*, eds. Steven Fink and Susan S. Williams. Columbus: Ohio State University Press, 1999.

———, ed. *Minnie's Sacrifice, Sowing and Reaping, Trail and Triumph: Three Rediscovered Novels by Frances E. W. Harper*. Boston: Beacon Press, 1994.

Fulton, Joe B. *The Reverend Mark Twain: Theological Burlesque, Form, and Content*. Columbus: The Ohio State University Press, 2006.

Gates, John Morgan. *Schoolbooks and Krags: The United States Army in the Philippines, 1898–1902*. Contributions in Military History Number 3. Westport, Connecticut: Greenwood Press, Inc., 1973.

Gatewood, Willard B. Jr., *Black Americans and the White Man's Burden, 1898–1903*. Urbana: University of Illinois Press, 1975.

Gilmour, David. *The Long Recessional: The Imperial Life of Rudyard Kipling*. New York: Farrar, Straus and Giroux, 2002.

Ginger, Ray. *William Jennings Bryan: Selections*. New York: The Bobbs-Merrill Company, Inc. 1967.

Go, Julian, and Anne L. Foster, eds. *The American Colonial State in the Philippines: Global Perspectives*. Durham, North Carolina: Duke University Press, 2003.

Goodrich, S. G. *The Young American: or Book of Government and Law; show their History, Nature, and Necessity. For the Use of Schools*. New York: Turner & Hayden, 1845.

Gordy, Wilbur F. *A History of the United States for Schools*. New York: Charles Scribner's Sons, 1898

Greene, Theodore P., ed. *American Imperialism in 1898*. Problems in American Civilization series. Lexington, Massachusetts: D. C. Heath and Company, 1955.

Greenberg, Amy. *Manifest Manhood and the Antebellum American Empire*. New York: Cambridge University Press, 2005.

Gribben, Alan. *Mark Twain's Library: A Reconstruction*. 2 vols. Boston: G. K. Hall & Co., 1980.

Griggs, Sutton E. *Imperium in Imperio: A Study of the Negro Race Problem*. New York: Arno Press and the *New York Times*, 1969. Originally published Cincinnati: The Editor Publishing Company, 1899.

Guillory, John. *Cultural Capital: The Problem of Literary Canon Formation*. Chicago: The University of Chicago Press, 1993.

Hagiioannu, Andrew. *The Man Who Would Be Kipling: The Colonial Fiction and the Frontiers of Exile*. New York: Palgrave Macmillan, 2003.

Hamilton, Richard F. *President McKinley, War and Empire. Vol. 1: President McKinley and the Coming of War, 1898*. New Brunswick, New Jersey: Transaction Publishers, 2006.

Harper, Frances E. W. *Iola Leroy, or, Shadows Uplifted*. Ed. Francis Smith Foster. Oxford: Oxford University Press, 1988.

Harrington, Fred Harvey. "Literary Aspects of American Anti-Imperialism, 1898–1902." *The New England Quarterly*, Vol. 10, No. 4 (December 1937), 650–667.

Harrington, Peter, and Frederic A. Sharf. *"A splendid little war": The Spanish-American War, 1898; the Artists' Perspective*. Mechnicsburg, Pennsylvania: Stackpole Books, 1998.

Healy, David. *U.S. Expansionism: The Imperialist Urge in the 1890s*. Madison: University of Wisconsin Press, 1970.

Hebard, Andrew. "Romantic Sovereignty: Popular Romances and the American Imperial State in the Philippines." In *American Quarterly*, Vol. 57, #3 (September 2005), 805–830.

Hess, Jean. "A French View of the War in the Philippines." In *The Public, and City and State* 72.2 (August 19, 1899), 13–16.

Hillard, G. S. *The Franklin Fifth Reader, for the Use of Public and Private Schools*. New York: Tainter Brothers, Merrill, and Co., 1871.

Hillis, Rev. Newell Dwight. Pastor of Plymouth Church, Brooklyn. "The Self-Propagating Power of Christianity." Annual Sermon before the American Board of Commissioners for Foreign Missions, delivered at Oberlin, Ohio, October 14, 1902. Published by the Board, Boston, 1902.

Hilton, Sylvia L., and Steve J. S. Ickringill, eds. *European Perceptions of the Spanish-American War of 1898*. Bern, Switzerland: Peter Lang, 1999.

Hitchens, Christopher. *Blood, Class, and Nostalgia: Anglo-American Ironies*. New York: Farrar, Straus and Giroux, 1990.

Hoganson, Kristin L. *Fighting for American Manhood: How Gender Politics Provoked the Spanish-American and Philippine-American Wars*. New Haven: Yale University Press, 1998.

Hunt, Michael H. *Ideology and U.S. Foreign Policy.* New Haven: Yale University Press, 1987.

Imperial, Reynaldo H. *Leyte: The Philippine-American War, 1898–1902.* Diliman, Quezon City: University of the Philippines Press, 1966.

Iser, Wolfgang. *The Act of Reading, A Theory of Aesthetic Response.* Baltimore: Johns Hopkins University Press, 1978.

Jackson, Gregory S. "'What Would Jesus Do?': Practical Christianity, Social Gospel Realism, and the Homiletic Novel." In *PMLA*, vol. 121, no. 3 (May 2006), 641–661.

Jacobson, Matthew Frye. *Barbarian Virtues: The United States Encounters Foreign Peoples at Home and Abroad, 1876–1917.* New York: Hill and Wang, 2000.

James, William. *Talks to Teachers on Psychology, and to Students on Some of Life's Ideals.* Cambridge: Harvard University Press, 1983.

———. "The Philippine Tangle." In *Boston Evening Transcript*, March 1, 1899. www.boondocksnet.com/ai/ailtexts/tangle.html.

Jelen, Ted. G. "Religion and Foreign Policy Attitudes: Exploring the Effects of Denomination and Doctrine." In *American Politics Quarterly*, vol. 22, no.3 (July 1994), 382–400.

Jernegan, Prescott F. *A Short History of the Philippines, For Use in Philippine Schools.* New York: D. Appleton and Company, 1905.

———. *Philippine Geography Primer.* Boston: D.C. Heath & Co., 1907.

———. *Philippine Question Books No 1, "1001" Questions and Answers on Philippine History and Civil Government.* Manila: Philippine Education, 1907.

Johnson, Edward A. *A School History of the Negro Race in America, from 1619 to 1890.* Raleigh, North Carolina: Edwards & Broughton, 1891.

Jones, Aled. *Powers of the Press: Newspapers, Power and the Public in Nineteenth-Century England.* Aldershot, England: Scolar Press, 1996.

Jones, Gavin. "Signifying Songs: The Double Meaning of Black Dialect in the World of George Washington Cable." In *American Literary History*, vol. 9, no. 2 (Summer 1997), 244–267.

Kaplan, Amy. *The Anarchy of Empire in the Making of U.S. Culture.* Cambridge, Massachusetts: Harvard University Press, 2002.

———. 1977. "Imperial Triangles: Mark Twain's Foreign Affairs." In *Modern Fiction Studies* 43.1 (1977), 237–248.

———. "Nation, Region, Empire." In Emory Elliott, ed. *The Columbia History of the American Novel.* New York: Columbia University Press, 1991, 240–266

Kaplan, Fred. *The Singular Mark Twain.* New York: Doubleday, 2003.

Kazin, Michael. *A Godly Hero: The Life of William Jennings Bryan.* New York: Alfred Knopf, 2006.

Kelly, Myra. *Little Aliens.* New York: Arno Press, 1975.

Kerber, Linda K. *Women of the Republic: Intellect and Ideology in Revolutionary America.* Chapel Hill: University of North Carolina Press, 1980.

Kern, Robert W. *Liberals, Reformers and Caciques in Restoration Spain, 1875–1909.* Albuquerque: University of New Mexico Press, 1974.

Koss, Stephen E. *The Rise and Fall of the Political Press in Britain: The Nineteenth Century.* Chapel Hill: University of North Carolina Press, 1981.

Krauth, Leland. *Mark Twain and Company: Six Literary Relations.* Athens, Georgia: University of Georgia Press, 2003.

———. *Proper Mark Twain.* Athens, Georgia: University of Georgia Press, 1999.

Krebs, Paula. *Gender, Race, and the Writing of Empire: Public Discourse and the Boer War.* New York: Cambridge University Press, 1999.

Lane, Christopher. *The Ruling Passion: British Colonial Allegory and the Paradox of Homosexual Desire.* Durham, North Carolina: Duke University Press, 1995.

Lears, Jackson. *Rebirth of a Nation: The Making of Modern America, 1877–1920.* New York: HarperCollins Publishers, 2009.

Levander, Caroline Field. "Confederate Cuba" In *Our Americas: Political and Cultural Imaginings*, eds. Sandhya Shukla and Heidi Tinsman, *Radical History Review* special issue, Duke University Press, 2005.

Lincoln, E. Eric. *Race, Religion, and the Continuing American Dilemma.* New York: Hill & Wang, 1984.

Lind, Mary Ann. *The Compassionate Memsahibs: Welfare Activities of British Women in India, 1900–1947.* New York: Greenwood Press, 1988.

Lodge, Henry Cabot, et al. *The United States and the Philippine Islands: Speeches in the United States Senate by Henry Cabot Lodge, George F. Hoar, Joseph L. Rawlins, and John C. Spooner.* The Brooklyn Eagle Library, no. 68. Vol. 17, no. 9 (June 1902).

Love, Eric. T. *Race Over Empire: Racism & U.S. Imperialism, 1865–1900.* Chapel Hill: University of North Carolina Press, 2004.

Lowell, Josephine Shaw. *Public Relief and Private Charity.* New York: Arno Press, 1971 [1884].

Mabini, Apolinario. *La Revolución Filipina (con otros documentos de la época).* Tomo segundo. Manila: Bureau of Printing, 1931

MacDonald, Robert H. *The Language of Empire: Myths and Metaphors of Popular Imperialism, 1880–1918.* Manchester: Manchester University Press, 1994.

Mahajani, Usha. *Philippine Nationalism: External Challenge and Filipino Response, 1565–1946.* St. Lucia, Queensland: Queensland University Press, 1971.

Malcolm, George A., assisted by Maximo M. Kalaw. *Philippine Civics: A Textbook for the Schools of the Philippines.* New York: D. Appleton and Company, 1920.

Mansfield, Edward Deering. *American Education: Its Principles and Elements. Dedicated to the teachers of the United States.* New York: A. S. Barnes, 1877.

Martí, José. *Obras Completas.* 20 Epistolario. La Habana, Cuba: Editorial de Ciencias Sociales, 1975.

———. *Selected Writings.* Edited and translated by Esther Allen. New York: Penguin Books, 2002.

Matos, Eliades Acosta. *Los Colores Secretos del Imperio.* Havana: Mercie Ediciones, 2002.

May, Glenn Anthony. *Social Engineering in the Philippines: The Aims, Execution, and Impact of American Colonial Policy, 1900–1913.* Westport, Connecticut: Greenwood Press, 1980.

McFerson, Hazel M., ed. *Mixed Blessing: The Impact of the American Colonial Experience on Politics and Society in the Philippines*. Westport, Connecticut: Greenwood Press, 2002.

McKnight, Douglas. *Schooling, the Puritan Imperative, and the Molding of an American National Identity: Education's "Errand Into the Wilderness."* Mahwah, New Jersey: Lawrence Erlbaum, 2003.

Messent, Peter. *Mark Twain and Male Friendship: The Twichell, Howells, & Rogers Friendships*. New York: Oxford University Press, 2009.

Millis, Walter. *The Martial Spirit*. Cambridge, Massachusetts: The Riverside Press, 1931.

Mitchell, St. Augustus. *Mitchell's School Geography: A System of Modern Geography, Comprising a Description of the Present State of the World, and its five great divisions . . .* 4th revised ed. Philadelphia: Cowperthwaite & Co., 1857.

Monroe, Lewis B. *The Third Reader*. Philadelphia: E. H. Butler and Co., 1873.

Morgan, John T. "What Shall We Do With the Conquered Islands?" In *The North American Review*, vol. 166, issue 499 (June 1898).

Moore, Edward Caldwell. *The World Crisis and Missionary Work. An Address at the 106th Annual of the Board, New Haven, Connecticut. October 26, 1915*. The American Board of Commissioners for Foreign Missions, Boston, 1915.

Moore, M. B. *The Geographical Reader, for the Dixie Children*. Raleigh, North Carolina: Branson, Farrer & Co, 1863.

Moreau, Joseph. *Schoolbook Nation: Conflicts over American History Textbooks from the Civil War to the Present*. Ann Arbor: The University of Michigan Press, 2003.

Morse, Jedidiah. *The American Universal Geography, or A View of the Present State of all the Kingdoms, States, and Colonies in the Known World*, vol. I, 6th ed. Boston: Thomas & Andrews, 1812.

Mulanax, Richard B. *The Boer War in American Politics and Diplomacy*. Lanham, Maryland: University Press of America, 1994.

Netzorg, Morton J. *Backward, Turn Backward*. Manila, Philippines: Metro Manila, 1985.

No author. *Cartoons of the War of 1898 with Spain from Leading Foreign and American Papers*. Chicago: Belford, Middlebrook & Co., 1898.

Noll, Mark A. *America's God: From Jonathan Edwards to Abraham Lincoln*. New York: Oxford University Press, 2002.

Packard, R. L. "Education in Cuba, Porto Rico, and the Philippines." United States Bureau of Education, chapter from the Report of the Commissioner of Education for 1897–98. Washington: Government Printing Office, 1899, 909–983.

Page, David B. *Our Dumb Animals*, vol. 31, no. 12 (Boston: May 1899), 146. Collection: Mrs. J. S. Cobb Printed Material, Massachusetts Historical Society.

Palma, Rafael. *The Pride of the Malay Race: A Biography of Jose Rizal*. Trans. Roman Ozaeta. New York: Prentice-Hall 1949.

Parker, Christian. "Christianity and the Cultural Identity of Latin America on the Threshold of the 21st Century." In *Social Compass*, 39(4), 1992, 571–583.

Parks, Leighton. "Christian Expansion, Ancient and Modern." In *Sermons and Addresses on the Spanish-American War*, no. 19. Boston, 1902 (microfilm).

Patterson, Rev. A.J. "Trial of St. Paul the Missionary before the American Board of Foreign Missions." Boston: Universalist Publishing House, 1888.

Peña, Yeni Castro. *El mito Roosevelt para América Latina (1901–1909)*. Quito: Universidad Andina Simón Bolívar, Sede Ecuador, 2007.

Perkins, Bradford. *The Great Rapprochement: England and the United States, 1895–1914*. New York: Atheneum, 1968.

Perry, Ralph Barton. *The Thought and Character of William James*. Nashville, Tennessee: Vanderbilt University Press, 1996.

Philippines Bureau of Education. *Course of Study for Intermediate Grades, with Suggestions for Teachers*. Manila: Bureau of Printing, 1917.

Phipps, William E. *Mark Twain's Religion*. Macon, Georgia: Mercer University Press, 2003.

Pierpont, John. *The American First Class Book; or Exercises in Reading and Recitation; Selected Principally from Modern Authors of Great Britain and America; and Designed for the Use of the Highest Class in Public and Private Schools*. New York: George F. Cooledge, 1835.

Pinney, Thomas, ed. *The Letters of Rudyard Kipling, Vol. 2: 1890–99*. Iowa City: University of Iowa Press, 2002.

Plaja, Fernando Diaz. *1898*. Madrid: Editora Nacional, 1976.

Porter, Bernard. *The Absent-Minded Imperialists: Empire, Society, and Culture in Britain*. Oxford: Oxford University Press, 2004.

———. *Critics of Empire: British Radical Attitudes to Colonialism in Africa, 1895–1914*. London: Macmillan, 1968.

Potter, Simon J., ed. *Newspapers and Empire in Ireland and Britain: Reporting the British Empire, 1857–1921*. Dublin: Four Courts Press, 2004.

Pratt, Julius W. *Expansionists of 1898: The Acquisition of Hawaii and The Spanish Islands*. Gloucester, Massachusetts: Peter Smith, 1959.

Putz, Manfred. 1990. "Mark Twain and the Idea of American Superiority at the End of the Nineteenth Century." In Serge Ricard, ed., *An American Empire: Expansionist Cultures and Policies, 1881–1917*. Aix-en-Provence: Université de Provence, 1990, 215–236.

Quibuyen, Florio C. *A Nation Aborted: Rizal, American Hegemony, and Philippine Nationalism*. Manila: Atenio de Manila University Press, 1999.

Quirk, Tom. *Mark Twain and Human Nature*. Columbia: University of Missouri Press, 2007.

Racelis, Mary, and Judy Celine Ick, eds. *Bearers of Benevolence: The Thomasites and Public Education in the Philippines*. Pasig City: Anvil Publishing, 2001.

Rafael, Vicente L. *The Promise of the Foreign: Nationalism and the Tecnics of Translation in the Spanish Philippines*. Durham, North Carolina: Duke University Press, 2005.

Raustiala, Kal. *Does the Constitution Follow the Flag?: The Evolution of Territoriality in American Law*. New York: Oxford University Press, 2009.

Ricard, Serge. *An American Empire: Expansionist Cultures and Policies, 1881–1917*. Aix-en-Provence: Université de Provence, 1990.

————. *Theodore Roosevelt et la justification de l'impérialisme*. Aix-en-Provence: Université de Provence, 1986.

Rizal, José. *El Filibusterismo (The Subversive), 1891*. Trans. Leon Ma. Guerrero. New York: W. W. Norton & Co., 1968.

————. *Noli Me Tangere* (1886). Trans. Soledad Lacson-Locsin. Honolulu: University of Hawai'i Press, 1996–97.

Robbins, Sarah. *Managing Literacy, Mothering America: Women's Narratives on Reading and Writing in the Nineteenth Century*. Pittsburgh: University of Pittsburgh Press, 2004.

Robertson, John M. *Patriotism and Empire*. London: Grant Richards, 1899.

Rodó, José Enrique. *Ariel*. Trans. F. J. Stimson. Boston: Houghton Mifflin Company, 1922.

Romulo, Carlos P. *Identity and Change: Towards a National Definition*. Manila: Solidaridad Publishing House, 1965.

Roosevelt, Theodore, and Henry Cabot Lodge. *Selections from the Correspondence of Theodore Roosevelt and Henry Cabot Lodge, 1884–1918*. Vol. I. New York: Charles Scribner's Sons, 1925.

Rotker, Susana. *The American Chronicles of José Martí: Journalism and Modernity in Spanish America*. Trans Jennifer French and Katherine Semler. Hanover, New Hampshire: University Press of New England, 2000.

Rowe, John Carlos. *Literary Culture and U.S. Imperialism: From the Revolution to World War II*. New York: Oxford University Press, 2000.

Salamanca, Bonifacio S. *The Filipino Reaction to American Rule, 1901–1913*. New Haven, Connecticut: The Shoestring Press, 1968.

Salazar, James B. *Bodies of Reform: The Rhetoric of Character in Gilded Age America*. New York: New York University Press, 2010.

Santiago-Valles, Kelvin. 1999. "'Still Longing for de Old Plantation': The Visual Parodies and Racial National Imaginary of U.S. Overseas Expansionism, 1898–1903." In *American Studies International*, 37.3, 18–42.

Schirmer, Daniel B. *Republic or Empire: American Resistance to the Philippines War*. Cambridge, Massachusetts: Schenkman Publishing Company, 1972.

————, and Stephen Rosskamm Shalom, eds. *The Philippines Reader: A History of Colonialism, Neocolonialism, Dictatorship, and Resistance*. Boston: South End Press, 1987.

Schoonover, Thomas. *Uncle Sam's War of 1898 and the Origins of Globalization*. Lexington, Kentucky: The University Press of Kentucky, 2003.

Scott, Arthur. *On the Poetry of Mark Twain*. Urbana: University of Illinois Press, 1966.

Schumacher, John N. *The Propaganda Movement, 1880–1895: The Creators of a Filipino Consciousness, the Makers of Revolution*. Manila: Solidaridad Publishing House, 1973.

Seed, Geoffrey. "British Reactions to American Imperialism Reflected in Journals of Opinion, 1898–1900." In *Political Science Quarterly*, vol. 73, no. 2 (June 1958), 254–272.

Serrano, Carlos. *Final del Imperio. Espana 1895–1898*. Madrid: Siglo XXI de Espana Editories, S.A., 1984.

Shaw, Angel Vlasco and Luis H. Francia, eds. *Vestiges of War: The Philippine-American War and the Aftermath of an Imperial Dream, 1899–1999*. New York: New York University Press, 2002.

Sheldon, Charles M. *In His Steps: "What Would Jesus Do?"* Shawnee County Historical Society, Bulletin No. 44, Winter, 1967. Orig. pub. in *The Advance*, first as a serial in the Congregationalist weekly by that name, beginning November 5, 1896, vol. 32, no. 1617; then in book form by the Advanced Publishing Co. Chicago, Illinois: The Advance Publishing Company, 1897.

Sheridan, Richard Brinsley. *The Filipino Martyrs: A Story of the Crime of February 4, 1899*. London: John Lane, The Bodley Head, 1900.

Silbey, David J. *A War of Frontier and Empire: The Philippine-American War, 1899–1902*. New York: Hill & Wang, 2007.

Slaughter, Anne-Marie. *The Idea That Is America: Keeping Faith with Our Values in a Dangerous World*. New York: Basic Books, 2007.

Smith, Angel. "The People and the Nation: Nationalist Mobilization and the Crisis of 1895–98 in Spain." In Angel Smith and Emma Davila-Cox, eds. *The Crisis of 1898: Colonial Redistribution and Nationalist Mobilization*. New York: St. Martin's Press, 1999, 152–179.

Smith, Ephraim K. "William McKinley's Enduring Legacy: The Historiographical Debate on the Taking of the Philippine Islands." In *Crucible of Empire: The Spanish-American War & Its Aftermath*. Ed. James C. Bradford. Annapolis, Maryland: Naval Institute Press, 1993, 205–250.

Smith, Willard H. *The Social and Religious Thought of William Jennings Bryan*. Lawrence, Kansas: The Coronado Press, 1975.

Sperry, Willard G. "Vision of the Kingdom, Annual Sermon before the American Commissioners for Foreign Missions. Delivered at Manchester, New Hampshire October 13, 1903." Published by the Board, Boston, 1903.

Stanley, Peter W., ed. *Reappraising an Empire: New Perspectives on Philippines-American History*. Cambridge, Massachusetts: Harvard University Press, 1984.

Startt, James D. *Journalists for Empire: The Imperial Debate in the Edwardian Stately Press, 1903–1913*. Westport, Connecticut: Greenwood Press, 1991.

Stewart, K. J. *A Geography for Beginners*. Richmond, Virginia: J. W. Randolph, 1864.

Storrs, Richard Slater. "Motives to Missionary Work: An Address Delivered at the Annual Meeting of the American Board of Commissioners for Foreign Missions at Toledo, Ohio, October 8, 1896." American Board of Commissioners for Foreign Missions: Boston, Massachusetts, 1896.

Taylor, S. J. *The Great Outsiders: Northcliffe, Rothermere and the Daily Mail*. London: Weidenfield & Nicolson, 1996.

Tessitore, Aristide. "Alexis de Toqueville on the Natural State of Religion in the Age of Democracy." In *The Journal of Politics*, vol. 64, no. 4 (November 2002), 1137–1152.

Theobold, Harry Couch. *The Filipino Teacher's Manual*. New York and Manila: World Book Company, 1907.

Tuckey, Sterling S., ed. *Mark Twain's Which Was the Dream? And Other Symbolic Writings of the Later Years*. Berkeley, California: University of California Press, 1966.

Twain, Mark. *A Connecticut Yankee in King Arthur's Court*. New York: Signet, 1963.

———. *Following the Equator: A Journey Around the World*. New York: Dover Publications, Inc. 1989.

———. *Roughing It*. New York: New American Library Signet Classics, 1962.

———. *Notebook* 44, 1901, Mark Twain Papers and Project, The Bancroft Library, University of California at Berkeley.

———. *What Is Man?* New York: Harper and Brothers, 1917.

Walker, Amasa. *The Science of Wealth: A Manual of Political Economy, Embracing the Laws of Trade Currency and Finance. Condensed and Arranged for Popular Readings and Use as a Text-Book*. Philadelphia: J. B. Lippincott & Co., 1872.

Waugh, Joan. *Unsentimental Reformer: The Life of Josephine Shaw Lowell*. Cambridge: Harvard University Press, 1997.

Webster, Noah. *The American Spelling Book; Containing the rudiments of the English Language, for the Use of Schools in the United States*. 90th Revised Impression, Philadelphia: Johnson & Warner, 1816.

———. *History of the United States; To Which Is Attached a Brief Historical Account of Our England Ancestors, from the Dispersion at Babel, to their Migration to America; and of the Conquest of South America, by the Spaniards*. New Haven: Durrie & Peck, 1832.

Welch, Richard E., Jr. *Response to Imperialism: The United States and the Philippine-American War, 1899–1902*. Chapel Hill: University of North Carolina Press, 1979.

Willard, Emma. *History of the United States, or, Republic of America; Designed for Schools and Private Libraries*. New York: N. & J. White, 1835.

Willson, Marcius. *Juvenile American History, for Primary Schools*. New York: Mark H. Newman & Co., 1847.

Wright, Henrietta Christian. *Children's Stories in American Literature, 1660–1860*. New York: Charles Scribner's Sons, 1896.

Young Men's Institute. *Catalogue of the Library of the Hartford Young Men's Institute*. Hartford, Connecticut: Young Men's Institute, 1873.

Zaide, Gregorio F. *José Rizal: Life, Works, and Writings*. Manila: Villanueva Book Store, 1957.

Zwick, Jim. *Confronting Imperialism: Essays on Mark Twain and the Anti-Imperialist League*. West Conshohocken, Pennsylvania: Infinity Publishing Co., 2007.

———. *Mark Twain's Weapons of Satire: Anti-Imperialist Writings on the Philippine-American War*. Syracuse, New York: Syracuse University Press, 1992.

INDEX

SUSAN K. HARRIS is the Joyce and Elizabeth Hall Distinguished Professor of American Literature and Culture at the University of Kansas. She is the author of several works on nineteenth-century literature including *19th-Century American Women's Novels* and *The Courtship of Olivia Langdon and Mark Twain*.